D1499474

SHAKESPEARE SURVEY

SHAKESPEARE SURVEY

AN ANNUAL SURVEY OF
SHAKESPEARIAN STUDY & PRODUCTION

II

EDITED BY
ALLARDYCE NICOLL

Issued under the Sponsorship of
THE UNIVERSITY OF BIRMINGHAM
THE UNIVERSITY OF MANCHESTER
THE SHAKESPEARE MEMORIAL THEATRE
THE SHAKESPEARE BIRTHPLACE TRUST

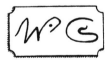

CAMBRIDGE UNIVERSITY PRESS

Published by the Syndics of the Cambridge University Press
Bentley House, 200 Euston Road, London, NW1 2DB
American Branch: 32 East 57th Street, New York, N.Y.10022

© Cambridge University Press 1958

ISBN: 0 521 06424 4

First published 1958
Reprinted 1974

Printed in Great Britain at the
University Printing House, Cambridge
(Brooke Crutchley, University Printer)

EDITOR'S NOTE

For the next, the twelfth, volume of *Shakespeare Survey*, the central theme will be 'The Elizabethan Theatre, Past and Present'. The thirteenth volume will be concerned particularly with '*King Lear*'. The latest date for consideration of articles for Volume 13 is 1 January 1959. Contributions offered for publication should be addressed to: The Editor, *Shakespeare Survey*, The Shakespeare Institute (University of Birmingham), Stratford-upon-Avon.

CONTENTS

[Notes are placed at the end of each contribution. All line references are to the 'Globe' edition, and, unless for special reasons, quotations are from this text]

LIST OF PLATES

SHAKESPEARE'S ROMANCES: 1900-1957

BY

PHILIP EDWARDS

It would be vainglory to suggest that recent criticism has succeeded in justifying the large claims it has made for Shakespeare's Romances. Though we may be convinced, because of the constant insistence, that the Romances are important, it is hard to point to the critic who has shown where the importance lies. At any rate, a retrospect of this century's work on the last plays has little progress to report. "We cannot enlarge our conceptions," said Hazlitt, "we can only shift our point of view." The chronological story of the changing attitude to the Romances is often told; to repeat it here would give a false impression of organic development. The views of Dowden, Strachey and Wilson Knight do not act out Tillyard's tragic scheme of Prosperity, Destruction and Regeneration. Although critics may see themselves as moving on from positions already reached, confounding the errors and enlarging on the hints of those who have preceded them, the chart of criticism over the years shows no continuous course, but a series of different vectors from different starting points. To make any sense out of the record of twentieth-century criticism of Shakespeare's last plays, with its bewildering disagreements on what the plays contain, it is essential to discuss criticism in the light of the assumptions the writers make about literature. This essay is more of an attempt to distinguish between the prevailing critical attitudes to the Romances in the last fifty years than an account of work done. I have chosen some two dozen studies in order to illustrate the four or five main critical approaches and the different conclusions which writers using a similar approach may come to. I am particularly sorry that this scheme, partly because it is rather arbitrarily selective and partly because it gives weight to criticism relating to the Romances as a group, does not allow me to discuss many important studies of individual plays.

The 'problem' of the last plays may be stated quite simply. *Cymbeline, The Winter's Tale, The Tempest*, with (sometimes) *Pericles* and (sometimes) *Henry VIII* as outriders, form a group with similar characteristics, incidents and endings. They seem more closely related than any other group of Shakespeare's plays. What they have in common makes them startlingly different from the plays which go before them. They are, moreover, written at the close of the author's writing career. So there is something of a mystery to be solved. The mystery is all the more interesting because the change in character appears to be a change away from the control and concentration which Shakespeare had achieved in the great tragedies. Construction and characterization seem to show not greater artistic maturity, but less. Inevitably, a good deal of the criticism we have to review is genetic criticism. The question, "Why should Shakespeare turn to writing these plays?" is inextricably entwined with the question, "What is the significance of these plays?" For some, the first question has been much more absorbing than the second, and, indeed, the second has only troubled them as a means of answering the first. But it is not curiosity alone that has led others, who set themselves no other object than the understanding of

I

the Romances, into a discussion of Shakespeare's motives. S. L. Bethell puts the point explicitly (*The Winter's Tale*, p. 20):

> Why does Shakespeare in the last phase of his dramatic activity turn to these naïve and impossible romances? And why is his dramatic technique apparently crude and incoherent? Was his interest waning —in the drama, or in life? Was his technical ability deserting him? These are the questions which every critic of the last plays must attempt to answer....

There is some danger of errors in critical logic when Shakespeare's motives, inferred from the nature of the Romances, are used to aid enquiry into the nature of the Romances, but the only point I want to make here is that in reviewing recent criticism it is impossible to separate discussion of the motives of the artist from artistic achievement. It is perhaps not a profitless speculation, however, to wonder what criticism would have made of these plays, or any one of them, if all Shakespeare's other plays had been lost.

THE POET HIMSELF

In the first decade of this century, most of the 'schools' of criticism we have to consider already existed in one form or another. But the dominant interest was biographical, and the search was for the poet himself. Poetry being the expression of a poet's feelings, discussion of poetry amounted to discussion of the poet. The re-creation of Shakespeare from the larva of his emotions took various forms. One was the reconstruction of personality. Lytton Strachey gives us a text: "Is it not thus that we should imagine him in the last years of his life?" ('Shakespeare's Final Period', *Independent Review*, III (1904), reprinted in *Books and Characters* and *Literary Essays*.) So little does Strachey question the duty of investigating the poet's state of mind, that, at the outset of his essay, he steam-rollers over his own doubts about the relations between an artist and his art, and "assumes the truth of the generally accepted view, that the character of the one can be inferred from that of the other". His masterful and entertaining onslaught was directed not at a method of enquiry, but at the conclusions which the enquiry usually led to. These conclusions he exemplified from Dowden and Furnivall, whose work lies outside my arbitrary limit of years. But in 1902, two years before Strachey's essay, Morton Luce had put forward strongly enough his own version of the "serene self-possession" remarked on by Dowden, in the old Arden edition of *The Tempest*. "Style is a revelation of soul" is his starting point—style in the largest sense. If *The Tempest* does not reveal the personal feelings of the author, it is "imposture", "subtle and despicable hypocrisy". *Cymbeline*, *The Winter's Tale*, *The Tempest* and part of *Pericles* represent a definite stage in the author's career. The structure of these plays shows, if not carelessness, a lack of "concentrated artistic determination and purpose", for the writing of plays is for their author now "more of a recreation". The spirit of the plays, however, is marked by a high morality of tone, and "they all tell of repentance and reconciliation, of pardon, love, peace". There is "a passionate return to nature", to "the happy, innocent life of hill and stream and field and flower"; there is "a reverent recognition of the supernatural", and "the thoughtful yet affectionate interest felt by maturer years in the woes and joys of youth". "He is now approaching his fiftieth year; and his experience, if it left him sadder when he wrote his great tragedies, has now left him wiser also." He is "kindlier with his kind". A good deal of the information for this picture of Shakespeare comes from an identification of Prospero with his creator.

There is a similar point of view in Walter Raleigh's chapter on 'The Last Phase' in his *Shakespeare* (1907). Shakespeare was weary of the business of drama and cared only to indulge his whim. The plays are the toys of serenity. The structure itself, then, is a reflection of the author's mood, and so are the incidents and situations—the pastoral scenes, for example, with their "peaceful round of daily duties and rural pieties". This mood is an all-embracing tolerance and kindliness, a mood or state of mind issuing from his mood during the tragic period. As he wrote his tragedies, Shakespeare was not aloof from the suffering and horror he portrayed. "His foothold is precarious on the edge that overlooks the gulf." Though "the smell of the fire had passed on him", he regained a perfect calm of mind.

Against this view of serenity and benevolence, Strachey rebelled. The happy endings of the plays showed, not Shakespeare's tranquillity, but that he knew how to end a fairy tale. "And in this land of faery, is it right to neglect the goblins?" Strachey points to the evil and the violence in the last plays, the infamy, the figures of discord, in Iachimo, Cloten, Caliban, for example. Shakespeare's powers of writing a good play, of creating interesting minor characters, of good-humoured tolerance, have all deteriorated. The reader is often bored—

It is difficult to resist the conclusion that he was getting bored himself. Bored with people, bored with real life, bored with drama, bored, in fact, with everything except poetry and poetical dreams....on the one side inspired by a soaring fancy to the singing of ethereal songs, and on the other, urged by a general disgust to burst occasionally through his torpor into bitter and violent speech.

Strachey's essay was, as they say, a 'useful corrective'. The vision of the mellowed and matured Shakespeare, sitting by the banks of the Avon, the wind playing gently with his white hair, submerged to reappear only furtively. But the essay has offended most succeeding critics, who, admitting the presence of evil and discord and acknowledging its importance, repudiate the idea that the plays are knitted out of boredom, disgust and poetic dreams. A view not unlike Strachey's, however, has recently been put forward in a pair of sharp and disconcerting essays by Clifford Leech (in *Shakespeare's Tragedies*, 1950), though Strachey's "impish account" is expressly rejected as respects dramatic care, thought and execution. Leech's account of the "new ethical attitude" of the last plays is something to which the biographical reconstruction, stressed here, is only incidental: no one would suggest that he reads the plays only for what he learns about their author. Leech discerns a "puritanic tinge" in the last plays, an urge to discipline man's unruly flesh. He finds forgiveness forced, or allowed only after severe punishment. "It is the more passionate nature that seeks in time for the curb upon itself." There is a tension between indulgence and restraint, between a love of beauty and a new asceticism in sexual matters. Strachey found Prospero a crusty middle-aged gentleman, and for Leech, too, he is no benign figure, but a disgruntled "schoolmaster-magician", lacking human sympathy, striving to discipline human nature, whose "tired and sententious epilogue...is significant of Shakespeare's own sense of the futility of castigation". It is a brave man who can talk of the concluding scenes of *The Tempest* in terms of "their recurrent harshness of tone and their burden of moral exhaustion" and a braver man still who can, in this post-war world of criticism, dare to attribute this tone to the emotional life of the dramatist. Shakespeare criticism would be the weaker without its dissentient voices.

A second type of biographical criticism uses the last plays as the material to create a chart of the dramatist's spiritual development. There is a clear distinction between this approach and the re-creation of the author's 'mood', though the two are often seen together. One must also make a distinction between criticism which goes no further than saying that a play expresses an attitude to life (or that the Romances as a whole express an attitude to life) and criticism in which the dominating interest is the consistent and gradual enlargement or alteration of the poet's attitude to life. Two studies of the last plays which illustrate this interest are discussed in a later section of this essay: D. G. James, 'The Failure of the Ballad Makers', in *Scepticism and Poetry* (1937), and G. Wilson Knight, *Myth and Miracle* (1929) and *The Crown of Life* (1947).

CONDITIONED ART

Throughout the century there have been critics fundamentally opposed to a 'subjective' solution of the problem of the Romances. Biographical criticism argues that they are plays which Shakespeare must write if he is to speak the truth about himself. Either his mood, or his vision of things, demands that *The Tempest* be written. In 1901 Ashley H. Thorndike had denied the propriety of such hypotheses (*The Influence of Beaumont and Fletcher upon Shakespeare*). He admitted that Shakespeare's mind was not the same at the time of writing *Hamlet* as at the time of writing *The Tempest*, that no one can disprove conjectures that personal circumstances may have accompanied his "varying creative moods". But he insisted that objective influences were decisive in the change of style towards the Romances. Shakespeare was an actor and a theatre-owner, with more than a detached interest in stage fashions and stage rivalries. His plays must pay, and he was determined to produce something which would gratify his public. Towards the end of the first decade of the seventeenth century, it was obvious that Beaumont and Fletcher had created a new type of drama, the heroic romance, which was immensely popular. Sensitive and obedient to the public demand, Shakespeare wrote his own tragi-comic romances. The happy endings of the plays are required by the form and the subject; Shakespeare may have wished to express the sweetness of forgiveness and reconciliation, but happy endings are naturally a feature of Beaumont and Fletcher also, and Shakespeare's mood may well have differed from those of the two younger men.

The thesis, then, is that Shakespeare imitated Beaumont and Fletcher. The whole theory depends upon the relative dating of Shakespeare's Romances and the work of Beaumont and Fletcher; in particular, of *Cymbeline* and *Philaster*, which certainly have incidents and passages which ring alike. The dating is an extremely uncertain business, and it is a marvel that so serious a theory can be built on very dubious foundations. Thorndike's arguments about the chronology of the relevant plays is highly conjectural, based upon probability and a sense of fitness more often than on fact. In addition, he does not take *Pericles* properly into account, and *Pericles* almost certainly precedes *Philaster*. *Pericles* is relegated to an appendix, and it is argued that it is not similar in tone and mood to the other Romances or to Beaumont and Fletcher. Another study of chronology might just as well show that Shakespeare was the pioneer and Beaumont and Fletcher the followers. There is also weakness in the insistence on the similarities between the work of Shakespeare and that of his young colleagues. On this, Thorndike has often been answered. (See, e.g., Harbage, *Shakespeare and the Rival Traditions*, p. 304.)

Another image of a Shakespeare bound to create what the public were clamouring for is seen in J. Q. Adams' *Life of Shakespeare* (1923), but now the change in the drama is caused, not by bright young men, but by the climate of the times: the enervating reign of James and the withdrawal of the theatre to a courtly audience. Adams notes a decline in seriousness and a vitiation of moral tone. Beaumont and Fletcher lead the new fashion, and Shakespeare must needs do his best to purvey what is required, finding his own style of play old-fashioned. But, reluctant and defeated though he may be, this Samson in Gaza will not totally destroy the spirit of his work; he meets the fashion half-way, so that the Romances are Shakespeare's attempt to hold fast to his moral tone in an alien world and an alien form of drama.

A much more attractive 'explanation' of the Romances in terms of theatrical conditions is in G. E. Bentley's 'Shakespeare and the Blackfriars Theatre' (*Shakespeare Survey*, 1, 1948). Here is a striking, vivid picture of Shakespeare as a man of the theatre, a picture which never belittles him, as Thorndike's does. Though Shakespeare is shown preoccupied with theatre-leases, engaging new dramatists, planning new plays in committee, concerned with finance, anxious to avoid box-office failure, we are not given a crafty impresario whose art is subdued to the main chance. Bentley's theory is simple. The King's Men acquired the lease of the 'private' theatre, Blackfriars, in the summer of 1608 (though playing hardly began before 1610). Here was a new, important and daring venture—a public company entering the world of the coterie-theatre, with its different type of audience and their different expectations in entertainment. Bentley suggests that there must have been earnest conversations amongst the leaders of the King's Men to make sure that their venture would be no failure, and that Shakespeare must have taken a chief share in these conferences. The King's Men, it is argued, decided to engage Jonson, Beaumont and Fletcher, with their experience in writing for the private theatre, and agreed that Shakespeare, their most successful dramatist, should turn his talents to providing a new sort of play for the Blackfriars audience, namely *Cymbeline*, *The Winter's Tale*, *The Tempest*, and, in collaboration with Fletcher, *Henry VIII* and *Cardenio*. Whether *Cymbeline* or *Philaster* came first no longer matters. "It is their common purpose and environment, not imitation of one by the other, that makes them similar."

One could wish that Bentley had dealt in his article with several possible objections. Again, there is the problem of *Pericles*, on the boards at the Globe by the spring of 1608 at the latest. Though Shakespeare may be responsible for only half of it, he undoubtedly enters the world of his Romances through that play. Secondly, there is no proof that the other Romances were not Globe plays. As J. M. Nosworthy points out (New Arden *Cymbeline*, p. xvi), Simon Forman saw *The Winter's Tale* and, presumably, *Cymbeline* at the Globe. Related to this is a deeper objection (for a play written for Blackfriars might also be played at the Globe where Forman could see it more cheaply) implied in Harbage's conviction (*op. cit.* p. 86) that the Romances are popular in type and do not belong to the moral world of the coterie-theatres. Harbage suggests that Shakespeare in his last plays is turning back to the popular adventure-drama of his youth. To this point we shall have to return.

The attractiveness of Bentley's thesis is that he does not trespass on what Shakespeare made of the challenge presented to him. He is in no danger of maintaining that, since the plays are written to order, they are, shall we say, 'insincere'. It is a foolish position to be at either of the extremes of 'subjective' or 'external' motivation. If theatrical circumstances influenced Shakespeare, he may still find freedom in his service. The saner criticism of the last plays, before and after Bentley, has been willing to accept the idea that there may well be 'pressure' of some kind on Shakespeare in these last years, but that his genius is not therefore subdued. The point is made with individual variations, as by Una Ellis-Fermor (*Jacobean Drama*, p. 268), or by J. F. Danby (*Poets on Fortune's Hill*, p. 106), who remarks: "A change of taste in the audience, a tiredness in the writer himself—any of a number of secondary causes would equally account for the shift of subject matter, without compromise to Shakespeare's integrity or his sincerity."

MYTH, SYMBOL AND ALLEGORY

By far the biggest and most influential school of criticism we have to consider is a school of many sects. Its members are united in the belief that the Romances are written in a form of other-speaking, and must be translated before their significance can be understood. There is little point at this stage in the waning of the century in speaking once more of the tremendous impact of anthropology and comparative religion on criticism, but it must be said that interest in the last plays would have been a shadow of what it has been in fact, if vegetation rites and royal deaths and resurrections, and the symbolic patterns in which the inner realities of human experience display themselves, had been less enthusiastically received into the small-talk of the age.

Allegory, of course, has been popular in *Tempest* criticism for a very long time, and it may help to make clear the spirit of the revelations that were yet to come to look at one specimen of allegory in the days of Edward VII. Churton Collins ('Poetry and Symbolism: A Study of *The Tempest*', *Contemporary Review*, January 1908) lacks the confidence which the findings of Miss Bodkin and Miss Weston gave to later interpreters; he is modest and humble. He found that Browning only laughed when he asked him if 'Hugues of Saxe-Gotha' were not symbolic of man's bewilderment before the divine providence. But he could not believe himself wrong to interpret the poem so; perhaps a poet is often unconscious that his work is an allegory of an experience deeper than it professes. If the inner significance of great poetry is not always defined in the author's mind, diffidence and tentativeness must accompany the criticism which would try to explain an inner significance. With all caution, Collins suggests that the island in *The Tempest* may be considered as the world, with Prospero as the controlling divinity. The characters are various aspects of humanity. The plot tells how those subjects who have sinned against and wronged a Power are at last brought before the Power. The wrong done is answered with forgiveness, "sealed and ratified by the marriage of the child of the wronged one with the child of the wronger". Like the last plays as a whole, *The Tempest* portrays the moral government of the universe in optimistic terms, Shakespeare being deeply influenced by the beauty of Christian belief. Whether we find an allegorical approach permissible or not, Collins is attractive, not only because he fears the rigid scheme, but because the play he is talking about is clearly the play of the same title which we have read. And critics who do not find allegory permissible have been content to summarize *The Tempest* on the text of *felix culpa* as Collins does: "The whole play is saturated with irony, an irony reversing the terrible irony of the tragedies: its very title is ironical—that tempest which was no tempest, that wreck which was no wreck, that salvation in loss, that harmony in discord."

If we jump over the years, the change in tone is sharp. Northrop Frye, for example, remarks: "With the disappearance and revival of Hermione in *The Winter's Tale*, who actually returns once as a ghost in a dream, the original nature-myth of Demeter and Proserpine is openly established" ('The Argument of Comedy', *English Institute Essays*, 1948 (1949)). No doubt one could push this kind of criticism further back than 1921, but it was in that year that Colin Still published his original study of *The Tempest* as *Shakespeare's Mystery Play*; it was "enlarged and clarified" in 1936 as *The Timeless Theme*. The titles together are admirably significant of his view that art is not what it seems, but "spontaneous reflections of the unchanging facts of mankind's spiritual pilgrimage". (This pilgrimage, a struggle out of darkness into light, is symbolized not only in art but in rituals, like, for example, the Eleusinian mysteries.) *The Tempest* is "a dramatic representation of the Mystery of Redemption, conceived as a psychological experience and expressed in mythological form". Only the critic who is himself a mystic can perceive the truths which great works of art reflect, and is able to interpret them. The office of hierophant is rarely assumed so candidly, but Still's conception of his role is not fundamentally different from that of other critics who take us through one or more of the Romances, explaining as they go, like Bunyan's Interpreter, what it all really means.

A few examples will illustrate Still's method and his wealth of comparisons. The story of the court party, for instance, reveals the pattern of the Lesser Initiation through Purgatory. The Ceremony of Water takes place when the courtiers are flung into the sea from their wrecked ship; as they emerge from the water their clothes are even finer than they were at first. This Ceremony takes place on a voyage from Tunis to Naples, almost identical with the voyage from Carthage to Cumae of Aeneas, at the end of which he too undertook his purgation in the descent into the underworld. The adventures of the court party, which include a banquet offered and removed, may be compared with the temptation of Christ as described by Milton in *Paradise Regained*. Stephano and Trinculo shadow forth the Fall. Ferdinand makes the ascent to the Celestial Paradise which constitutes the Greater Initiation. Prospero, as the initiating priest, may also be considered as the God whom the priest represents.

There are several 'anthropological' studies of the last plays: two on *The Winter's Tale* may be mentioned. F. C. Tinkler was himself an anthropologist; his interpretation of *The Winter's Tale* appeared in *Scrutiny* in 1937. Much of the article is about a synthesis of the rural and court 'modes', which I shall discuss later. But "the larger rhythm of the play" is "the association between the idea of a divine king and the rhythm of the seasons". Mamilius is the concrete symbol of the spiritual health of his father, Leontes, and his death is always talked of in terms of its effect on other people. Perdita and Florizel are "almost vegetation deities" and in the final reunion "the rhythm is complete and the Waste Land is made fertile once more". F. D. Hoeniger's discussion of the play in 1950 (*University of Toronto Quarterly*) was put forward as "a revaluation based on a new and revolutionary interpretation of its meaning". Hoeniger justifies his parabolic reading of the play as being in the medieval tradition of anagogy. His essay is not so much on how one may perceive in *The Winter's Tale* the age-old vegetation myth of rebirth, but on the play as an allegory of that deep scheme. He notes the significance of references to the seasons, and to the similarity of children and parents. He then draws the parallel between

Perdita and Proserpine, and Hermione and Demeter. "The Persephone of the one year becomes the Demeter of the next. By analogy, we can understand the close similarity between Perdita and Hermione." The myths and mysteries of the vegetation cycle also expressed "man's hope in a blissful immortality". "Leontes' paradise at the end of the play is not, like Perdita's, that of a garden, but of a city and a temple, corresponding to the Heavenly City in the New Testament, the Temple of God. There he remarries Hermione, just as Dante meets Beatrice again, and Faust the eternal form of Gretchen."

The most vigorous exponent of the theory that the last plays are myths, bodying forth man's apprehension of the mystery of salvation and immortality, is, of course, Wilson Knight. In his essay on *The Tempest*, Knight makes a most important statement of belief about the nature of drama (pp. 226–7). "Fundamental verities of nature, man and God do not change." For these verities there is "a certain common language of symbol", found in mythology, ritual and poetry. In the Middle Ages the dominating ritual was the Mass. "The medieval system losing its hold, the way was open for a far more richly varied drama, with manifold dangers but also new possibilities of illumination."

A common store of racial wisdom for centuries untapped is now released, as Prospero releases Ariel; and the highly responsible artist has himself to explore and exploit the wide area of imaginative truth apparently excluded (though perhaps in some sense surveyed and transcended) by Christian dogma.

The vision of "fundamental verities" which the last plays symbolically express is one towards which Shakespeare's plays have been remorselessly working, and this unfolding vision it is the office of the critic-priest to mediate to the public. There is a remarkable consistency and symmetry in Knight's account of the development of the Shakespearian vision, and of its relation with the increasing understanding of truth to be found in the work of other great seers: Tolstoy, Dostoievsky, Keats.

The progress from spiritual pain and despairing thought through stoic acceptance to a serene and mystic joy is a universal rhythm of the spirit of man....As for my contention that the Final Plays of Shakespeare must be read as myths of immortality, that is only to bring them into line with other great works of literature. Tragedy is never the last word.

Another comparison is made with the three books of *The Divine Comedy*, and then this three-stage development is to be seen as a reflection of "that mystic truth from which are born the dogmas of the Catholic Church—the incarnation in actuality of the Divine Logos of Poetry; the temptation in the desert, the tragic ministry and death, and the resurrection of the Christ" (*Myth and Miracle*, reprinted in *The Crown of Life*. See pp. 29–31). It is a sign of the times that one's response to patterns of this kind is not exaltation but considerable nervousness.

It is impossible for a summary of Knight's book to do more than indicate very sketchily the direction of his arguments. *Pericles* stands on the threshold of the Romances, as the Romances stand on the threshold of *Henry VIII*. "We are watching something like a parable of human fortune, with strong moral import at every turn." Pericles is less a tragic hero, related by his own deeds to his disaster, than a suffering Everyman, though he may be said to endure "a fall in the theological sense" in his immoderate desire for Antiochus' daughter. The movement of his career ends beyond tragedy, in some "higher recognition and rehabilitation" with the recovery of the supposedly dead Marina and Thaisa. *The Winter's Tale* shows suffering and its transcendence with a more intimate relevance to the acts and thoughts of the tragic hero.

Our drama works...to show Leontes, under the tutelage of the Oracle, as painfully working himself from the bondage of sin and remorse into the freedom of nature, with the aptly-named Paulina as conscience, guide and priestess. The resurrection [of Hermione] is not performed until (i) Leontes' repentance is complete and (ii) creation is satisfied by the return of Perdita, who is needed for Hermione's full release....Nor is it just a reversal of tragedy; rather tragedy is contained, assimilated, transmuted; every phase of the resurrection scene is soaked in tragic feeling, and the accompanying joy less an antithesis to sorrow than its final flowering.

Cymbeline is made to follow *The Winter's Tale* on the argument not of external evidence but of the likelihood of a pattern of Shakespeare's development. Knight argues that the Vision of Jupiter is indispensable to the play—and Shakespeare's. In *Myth and Miracle* also, the great significance of this expression of divine guidance and control had been stressed. In the later study he writes, "Our apocalypse...stands central among Shakespeare's last plays....It is our one precise anthropomorphic expression of the beyond-tragedy recognition felt through the miracles and resurrections of sister-plays and reaching Christian formulation in *Henry VIII*." *The Tempest* is to be seen as an allegory once more ("Prospero, Ariel, Caliban, Miranda: all are aspects of Shakespeare himself") and it is also "a myth of the national soul"; in spite of the play's virtues, the themes of Shakespeare's work tend to dissolve "into a haze of esoteric mysticism". *Henry VIII* gives the finest and highest expression of what all Shakespeare's plays have been leading towards. The three 'falls' of Buckingham, Wolsey and Katharine express perfectly the Christian humility, forgiveness and charity not fully achieved by Prospero. The vision afforded to Katharine, in its "silent ritual" is "the most satisfying projection" of the other-worldly intuitions found in the Romances. The completion of the tragic pattern in patience and forgiveness, and a vision of a world beyond this, is set in a national play, making much use of ritual. Cranmer's prophecy at the close of the play unites the themes of tragic mysticism and national greatness.

For Knight, Shakespeare succeeds in finding a local habitation and a name for his perceptions of what lies beyond human experience. D. G. James' extremely lively and stimulating essay, 'The Failure of the Ballad Makers' (1937), is a study in failure, the story of the struggle to find a myth to pronounce the unpronounceable. The essential myth in the last plays is the finding of what is lost. But this myth is complicated by the presence of others: the bringing of the dead to life, the recovery of a lost royalty, the search for what is lost by a royal personage, the helpless situation of the lost person (who is also royal). These myths combine in stories "which issue from a state of peace and love, into which, after suffering and disloyalty, they again pass". Royalty symbolizes a spiritual supremacy and beauty. The person lost, of incomparable worth, symbolizes the loss by man, through his own evil, of his most treasured spiritual possession. When in the plays the lost person is found, the loser finds his highest spiritual state and is redeemed.

But the last plays, says James, are "tortured by a sense of inexpressiveness and failure". The myths are inadequate for Shakespeare's apprehensions. In the first place, the symbolism is inconsistent, contradictory, confused. In the second place, by using human symbols to convey a sense of what lies beyond humanity, Shakespeare puts an impossible strain on dramatic credibility. "We alternate throughout the plays between a sense of Shakespeare's high metaphysical symbolism and a sense of the silly." The raising of the dead is monotonously repeated and dramatically embarrassing. Thaisa is "incredibly stupid" not to seek for Pericles after Cerimon has restored her; the deception practised by Paulina on Leontes is "preposterous". In the third place, and for him most conclusively, James holds that Shakespeare is trying to go where art cannot go. His struggle is doomed to failure. The imagination of the poet (we have to draw on the whole of *Scepticism and Poetry*) is always labouring to encompass the whole of life, and to achieve a unity. Sometimes, if the poet's own experience can no longer provide the harmony, there comes to him the dim apprehension of our life as but a fragment of a transcendent reality. But poetry does not have the means of bodying forth this transcendent reality. Art and religion do not overlap; it is to stretch art to its breaking point to try to express what lies beyond human life. "The ship of poetry must, to use a famous phrase, suffer shipwreck at the entrance to harbour."

No one can re-read the last plays after studying James without being made watchful for new possibilities and new subtleties. But there are several serious objections to his work, the greatest of these being the dangers of systematization. For James as for Knight, the last plays illustrate an ideal pattern of the development of an artist's understanding of life. The description of Shakespeare's period of "maiden thought" sounds odd to anyone who has read the early histories with Sisson's *Mythical Sorrows* in mind, and it hardly helps to be told that a time of intense and unclouded human joy was possible for Shakespeare because of the unique period of history in which he lived. The neatness of the progress through "the time of crisis" to the ultimate perception is not convincing. James' mythological framework is also narrow and inflexible: either the plays are distorted to fit the framework (particularly *Cymbeline* and *The Tempest*), or worse, Shakespeare is belaboured for the confusion of his symbols. This is particularly clear in James' discussion of the symbol of royalty. Shakespeare is at fault for not having done what James thinks he is trying to do. When we read that "in *The Tempest* Shakespeare made a last and desperate effort to cope with his impossible task", we may unkindly wonder if the desperate effort and impossible task do not refer to the critic who would reduce the plays to his own orderly scheme.

Again, the "silliness" of the plays is not so apparent to readers more at home in fairy-tale than James appears to be. His resentment at the lack of realism in the last plays is strange. It seems an extraordinary thing to require of drama and of Romance in particular that its characters, motives and incidents should give a direct image of real life. And once it is granted that "human symbols" do not need to behave as our neighbours do, then the thin end of the wedge is driven into the notion of a failure to communicate the incommunicable.

Finally in this section, D. Traversi's *Shakespeare: The Last Phase* (1954). The plays here are held to be "expanded images", and realism has been deliberately abandoned by Shakespeare. The movement of the plays is towards the healing of divisions; "at the heart of each...lies the conception of an organic relation between breakdown and reconciliation". For Traversi, rebirth and reconciliation involve experiences much less transcendental and otherworldly than they do for Still or Knight or James, and it is one aspect of the spiritual fruition in the plays as seen by Traversi that I wish to isolate.

The plays reveal the acquirement of "maturity". "The romantic love of Posthumus...needs to be subjected to a destructive process which will eventually bring it to a full maturity." The development of the character of Miranda is a progress towards maturity; her father's reminiscences place her "on the threshold of a decisive broadening of her own experience".

We have seen already, in *Cymbeline* and *The Winter's Tale*, that the relationship between natural simplicity and the civilized life is a constant theme of the last plays. It is not...presented in the form of a simple contrast. The state of nature...safeguards virtues which need to be taken into account in any balanced view of life, virtues, moreover, which are deliberately contrasted to the corruption, emptiness and insecurity which the surface polish of court life so imperfectly conceals; but these virtues, left to themselves, abstracted from their full human context, languish and reveal their essential incompleteness. They need, in other words, to be assumed into a complete scale of civilized values, and this necessity is at once social and, as far as the individual is concerned, maturing [p. 223].

A "balanced view of life" becomes the mist-hidden crag which is the goal of human striving. The problem of maturity, Traversi remarks, is a problem inherent in the development of life and in no way to be evaded. It is certainly not easy to escape from it. It appears in Tinkler: Sicilia and Bohemia are "almost symbols" of the "contrasted modes" which must be balanced. The fusing of pastoral and court values represents the fusing of Reason and Intuition, and the play reveals a "significant synthesis" of the various disparate elements of a culture. Bethell's study of *The Winter's Tale* (see below, p. 13) also plays with the notion that the wedding of the values of court and country presents "an acted parable of social regeneration".

The reduction of the complexity of Shakespeare to a striving towards a balanced view of life seems to me typical of the pallidness of all interpretations of the last plays which insist that they are symbolic utterances. There is an appearance (there is certainly a claim) that the depths are being opened, riches are being revealed. But it is an appearance only. It is a disservice to Shakespeare to pretend that one is adding to his profundity by discovering that his plots are symbolic vehicles for ideas and perceptions which are, for the most part, banal, trite and colourless. The 'symbols' are so much more fiercely active, potent, rich, complex as themselves than as what they are made to convey. When they are translated, they do not have a tithe of their own magnitude. It was well said, in this connection, that "one of the most important things an apple can mean is simply itself" (J. F. Danby, *Poets on Fortune's Hill*, p. 99). Sentimental religiosity, in the sense of a vague belief in a vague kind of salvation, and vague tremors at the word 'grace'— so long as it is decently disengaged from Christianity; platitudinous affirmations of belief in fertility and re-creation; an insistence on the importance of maturity and balance: these are the deposits of Shakespeare's last plays once the solvent of parabolic interpretation has been applied, but these are not what the reader or the audience observes in Pericles' reunion with Marina, the Whitsun pastorals, Leontes' denial of the oracle or the wooing of Ferdinand and Miranda. The power of suggestion, which is one of the striking features of the last plays, is positively decreased by the type of criticism we are considering. There are many moments when the stage seems to become the whole universe. "Thou that beget'st him that did thee beget", Perdita's "One of these is true..." with Camillo's "Yea, say you so?"—but it is futile to seize them from their contexts. The moments of mystery and power quite lose their force when they are seen, not as

shafts of light going out from the play, but overt statements of themes which the play allegori-
cally presents.

Of course, Shakespeare's dramatic art uses symbols: no play of his could exist without them.
Of course, his plays reverberate far beyond the particular stories they tell. But to admit the
presence of symbolism in drama, to admit a universal application in his plays, is a very different
thing from accepting the principle that plays are symbolic presentations of the occult regions of
human experience.

Many warning voices have been raised against symbolic and allegoric readings, though the
protests have sometimes been made for the wrong reasons. Stoll's essay on *The Tempest* (*PMLA*,
XLVII, 1932) is still worth reading, though he was attacking chiefly the older allegorists. He
makes a good case that Ariel and Caliban *need* to symbolize nothing; they were creations of a
kind recognizable to the audience and their parts in the play are totally explicable in those terms.
If they are seen as symbols, their function is *diminished*: the artistic effect of the play is reduced
when characters become labels attached to "meanings". Danby has also remarked on the
diminishing effect of symbolic interpretation; anthropology, he remarks (*op. cit.* p. 97) "tends to
silt over" the clear outline of the moral world of the plays. Perhaps this may be the place to
mention also F. R. Leavis's most important "Caveat" concerning criticism of the last plays
(*Scrutiny*, X, 1942). Although it did not attack symbolic interpretations as such, his strictures
touch the main errors of the mythopoeists. He insists that each of the last plays be taken separately,
and judged in the manner appropriate to it and on its own merits. And the play as a whole must
be judged before comments on its significance, derived from its imagery or a study of its themes
in isolation, can be permitted. The danger of anti-Bradleyism is that it may lead a critic away
from looking at the play as a whole. In *Cymbeline*, it is suggested, it is a waste of time to look
for themes revealed in the imagery of commanding significance, since in that play Shakespeare
did not transmute the romantic convention. *The Winter's Tale is* a masterpiece, but the same
method of interpretation will not serve this play, in which unreality is all, and *The Tempest*, a
'realistic' play.

The Pattern of Tragedy, and a Christian Interpretation

How deeply rooted the symbolic approach to the Romances is, is apparent in the way it has
coloured the work of those whose criticism as a whole obeys different principles. E. M. W.
Tillyard's *Shakespeare's Last Plays* (1938) is based upon an assumption that the scheme of tragedy
is of three stages: prosperity, destruction and regeneration. He suggests that the final stage is
only hinted at in Shakespeare's tragedies, and that the Romances complete the tragic pattern.
In discussing his tragic scheme, Tillyard calls upon Miss Bodkin's work, and emphasizes that
tragedy is a symbolic rendering of our most elementary life-processes, of the destruction and
re-creation found in all growth, material and spiritual. Besides so general an assumption about
the symbolic mode of the Romances, particular symbolism is pointed out in the course of the
work. Perdita is to be seen as both human and a "symbol both of the creative powers of nature,
physical fertility, and of healing and re-creation of the mind". The end of the book brings us on
to Wilson Knight's ground: "It is not fantastic to see in *The Winter's Tale*, Shakespeare's attempt
to compress the whole theme of The Divine Comedy into a single play."

In spite of this language, there is little 'translation' of the characters and the incidents at the heart of Tillyard's arguments, and, essentially, his criticism does not seem to me to be subterranean. He succinctly announces his thesis about the three Romances (he excludes *Pericles*):

We find in each the same general scheme of prosperity, destruction and re-creation. The main character is a King. At the beginning, he is in prosperity. He then does an evil or misguided deed. Great suffering follows, but during that suffering or at its height, the seeds of something new to issue from it are germinating, usually in secret. In the end, this new element assimilates and transforms the old evil. The King overcomes his evil instincts, joins himself to the new order by an act of forgiveness or repentance: and the play issues into a fairer prosperity than had first existed.

It is essential to Tillyard's thesis that the plays hang together as a group and show Shakespeare's attempt, fumbling at first in *Cymbeline*, to express this one scheme. Only if they are interlocking is the critic justified in creating an 'overall' pattern, made up of elements taken from each play. For nothing is more certain than that only one of the plays, *The Winter's Tale*, answers Tillyard's description. And it is only if we grant Tillyard's bold assumption that we can tolerate his sharpness with *Cymbeline* for not being *The Winter's Tale*; Shakespeare is, apparently, not at ease with his new material and method, and Tillyard says that his pattern can only be seen "by making an intellectual abstract of the play". It is also necessary, to make *The Tempest* fit into the scheme, to see Prospero as a tragic figure with the accustomed burden of *hamartia*. One may well be dissatisfied both with Tillyard's view of tragedy and the relevance of his ideal pattern in the Romances to the individual plays. But in stressing the continuity of the Tragedies and the Romances, *Shakespeare's Last Plays* did important work, and it is interesting, too, that Tillyard was one of the first to emphasize the conventions of Romance in which Shakespeare was working. "We shall not understand", he remarks, "what Shakespeare's contemporaries expected from the romantic material and what types of feeling they thought it capable of treating, unless we remember what they thought of the *Arcadia*."

S. L. Bethell's study of *The Winter's Tale* (1947) also has one foot in the anagogical camp, and it plays rather rashly with "unconscious purposes". But Bethell kept a firm rein on the temptation to "catch the sense at two removes". He has important strictures to make about James' essay; especially, that James, in abstracting certain themes, has removed the flesh and blood of "the full poetic context" which really must settle the significance of any such themes. "It is not a new mythology that the play presents—not a new interpretation of human experience but the old interpretation newly translated into terms of the romance."

The "old interpretation" is for Bethell a Christian interpretation. Bethell has been attacked for creating Shakespeare in the image of his own beliefs. His own introduction forestalls such criticism: admitting that the 'real truth' is inaccessible and that critics will tend to stress those aspects of it which most interest them, Bethell asks if it is only churchmen whose criticism is warped by their beliefs (or, one might add, by their absence of any beliefs).

Bethell shows how important is the avoidance of realism in *The Winter's Tale*. By using fairy-tales and marvels, by including the old joke about the sea-coast of Bohemia, by anachronisms and antiquated techniques, Shakespeare liberates the story from one kind of reality in order to empower it to express another. The "beneficent ordering of the universe" could not be shown so well in a drama which copied real life. Bethell discusses Leontes' crimes in terms of sin, original sin, innocence and grace, and the oracle of Apollo as suggesting that all things are under the control of God. Shakespeare opposes Leontes' life-denying passion with the life-affirming quality of the love of Perdita and Florizel. In the frankness and fullness of this love, Bethell perceives a dovetailing of the natural and the supernatural, and a resolving of the old ascetic tensions of Christianity; "the original plenitude of the Christian way of life" is restored. The restoration of Hermione expresses the future life in terms of the present; the statue-scene is "a carefully prepared symbol of spiritual and actual resurrection, in which alone true reconciliation may be attained".

Although there is a good deal in Bethell's study which is unconvincing, although the dangers of symbolic interpretation (as in the last sentence quoted) are sometimes serious, Bethell approaches his play with all the insight into the nature of drama which he showed so well in his book on Shakespeare and the popular tradition. He may over-interpret, but he knows what manner of thing he is dealing with. His death was a loss to English studies.

How the tradition that the Romances are myths or symbolic patterns may weaken and deflate them for readers is evident in R. A. Foakes' introduction to the New Arden *Henry VIII* (1957). Foakes accepts the prevailing view and is not unnaturally dissatisfied with what it is claimed Shakespeare has contrived. In his last plays, including *Henry VIII*, Shakespeare wished to portray "a sweep of life shaped in a restorative pattern". Each of the Romances fails in a different way; each lacks dramatic power. The profundity is there, but "the profundity is not easily revealed in action". The audience watches "a ritual that is only partly comprehensible, because its terms are not wholly dramatic; they suspect a philosophy of life, recognising tolerance, benediction, the joy of restitution, but are not given the key to it all". Small wonder that Foakes makes Shakespeare grow impatient with his parables and break the staff of symbolic utterance in order to "turn to real life again" in *Henry VIII*. In this last play, he can give full dramatic life to the themes of his final years—the restoration of what has been lost, the winning of self-knowledge, the compensations for suffering, the vitality of the young, forgiveness, patience in adversity. Foakes' excellent criticism of *Henry VIII* is not affected by his low opinion of the Romances, but it may be worth saying that the next step, after becoming dissatisfied with the Romances as they are described by recent critics, is to realize that the Romances have in fact been wrongly described.

THE SHAPE AND MEANING OF ROMANCE

Some recent critics, who are very far from forming a school, are united in eschewing biography, comparative religion and theatrical history, and see their way into the 'meaning' of the Romances by examining their form. There is a claim that the conventions and uses of the romance as understood and practised by the Elizabethans can give immediate help in the struggle of knowing what Shakespeare was up to in his last plays.

The revival of interest in romance is dealt with at some length by J. M. Nosworthy in the New Arden edition of *Cymbeline* (1955). The revival of that poor play, *Mucedorus*, shows at the same time the interest in tragi-comic romance and the poverty of existing material. Shakespeare and Beaumont and Fletcher were engaged with something not new but very old. The difference between *The Rare Triumphs of Love and Fortune* (performed in 1582) and *The Tempest* is one of quality and not of kind. J. F. Danby, in *Poets on Fortune's Hill* (1952) stresses the great influence on Shakespeare's Romances of Sidney's *Arcadia*. F. Kermode (New Arden *Tempest*, 1954) discusses, for their relevance to Shakespeare, both the native traditions of romantic drama and the literary conventions of pastoral romance, especially the 6th Book of *The Faerie Queene*. E. C. Pettet (*Shakespeare and the Romance Tradition*, 1949) emphasizes the *Arcadia*, and usefully points out what is often forgotten, that Shakespeare's interest in romance was always with him, from the time he surrounded the classical plot of *The Comedy of Errors* with the story of Aegeon and Emilia—to be used again in *Pericles*.

That Shakespeare's last plays are 'romances' "in the restricted and historical sense of the word", as Pettet puts it, does not seem to be a matter for doubt. The wanderings, disguises, and surprises, the abundance of incident, the lack of verisimilitude, the pastoral settings, the dangers and escapes, the treatment of love—all these in Shakespeare have been related to the stock features of romance. It may be useful to concentrate on characterization in the light of the requirements of romance; it is a good subject for demonstrating the importance of the question, "What *kind* of a play is this?" Pettet and Nosworthy remark that the extravagant and improbable adventures of romance make realistic and consistent attitudes of mind and patterns of behaviour out of place. By the side of Shakespeare's earlier characterization, the character-drawing of the Romances will seem superficial and sketchy, but that is what romance requires. Pettet notes the tendency to divide characters into rigid categories of black and white, and this aspect is developed by Danby and Kermode. Danby rejects the notion that the simplified technique indicates a symbolic approach, and prefers to talk of a "schematic" technique. Kermode stresses the "ideal clarity" of characterization in pastoral romance which Shakespeare achieves. The in-between shades of real life are rejected by romance, which produces a Sidneian golden world, making clear by selection what "actuality" obscures, as Shakespeare makes in Miranda a shining and unqualified image of chastity.

Why did Shakespeare turn towards the new discipline of undisciplined romance, and what did he make of his material? Nosworthy suggests that he turned to it because it was there, and a challenge to his art. There was a need for new plays to meet the interest in tragicomic romance; Shakespeare recognized "that he had said all he could say, and all that any man could say, in tragic form" and willingly turned in a new direction. But there was little to guide him in new fields. "*Pericles, Cymbeline* and, to a certain but insignificant extent, *The Winter's Tale* were the pioneer colonizing efforts of a Shakespeare more completely without a reputable model than he had ever been." In turning into drama the accepted features of romance, Shakespeare met difficulties which he could only solve by trial and error.

The sustaining of a satisfactory tragi-comic balance is one of the problems implicit in romance material, and the achievement of a perfectly happy ending is another.... Above all, perhaps, there is the structural challenge implied in the romance's demand for alienation and subsequent reconciliation. "Once upon a time...", "Far away and long ago...", formulas so simple and so current in fairy-tale, impose problems of space and time which sorely tax ingenuity when they are transferred to the stage [p. xxxi].

[*Cymbeline* is] the creation of a man perpetually fascinated by his dramatic experiment, surprised and exhilarated by the new sensations and discoveries which the elaboration of his unfamiliar material has yielded [p. xliii].

There is something in these comments reminiscent of the image of the artist Shakespeare to be found in the best chapter (XI) of Quiller-Couch's *Shakespeare's Workmanship* (1918), though, of course, Quiller-Couch was not concerned with the conventions of romance. Quiller-Couch remarked that "every artist of the first class tires of repeating his successes, but never of repeating his experiments". Shakespeare had taken drama as far as it could go in his great tragedies. "Having triumphed in the possible, the magnificent workman has grown discontented with it and started out to conquer the impossible, or the all but impossible." Shakespeare tries to portray dramatically the slow growth of repentance and forgiveness, with its great problem of time. Here is "the same excellent workman passing on to attempt a far more difficult thing than any justification, by a stroke, of the ways of God to man; passing on to attempt the reconciliation, by slow process, under God, of man with man". "Shakespeare's aim in these last plays has brought him at last 'up against' the limitations of his art."

To return to more recent critics, and the limitations of romance, Kermode presents us with a more cerebral Shakespeare than Nosworthy does, an intellectual more occupied with a "conscious philosophic structure" than an artist delighting in the virtuosity of solving in the last acts of his romance all the difficulties he has set himself. "The formulation of poetic propositions concerning the state of human life" is most easily made in certain fables treated in popular tragi-comic form. Here is a popular fashion, here also is the accepted content of ideas of literary romance, and here is Shakespeare ready to carry out (in *The Tempest*) "his last poetic investigation into the supernatural elements in the human soul and human society". Pastoral tragicomedy is a mode of poetic inquiry: to understand the ideas in *The Tempest* we need to understand the conventions of this genre, for *The Tempest* is "a play of an established kind dealing with situations appropriate to that kind". Like all serious pastoral poetry, it "is concerned with the opposition of Nature and Art"; Shakespeare, with his "richly analytic approach to ideas" explores nature and nurture, ignorance and knowledge, lust and self-control, each aspect of human potentiality glancing off the tough hide of Caliban's "nature without benefit of nurture". The play as a whole presents the larger idea of the providential disaster, a "happy misfortune, controlled by a divine Art".

Danby spends little time on the motivation towards romance. Nervous breakdowns and religious illuminations are unnecessary to account for a decision to use a different subject matter, for it is a means of exploring another part of the same moral country to be seen in the tragedies. An earlier chapter of his book has described the *Arcadia* as a "compendious" work, all the features of which are directed towards the great moral end of exemplifying patience and magnanimity. In bequeathing the form of romance, Sidney is inevitably bequeathing the philosophy which the art-form implies. The romance is "orientated towards perfection". Its "interlocked spheres" are

the sphere of virtue and attained perfection; then the sphere of human imperfection, political and passionate, surrounding and likely at any minute to threaten the first; around these again, the sphere of non-human accident, chance, or misfortune, the sphere of the sea and storms; and finally, enclosing all, the sphere of the transcendent, guaranteeing after the 'storm or other hard plights' that the ending will be a happy one—granted patience [p. 80].

Shakespeare responds to the "inward theme" of the romance with almost lyrical excitement in *Pericles*, and treats it with increasing complexity in the later plays. "It is the inwardness which is important: the externals alone would never explain either Shakespeare's excitement or the individuality of his accent." Shakespeare, then, inherits from Sidney a means of portraying certain attitudes which are Sidney's, his own, and also traditional. The vision is both personal and impersonal, a personal recognition of features in a moral landscape which is public.

This public landscape is that of Storm and Adversity, and of Virtue, and Patience, and Charity—a landscape shaped and weathered by the general Christian tradition of the west from Boethius onwards, shaped too (immediately) by the contemporary literary means of depicting this landscape in the Romance.

There are obviously differences of approach among these last three critics and different findings, not to be attributed to the different area of Shakespeare's art they are concerned with. Individual differences apart, there is in Danby and Kermode a similarity in their concern for "ideas-in-poetry" (Kermode's phrase) which romance is capable of expressing. Nosworthy's position (concerning *Cymbeline* alone) is a little different. I find his final introducing of the Phoenix myth, and the Peace which passeth all understanding, very hard to justify (pp. lxxxi–lxxxiv), but up to that point he is governed by a simpler conception of romance, allowing less room for poetic philosophy, than Danby or Kermode. His concern is Shakespeare's solving of certain artistic problems. Romance moves from separation to union, from promiscuity to singleness. In meeting the challenge of romance, Shakespeare sublimates what he is given; in the very structure of the dramatic romance he creates is to be found his own voice. The confusion of the play, its hopelessly varied multiplicity, is itself a recognition "that life itself is not a coherent pattern leading by orderly degrees to prosperity, as in comedy, or to destruction, as in tragedy, but a confused series of experiences, good and evil, grave and gay, momentous and trivial". The great act of union of those who have been parted acquires a spiritual value, it is Shakespeare's "most complete and triumphant vision of unity".

AGENDA

The irresponsibility of judging the work of others, without standing in the dock oneself, will not be lessened by suggestions about the paths which criticism might usefully take. We can probably afford some fallow years in discussions concerning the seriousness of the Romances; at least until the manner in which they may be said to be serious has been rather more carefully defined. Those who have investigated the relation of Shakespeare's last plays to the conventions and potentialities of romance have brought illumination where before there was so much darkness, but even so it might be said that they sometimes attribute the wrong kinds of profundity to these plays. Danby sounds a cautionary note when he remarks that over-anxiety about the greatness of Shakespeare's last plays may lead to a distortion of their tone. "Shakespeare's last plays are not conceived at the same level of seriousness as Dante's *Paradiso*. They have an *ironia* of their own." They are "adjusted to the level of entertainment, controlled by an intention 'which was to please'." 'Controlled' is a better word than 'adjusted', but the notion is obviously true. But the question which too few ask is, what kind of emotional response were the Romances designed to arouse? Has not the 'delight' of romance been rather neglected? Romance surely has its own catharsis in the satisfaction of those who witness the reconciliations and reunions which close each of the plays: Marina restored to Pericles, Imogen to Posthumus, Hermione to Leontes, Perdita joined to Florizel, Miranda to Ferdinand, and Prospero restored to his dukedom. It is, primarily, the satisfaction which these triumphs bring to the audience which is the aim of the Romances—and of all romance. It is an end in itself. It seems, perhaps, something of a licence to extend this satisfaction into a recognition that the author was, in life, an optimist; a recognition that Shakespeare made any general statement about the triumph of good over evil in this world or the next, about the continuity of things, or even about the power of forgiveness to subdue the erring and to change them. At the end of *Henry V*, a play of war, the invader is betrothed to the daughter of his enemy, and the two stand together while their union is blessed with all dignity and ceremony. Here is a happy ending, unity out of disunity, the hope for the future, the old blessing the young, the sense of divine guidance and promise. But as the stage clears, the Chorus reminds us of what the future holds in store *in fact*. He tells us that the fruit of the union will be Henry VI, in whose reign the kingdoms now united will be torn apart and England itself bleed. No one suggests that at the close of *Henry V* Shakespeare is making a serious comment on the condition of human life, either optimistic (before the Chorus speaks) or cynical (after the Chorus has spoken). The play of *Henry V*, like each of the Romances, is an action "complete in itself"; it is a single and entire experience, ending in triumph, concord and peace. The reign of Henry V also existed in history; as the play is rounded off with the completion of the action in marriage, so (since it is also a piece of history) it is necessary for Shakespeare to remind his audience of what really followed for the historical personages. The play is a nice moral of the slipperiness of the relations between life and art.

To criticize the last plays in terms of the formal requirements of romance and the emotional response of the audience seems to me a very strenuous task considering the temptations we are exposed to of taking short cuts to Shakespeare's vision. But it is probably the only way of not falsifying those moments in these fantastic plays when Shakespeare's verse rarefies the air and we know perfectly well that something important is being said. But, as I have suggested, criticism might for the moment ignore the illumination and the universality in the last plays. If the light which has been the main attraction of the Romances seemed rather pitifully dimmed while more mundane investigations were made into the nature of romance, we might at least have the hope that from modest beginnings, and taking each of the plays on its own, we might learn a critical language capable of interpreting the Romances.

THE STRUCTURE OF THE LAST PLAYS

BY

CLIFFORD LEECH

The experience of time makes us aware of both cycle and crisis. On the one hand, today repeats yesterday's pattern and foreshadows tomorrow's, the seasons revolve, and the life-patterns of the generations are at one with each other. On the other hand, we have the notion of the decisive happening, the moment of truth and of choice, beyond which there is no going back, no re-currence of what preceded that special point of time. In forms of art that make use of the time-dimension—literature, music, drama, film—both these aspects will potentially exist, and either may receive the greater stress. The opposing extremes can be illustrated in the news-reel (for cinema or television) and the documentary film. In the first, there is the record of a unique event, the coronation of a queen, the marriage or burial of a popular figure, a conflagration, or an incident from war: each of these is presented to us as a moment with interesting causes and effects, a key-moment in a series. In the second, there is the suggestion of a recurrent pattern, the making of a particular product, the general habit of life of a community, the passing of the seasons within one spatial context. Dylan Thomas' radio-play, *Under Milk Wood*, is an obvious example of this cyclic representation, despite the poet's highly individual interpretation of life in Llaregyb; so too is Georges Rouquier's film *Farrébique, ou les quatre saisons*; and Vladimir and Estragon, in Samuel Beckett's *Waiting for Godot*, spend each day in the same pattern of waiting and improvised stratagem. On a different scale, we find a similar phenomenon in the long novel that merely narrates a hero's adventures, suggesting both the variety within the individual life-pattern and the near-repetition of that pattern within a particular community. Jack Wilton and Nicholas Nickleby are not individualized and are basically unaffected by event: their stories are only nominally theirs. But in the generality of writing the cyclic representation tends to be less extreme. However firmly the cyclic pattern may be underlined, there is a tendency to suggest a uniqueness in the action presented, to find special moments of beginning and ending, which shall hint at, even if they do not affirm, the idea of crisis. Indeed, this is common even in the films of the Italian neo-realist school. Federico Fellini's *I Vitelloni* is a study of a group of young men who are drifting through the post-war years, living on their relations' help, having neither firm purpose nor, it appears, the chance of decisive action. Yet the maker of this film chooses a dramatically striking moment—a girl's realization that she is pregnant—to begin his account of the matter, and concludes by suggesting that one of the young men has come to some realization of his responsibilities and that another has made a break with the environment in which he rotted. Yet there is an admission that, for the rest of the group, things will go on as before, and we in the audience are not perhaps made to feel confident that anything decisive has happened.

This example from contemporary cinema is not without point in a discussion of Shakespeare's final plays. We shall find in the first and the last of them an approximation to the purely cyclic representation of time, and in the others an attempt to reconcile the notions of cycle and crisis. That the attempt to suggest crisis, in the middle plays of the group, is not in every instance successful does, I think, depend on the fact that, in the ultimate sense, the only true form of crisis is death (and resurrection, if you will) or enduring madness or a sin beyond mercy or a longing finally frustrated. Comedy may choose to present marriage as its point of resolution, but we can accept that only for pleasure's, not truth's, sake. The realization that one will never get to Moscow is, on the other hand, a valid terminal point.

It is normal for the major plays of ancient, medieval and modern times to depend primarily on the notion of crisis. Oedipus comes to know his sin and blinds himself; Christ is crucified, and rises from the dead; the terrified Everyman is brought to the point of recognizing vanity and of final submission to God's will; Hamlet knows himself poisoned and gives Claudius his death-thrust; the Lady from the Sea makes her choice, in freedom and on her own responsibility, and a new pattern of life is established for her. The fact that this last example does not convey complete conviction, does in fact remind us of the endings of Shakespeare's last plays, does not lessen the emphasis that Ibsen has put on the notion of crisis. In all these instances, of course, there is a suggestion of the cyclic behind the sense of the unique. Oedipus and Hamlet and Ibsen's Ellida are symbols of humanity in general, and their sudden enlightenments are not foreign to us; Everyman is presented as a model for us to emulate; and Christ's passion and resurrection are understood as co-existing with man's sin and prayer for forgiveness. But the immediate emphasis of these representations is on the uniqueness of the event, its special relevance to the figures immediately before us, who have no going back, no possibility of covering again the same ground. On the other hand, we can find drama, in the Elizabethan age and at other times, where the emphasis is rather on the possibility of repetition. A likeness between *Cymbeline* and the anonymous play *The Rare Triumphs of Love and Fortune* (*c.* 1582) has recently been mentioned by J. M. Nosworthy,[1] and indeed we may bear this play in mind in relation to the last plays as a whole. In Act I we are on Olympus, where we learn of a quarrel between Venus and Fortune, each wishing to exercise the greater influence on human life; the remaining four Acts present the story of the lovers Hermione and Fidelia, who are made subject in turn to the favour of Venus and the hostility of Fortune. The alternations of good and ill come to an end when Venus and Fortune agree no longer to exercise contrary influences. This resolution came in Act V because that was the point where a play had to end: clearly there was nothing inherent in the situation to cause the reconcilement, no reason why the good and bad luck for the lovers should not continue to alternate. The ending is a mere patching-up, and the dominant impression left by the play is one of flux and reflux, of an action which, of its nature, could not have its point of crisis unless the operations of Fortune led the lovers to death. In a less immediately obvious way, a sense of the cyclic is given by Thomas Heywood's *1 The Fair Maid of the West* (before 1610). Here, too, we have alternations of fortune and misfortune and a final assertion of the married happiness of Bess and her gentleman lover Spencer. Before that is achieved, we have their avowals of love, despite the difference in their rank, Spencer's reported death in battle, Bess's valiant sailing against the Spanish enemy in the ship she has purchased with her inheritance from Spencer, her adventures on the high seas, and their meeting again in Morocco, where the Sultan smiles on their love and presides over their marriage. This is an arbitrary point of termination, and when Heywood took up the story again, perhaps twenty years later,[2] he was able to show how further trials and adventures could befall them, how good and bad luck could indefinitely take their turns with Bess and Spencer as with the lovers of *The Rare Triumphs of Love and Fortune*. Even if the Second Part had not been written, we could see that the wedding is an emphatic, rather than a decisive, moment in their life-patterns: if separation and reported death could come before, they could as well come later.

During the Elizabethan years the idea that a play should have five Acts had a wide currency. We do not know for certain whether at the public theatres around 1600 there were four pauses in the action, but certainly there is good evidence for the practice at the private theatres. In any event, many of the public theatre plays of that time were given a five-Act division when they were printed, and it is evident that, at least in some cases, this represented a five-phase structure that was in the dramatist's mind during composition. There can be no doubt, too, that this form of structure became general not long after the beginning of the seventeenth century. It was a structure that, as T. W. Baldwin has shown, derived from the medieval and Renaissance commentators on Terence.[3] This was subject to considerable variation, both because it was adapted for tragic writing and because individual dramatists experimented freely in their choice of subject-matter and their placing of emphases within the structure. Nevertheless, a departure from the inherited pattern was, in most cases, likely to be a conscious departure, and the idea of the pattern remained more or less constant in the drama before the Civil War. It is possible, therefore, to present a generalized picture of Act-structure which the dramatists appear to have had before them as a norm. The first Act would present a situation, indicating tensions and oppositions, hopes and plans, a ranging of forces one against another. The second would show these forces becoming active, so that in the third there would be open conflict. Yet this would bring no resolution: rather, it would appear that a momentary *impasse* was reached, a height of complication ("the *Epitasis*, or busie part of our subiect", as Jonson described it[4]) which could not be resolved without a new movement in the action. This new movement would be initiated in Act IV—as when Lucius goes to the Goths in *Titus Andronicus*, or when Malcolm is seen among the English in *Macbeth*, or when the scene changes to outside the city in *Timon of Athens*, or when Sebastian meets Olivia in *Twelfth Night*—and would achieve its consummation in Act V. This disposition of material inevitably implies an emphasis on the notion of crisis. What is involved in such an action is the presentation of a unique conflict of forces, with first an indecisive and finally a decisive encounter. If the play is a comedy, we may feel that the ending is provisional, but we are discouraged from feeling that it is a mere point of rest. There is, moreover, a strong sense of determinism in such an action: with such characters and such a situation given, there can be only this result. To follow Horace's advice to plunge *in medias res*—and in some measure the plays on this pattern recognize the wisdom of the precept—is to accept the notion that a particular life-process is, after its initiation, unalterable.

All of Shakespeare's last plays that were included in the First Folio were there divided into five Acts, and W. W. Greg has pointed out that this is what we should expect of plays of their date.[5] *Pericles*, not in the Folio, is the only one of the group to appear in a Quarto edition: there, as almost invariably in Shakespeare Quartos, there is no indication of Acts. Nevertheless, the play manifestly falls into five separate sections, corresponding to the five Acts of the modern editors.[6] The first section gives us the adventures of Pericles at Antiochus' court, his flight to Tyre and then from it, and his arrival at Tharsus with the corn for the city of famine. Clearly there is here no plunging *in medias res*, no opposition of forces that will be demonstrated throughout the play: Antiochus plays no part in Act II, and his death is reported in Gower's speech before Act III. Though the Quarto has no Act-headings, it has a line across the page after the scene of the arrival in Tharsus, and another after the scenes in Pentapolis that we now call Act II. The Pentapolis scenes do, in fact, constitute a playlet in themselves. A knowledge of Act I is not needed for their understanding: when the play was performed at Stratford in 1947, the omission of the opening Act seemed to cause no uneasiness or puzzlement. And Act II ends with the marriage of Pericles and Thaisa and their departure for Tyre. There is not this extreme degree of separateness in Act III, yet it manifestly constitutes a phase in the action: it begins very much as Act II did, with a dumb-show inserted within Gower's speech, showing Pericles called back to his kingdom; then we are shown how Thaisa apparently dies, is revived by Cerimon and finds refuge in Diana's temple, and how Marina is born, and left in the care of Cleon and Dionyza. At the beginning of Act IV Gower indicates that time has passed, enough of it to allow Marina to grow up, as Perdita was to grow up between Acts III and IV of *The Winter's Tale*. This Act presents the adventures of Marina up to her escape from the brothel in Mytilene. Her story is interrupted in IV, iv, where Gower shows us, in dumb-show, Pericles' grief at the report of her death. This is the first time Gower has appeared within an Act, and it is his first speech consistently (apart from the opening lines of Marina's epitaph) in decasyllabics: we may suspect some revision of the text here, to insert a fitting prelude for Pericles' distraught condition in Act V, but the unity of the Act is not impaired by this, since Marina is still its focal point. The fifth Act is wholly given up to the two reunions, at Mytilene with Marina, at Ephesus with Thaisa. Thus we have a manifest five-Act structure, but one quite different from the general pattern outlined above. There is no reason why further adventures should not have taken place, demanding their separate phases in the action. The possibility of internal strife at Tyre is hinted at in Act II: this could have been used to fill an Act of its own, with Pericles returning from Pentapolis to make all right, and then losing Thaisa on a subsequent voyage. Or Marina might have married Lysimachus at the end of Act IV, have been separated from him and endured further hardships in another Act, before meeting her father and coming to her story's end. Certainly such things were not in the source-books, but what matters is that the five-phase division is not inherent in the nature of the story, but is imposed on the story because of its traditional authority.

More important is the fact that the ending of the play is not truly a point of finality. Certainly Shakespeare has done much to make us accept it as such. A goddess has intervened, instructing Pericles to travel to Ephesus (though only chance has led him to Mytilene), and the reunion at the end, coming after a long double separation, has the effect of establishing a new condition of things. But basically this is no more stable than the union of Bess and Spencer at the end of *1 The Fair Maid of the West*. A substantial part of an individual's life-story has been presented, with no cause-and-effect relationship between most of its happenings. Fortune alternately frowns and smiles, and there is no immunity won, no journey to a point outside Fortune's range. The play has the character of a novel in which the hero's fortunes are traced from an early moment in his life to a convenient halting-place some years later. We have the sense of a life-cycle, which can be repeated both in other lives, and, in its essentials, in the same life if our vision is extended. There is no need for us to consider how Shakespeare came to handle such a story, or whether *Pericles* is wholly his. The important thing is that it is a new departure in his work.

In the early and middle history-plays, as well as in the comedies and tragedies, there had previously been a strong sense of cause and effect. Accident could play a part, a considerable one in *Romeo and Juliet*, but the dominant impression was always that of a process developing—and, in its main outlines, inevitably—from the premisses of the exposition. And from this new departure in *Pericles* there was to be no turning back. The structural patterns of the plays that followed were to be more complex, and indeed in *The Winter's Tale* and *The Tempest* there is manifestly an attempt to fuse the notions of cycle and crisis, but the impress of *Pericles* is in some measure on each of its successors.

Cymbeline, though divided into Acts in the Folio, shows a remarkable independence of the traditional pattern. The initial situation—comprising Imogen's marriage to Posthumus, his banishment, her father's anger, her step-mother's veiled hostility, Cloten's desire—is simply a starting-point, like Pericles' wooing of Antiochus' daughter: there is no preparation here for the wager-plot or for the conflict with Rome. The first Act takes us up to the scene in Imogen's bedchamber, where Iachimo emerges from the chest and collects evidence that will convince Posthumus of his wife's infidelity. The second is principally concerned with the continuation of the wager-plot, but contains the first hint of the conflict with Rome and displays Cloten's pursuit of Imogen more fully: there is a striking end here, with Posthumus' outcry against women. In the third Act we have the development of the political strife, and the arrival of Imogen in Wales. This introduction of a new locality, with developments that will materially affect the ending of the play, is characteristic of a fourth Act of the usual sort: here it seems introduced with no regard for the traditional pattern. At the end of this Act, however, we have a scene in Rome where a Senator announces the levying of a fresh army to support the one in Gallia. J. M. Nosworthy has suggested that this scene may have got into the wrong place,[7] but it does provide a means of bringing all the characters together, and in that way is an acceptable linking-scene with the following Act. Then, in Act IV, we have careful preparations for the *dénouement*: Imogen becomes the servant of Lucius, Iachimo is mentioned as joining the Roman force against Britain, Bellarius and the sons of Cymbeline decide to join in the fighting. But there is no new development here, no respite from action (as in the fourth Acts of *Hamlet*, *1 Tamburlaine*, *Othello*). The last Act is a separable unit, with its fifth scene a remarkable series of discoveries, reconciliations, and disposals of the inconvenient.

It will be evident that we have no determined or patterned growth throughout the play. Posthumus' exile does not necessarily lead him to a meeting with Iachimo. Imogen's danger from her husband's wrath is accidentally relieved by her encounters with her brothers and with Lucius. The coming together of all the characters in Act v, with Iachimo's repentance and confession, the Queen's death and confession, and Cymbeline's decision to make a peace favourable to his conquered enemies, is the contrivance of Fortune or of Providence, not the simple conclusion from the play's premisses. Certainly Shakespeare was at some pains to suggest a finality, something more decisive than a mere tale's ending. He brought Jupiter on to the stage, and the god prophesied the happiness of Imogen and Posthumus and the discovery of Cymbeline's sons; and the Soothsayer's vision, reported in Act IV, presages peace between Rome and Britain. Indeed, we are told:

> The fingers of the pow'rs above do tune
> The harmony of this peace.

(v, v, 466–7)

Because the ending is so thorough in its discoveries and reconciliations, because the gods have spoken, because the war is ended with good will on both sides, we may feel that finality has been achieved. Nevertheless, the action remains one of alternation between Fortune's smiles and frowns. At the end the things of woe are banished, but we have no certain sense that the putting to rights is final. Cymbeline (however much he will blame his Queen for his hostility to Posthumus and to Rome) may be temperamental yet; Posthumus, once so easily misled concerning his wife, may entertain doubts again. This tale is over, but the characters have not reached a point of no return. The play echoes *Pericles* in its loose narration, in its final reunions, in its occasional brutality (as in Imogen's disregard for Lucius' life, despite his expectation, when Cymbeline offers her any boon she may choose), in its employment of a divine appearance. But it has not the neat five-phase structure of the earlier play, the writer being content to let the story develop with little reference to Act-division: he seems, in fact, to be concerned only to end an Act at a striking or an anticipatory point of the story.

In so far as *Cymbeline* is the story of Imogen, it is close indeed to *Pericles*. But it is also the story of Posthumus, and in that respect it looks forward. Here we have guilt, punishment, repentance, and a final mercy. That was to provide the central pattern for *The Winter's Tale*, which shows an altogether firmer structure, and a return to the traditional arrangement of Acts.

Here indeed the first Act presents us with a firm exposition: Leontes' suspicion and Polixenes' flight from Sicily give us the groundwork for the later developments. Then Act II shows us the arrest of Hermione and the preparations for her trial. Yet, despite the threat, it seems difficult at this point to assume that the course of action will be disastrous. It is Leontes who determines to consult the oracle—in Greene's *Pandosto* it was the innocent wife who made the appeal to the god—and in other ways he shows himself not without mercy, modifying his first order to Antigonus that the new-born child must at once be killed. The first scene of Act III seems to confirm our confidence that the danger will be averted, as Cleomenes and Dion report their experiences at Apollo's shrine and emphasize, as it were, the benevolent intent of the god. But the next scene brings the *epitasis*, when Leontes refuses to credit the god's word and is immediately punished by the death of Mamillius and the apparent death of Hermione. Finally in this Act Antigonus leaves the child Perdita on the Bohemian sea-coast, and is devoured by the bear: the Shepherd and the Clown find the child, and in their easy talk provide a link with the following Act and once again prevent us from feeling over-seriously concerned. The new departure characteristic of fourth Acts, but here much more firmly underlined, is introduced by the chorus-speech of Time: this casual presentation of time-healing helps us to come to terms with the new development, both because of the time-lapse and because of the relaxed tone of the speech. At the end of Act IV, the *dénouement* is thoroughly prepared. Florizel and Perdita are on their way to Sicily, Camillo has told us that he will get Polixenes to follow them, and we know that Perdita's identification papers will accompany her. Yet the main concern of Act V, Hermione's reappearance, is not prepared for. Indeed in III, ii Leontes had spoken of going to view her dead body; in III, iii Antigonus reported seeing her in his dream and deducing her death from that; the oracle in III, ii gave no hint of her survival (it could easily have included the words "the king shall live without a wife" instead of "without an heir"); and in the play's source Greene did not resurrect the King's wife. Moreover, Hermione's survival, in being kept secret from the audience as well as from Leontes, is unique in Shakespeare's work. It looks as if Shakespeare's original intention in this play was that Hermione should really die in the third Act, and that the reunion in the fifth should concern only Leontes, Perdita and Polixenes.[8] When, however, he came to Act V, he may have realized that he had left himself hardly enough material for a satisfactory final Act: Perdita had only to be identified, and all would be put right. He would not want to continue the story as in Greene, with Leontes contracting a passion for his unknown daughter: this is no matter for a final Act, and it would not fit into the pattern of sin, repentance, punishment and mercy that informs the play. It was perhaps only when nearing the end of the play's composition that he remembered Thaisa. Having decided that Leontes, like Pericles, should find his wife as well as his daughter, Shakespeare profited from his earlier handling of this sequence of events. In *Pericles* the stress is on the finding of Marina, and the reunion with Thaisa is, in comparison, summarily handled. Here the last Act skilfully leads up to Hermione's resurrection, the reunion of Leontes and Perdita being narrated by some excited gentlemen of the court. If, however, there was a change of plan in *The Winter's Tale*, it did not affect the Act-structure, which is firmly made and in the traditional mode.

This structure is related to the thought-pattern of the play. It is, at first glance, the "sad tale" that is "best for winter" mentioned in II, i, yet it achieves a sense of finality that is altogether absent, despite the gods' interventions, in *Pericles* and *Cymbeline*. This, after all, traces the pattern of a generation's irreparable loss. Time, for all his jocularity in IV, i, will not have his sands pushed back. On seeing the statue that is Hermione, Leontes exclaims:

> But yet, Paulina,
> Hermione was not so much wrinkled, nothing
> So aged as this seems. (v, iii, 27-9)

When he has his wife again, their story is virtually over: we cannot envisage his raging with jealousy again, now that time and its long sorrow have operated on King and Queen alike. It is the young whose story is not yet ended, but Florizel and Perdita are not central figures in the play. They suggest the flux of things within which the story of each generation fulfils itself. The peace at the end of *The Winter's Tale* is sad as well as solemn, and the more definitive for that. Despite what appears to have been a change of plan during composition, this is the most fully articulated of the Last Plays. The suggestion of flux in the unfinished story of Florizel and Perdita combines with the apprehension of crisis for Leontes and Hermione, with its ultimate resolution after many years. Strangely, it is the apparently unforeseen resurrection of Hermione that allows Leontes to hold the central position in Act v, and for the ending of the play to suggest a true, a by no means factitious, finality: if the statue-scene were missing, we should indeed still have a sense of finality in Leontes' loss, but the stress would be on the younger generation and its unfinished story.

The accidents of composition may have played their part in the structural achievement of *The Winter's Tale*, but there can be no doubt that Shakespeare in *The Tempest* aimed from the beginning at a firm articulation. This time the central figure was to be, not the offender who comes to repentance, but the sufferer who is also an incarnate Providence, measuring with care his punishments and mercies. Prospero is the dream-figure of ourselves which we all from time to time imagine, elevated by a special dispensation to a position of full authority over our enemies and even our friends, able with a nod to perplex, to chastise, to pardon. He may remind us of Baron Corvo's strangely elevated hero in *Hadrian VII*, who within a short time from the novel's beginning is seated in the papal chair. There is no need for a theophany in this play, for Prospero has himself the divine capacity: when the figures of Juno and Ceres appear in the masque, they are Prospero's spirits, to be invoked and banished at a word. The play will, like *The Winter's Tale*, show sin and punishment and repentance and pardon, but it is lesser figures who will suffer this chain of experiences: in the centre is the deprived Duke of Milan, who will impose his law and finally resume his princely status. But a difficulty lies in the fact that Prospero is indeed a dream-figure. Once he moves back into the society of men, he re-enters the world of flux. Abandoning the authority of magic, he is subject once again to the dangers that he knew, years before, in his duchy. Moreover, there is no sense of finality in the stories of those he punishes and pardons. Antonio and Sebastian receive their rebuke, for their planning of Alonso's murder, in a mere aside; Caliban will "sue for grace" because Prospero is more imposing in his ducal robes, as well as evidently more powerful, than the drunken Stephano in his borrowed finery; Miranda's dazzlement at the "brave new world" (which includes Antonio and Sebastian among its "goodly creatures") suggests the reverse of finality in her story. Prospero at the play's end, implying Alonso's responsibility for Trinculo and Stephano, admits his own responsibility for Caliban:

> Two of these fellows you
> Must know and own; this thing of darkness I
> Acknowledge mine. (v, i, 274–6)

In this there is surely a hint of his power's limits, of his belonging (despite all the authority of magic in the past, of ducal status in the future) to Alonso's world. Certainly a suggestion that a process is complete is contained in the assertion that henceforth "Every third thought shall be my grave". The sense of tiredness that is implied here is indeed not unlike that that finally oppressed Corvo's Hadrian, who, however, was allowed assassination when the dream of power faded. But we cannot feel a sense of true completion in Prospero's story: what Antonios will intrigue against him yet in Milan, what Calibans will resist his teaching, remain unidentified yet ever potential. His books, now drowned, have enabled him to discomfit his enemies within the play. The future stretches ahead for him as it did for Pericles and Imogen, with the possibility that the play's pattern of events can recur.

Yet it is obvious that Shakespeare in his planning of this play aimed at conveying a sense of crisis, of the achievement of a decisive moment in the lives of Prospero and his subjects. The Unities are preserved, and the play contains frequent time-references that indicate the total duration of the action as four hours and the rapid sequence of the several happenings. Moreover, there is a firm Act-structure, not quite according to the traditional pattern but fairly close to it. It cannot exactly preserve the pattern, because on the enchanted island there can be no serious conflict: nevertheless, Shakespeare has arranged for the opposition to Prospero to reach its fullest development in Act III, and for the assertion of his power to be increasingly displayed in the succeeding Acts. The total argument, moreover, is presented in five separately apprehensible units.[9] The first Act is a long exposition (more than a quarter of the play), and takes us up to Ferdinand's meeting with Miranda and his immediate subjection to Prospero. Within this Act we have Ariel's fit of rebelliousness, and Prospero's stern handling of this is an image of his handling of the three other rebellions that will be more fully developed in the play. The two scenes of the second Act show us the arrival of Alonso and his company, and of Trinculo and Stephano: in each instance there is exhibited matter for correction. Then in Act III the three rebellions are handled in turn: Miranda, defying her father's injunctions, visits Ferdinand and confesses her love; Caliban, with Trinculo and Stephano, plots against Prospero; Alonso and the rest, whose rebellion lies in the past, are driven to desperation by the vision of the banquet and of Ariel as a harpy, and Alonso is ready to kill himself. Two of these rebellions are disposed of in Act IV, as Prospero releases Ferdinand from toil and consents to his betrothal, and then employs Ariel and the dog-spirits to chasten Caliban and his allies. The famous lines on the mutability of man's works and of Nature herself come between these two assertions of Prospero's power: they provide a commentary on it which does indeed foreshadow the play's final suggestion that the crisis is not yet, is not within the play's ambit. The last Act gives us the end of the remaining rebellion, and puts loose ends into place. It is noticeable that Prospero's words on his abandonment of magic—"deeper than did ever plummet sound I'll drown my book"—remind us of Alonso's decision in III, iii to follow his son to death:

> I'll seek him deeper than e'er plummet sounded,
> And with him there lie mudded.   (III, iii, 101–2)

The abandonment of magic power is, indeed, a kind of death for Prospero. But this ending is a mere re-entry into the flux: as a Duke of Milan, he will become Fortune's subject again. This is part of the undercurrent of the play, in contrapuntal relationship to the Act-structure and the overt affirmation of Prospero's triumph. This undercurrent moves towards the surface at the play's end, and makes it appropriate that, in the Epilogue, Prospero no longer summons elves and demi-puppets but speaks of prayer that may yet bring mercy and pardon.

The sense that nothing is yet completed is perhaps strongest of all in *Henry VIII*. The Prologue indicates that this play will excite pity, and present truth with some spectacle; it will, however, avoid bawdry, battles and clowning; its substance will be the falls of great persons:

> Think ye see
> The very persons of our noble story
> As they were living; think you see them great,
> And follow'd with the general throng and sweat
> Of thousand friends; then, in a moment, see
> How soon this mightiness meets misery.   (Prol. 25–30)

In the first Act we are given the story of Buckingham's fall, which is almost completed; the Queen's, too, is hinted at, as we find Henry meeting Anne; Wolsey is shown in his splendour, with indications of his lack of scruple and the hostility he arouses. There is a striking end to the Act, when Anne takes Henry's fancy at the masque: we can anticipate at this point the execution of Buckingham and the royal divorce. Act II completes Buckingham's story and develops Katharine's to the trial-scene. It ends with an anticipation of Wolsey's fall, as Henry turns from him to Cranmer. There is, moreover, a hint in II, iii of the birth of Elizabeth, as the Lord Chamberlain conjectures, aside:

> and who knows yet
> But from this lady may proceed a gem
> To lighten all this isle? (II, iii, 77–9)

Here, as so often in the play, our attention is directed to events beyond the play's scope, and this particular matter will, of course, be returned to at the end of Act v. Act III completes the falls of Katharine and Wolsey. There is a strong irony in the first scene, where Katharine, feeling baffled by her enemies' power, is unaware that the two Cardinals are attempting to save Wolsey and Rome from the disasters that threaten. Wolsey's fall is not for his demerits: it comes from Henry's impatience to have Anne by his side and from Wolsey's carelessness concerning the inventory. When he knows that greatness for him is past, he is made to think of More, Cranmer, Anne and Cromwell, who are now rising:

> *Cromwell.* . . . Sir Thomas More is chosen
> Lord Chancellor in your place.
> *Wolsey.* That's somewhat sudden.
> But he's a learned man. May he continue
> Long in his Highness' favour, and do justice
> For truth's sake and his conscience; that his bones,
> When he has run his course and sleeps in blessings,
> May have a tomb of orphans' tears wept on him!
> What more?
> *Cromwell.* That Cranmer is return'd with welcome,
> Install'd Lord Archbishop of Canterbury.
> *Wolsey.* That's news indeed.
> *Cromwell.* Last, that the Lady Anne,
> Whom the King hath in secrecy long married,
> This day was view'd in open as his queen,
> Going to chapel; and the voice is now
> Only about her coronation. (III, ii, 393–406)

Here certainly we must assume that the audience is expected to look beyond the end of the play: each one of these will perish at the executioner's hands. Wolsey sees the danger of ambition, and of pride, but it does not occur to him to express regret for his actions against Buckingham, Katharine and the English people. His fall comes through the rotation of Fortune's wheel:

> This is the state of man: to-day he puts forth
> The tender leaves of hopes; to-morrow blossoms
> And bears his blushing honours thick upon him;
> The third day comes a frost, a killing frost,
> And when he thinks, good easy man, full surely
> His greatness is a-ripening, nips his root,
> And then he falls, as I do. (III, ii, 352–8)

It was a mistake to aspire, but his fall, as he sees it, has not come from wrong-doing, and indeed the things in the play that immediately occasion his fall are not among his moral blemishes. At the end of Act III, all we are told to anticipate is Anne's coronation. That insecure exaltation apart, the play seems over. When, in the first scene of Act IV, the coronation is described, the two gentleman commentators bring Buckingham and Katharine and Wolsey to our minds. At the end of the coronation procession, we are told that the falls of the great are always to be anticipated:

> 2 Gentleman. . . . These are stars indeed,
> And sometimes falling ones.
> 1 Gentleman. No more of that. (IV, i, 54–5)

Again our attention is directed to a cyclic process. From this scene we also learn that intrigues at court continue, and that Cromwell's star is yet rising. The one other scene of the Act shows us Katharine's vision before her death. Certainly this is offered as a deliberate contrast to the coronation of Anne: the garland placed on Katharine's head is evidently a promise of something more durable than the crown that Anne has won. This Act has been carefully planned, but again we may wonder, if we have not taken up the hint from II, iii noted above, what is left for a following Act. And even the christening of Elizabeth is obviously not matter enough for that. With a most attractive irony, Shakespeare shows us in the greater part of Act v how Cranmer is saved by Henry from the fall that almost comes upon him. Gardiner looks forward, indeed, not merely to Cranmer's overthrow but to Anne's and Cromwell's too—and we know that all will in time come about. Cranmer is saved by the good luck of Henry's friendship, and Buckingham and Katharine and Wolsey have fallen through bad luck, as Cranmer himself and Anne and Cromwell and More will also, in time, fall. The Act ends, it is true, with the christening of Elizabeth and Cranmer's prophecy of her greatness and even of her successor's. But during this play we have heard too much of the insecurity of man's estate to feel that a new order could ever be firmly established. Indeed, the Epilogue turns our thoughts away from Anne's triumph and from any glory that Elizabeth and James can reflect on her. We are taken back to Katharine, who fell as Anne rose:

> All the expected good w'are like to hear
> For this play at this time is only in
> The merciful construction of good women;
> For such a one we show'd 'em. (Epil. 8–11)[10]

There could be no tight structure in this play, for it is truly a chronicle, beginning arbitrarily with the fall of Buckingham and ending arbitrarily with Anne's moment of splendour. More-over, our attention is repeatedly drawn to events outside the time of the play, and these (apart from the sanguine references to England's condition under Elizabeth and James) concern events of the same kind as we have witnessed in the action. There could be no question of the traditional pattern being used, but Shakespeare has nevertheless taken over the idea of a five-phase structure, and has seen to it that the separate Acts end at impressive moments. Of all the last plays, it is the one that most clearly indicates the cyclic process. Nothing is finally decided here, the pattern of future events being foreshadowed as essentially a repetition of what is here presented. Whether or not this play is wholly Shakespeare's, it brings to a full development an attitude towards life that is inherent in *Pericles* and *Cymbeline* and *The Tempest*, despite Shakespeare's attempts to suggest a definitive moment in each. Only *The Winter's Tale*—his major achievement, surely, at this time of his life—successfully combines the sense of flux, of cycle, in its presentation of Florizel and Perdita, with the sense that some actions are uniquely determining, are matters of crisis, as was Leontes' rejection of the oracular word. Only *The Winter's Tale* faces the realization that repentance is not enough, that 'reunion' is a bogus word, that the only finality (within the world around us) is loss.

NOTES

1. *Cymbeline*, ed. J. M. Nosworthy (*New Arden Shakespeare*) (1955), pp. xxiv–xxviii.

2. On the dating of the two Parts, see G. E. Bentley, *The Jacobean and Caroline Stage*, IV (1956), 568–71.

3. *Shakspere's Five-Act Structure*, Urbana, Ill., 1947: see, especially, the quotations from Landino (p. 112) and Willichius (pp. 231–2).

4. *Every Man Out of his Humour*, III, viii, 102.

5. *The Shakespeare First Folio* (1955), pp. 414, 418, 425.

6. In the Third and Fourth Folios, Act III begins at the modern III, iii, Act IV at the modern IV, iv, and Act V at the modern V, i, 241 (the appearance of Diana).

7. *Cymbeline*, ed. J. M. Nosworthy (*New Arden Shakespeare*) (1955), p. 120.

8. W. W. Greg, *The Shakespeare First Folio*, p. 417, n. 6, has drawn attention to a letter by J. E. Bullard and W. M. Fox in *The Times Literary Supplement*, 14 March 1952, in which it is argued that our Act V is not the original conclusion of the play.

9. W. W. Greg, *op. cit.* p. 418, n. 1, has suggested that the Act-division in the Folio is not only original but indicative of the manner of performance: Prospero and Ariel, he points out, leave the stage at the end of Act IV and are required again at the beginning of Act V. Frank Kermode, *The Tempest* (1954) (*New Arden Shakespeare*), pp. lxxiv–lxxvi, claims that the play follows the traditional Act-pattern, ingeniously suggesting that Prospero's perturbation at Caliban's rebellion in Act IV, and his apparent response to Ariel's counsel of forgiveness in the last Act, are signs of the play's material being forced into the traditional pattern. But Prospero's perturbation is bound up, I think, with his later hint of his responsibility for Caliban, and his prompting by Ariel is needed to bring him to the actual abandonment of magical power (for its prior planning can go along with a comprehensible reluctance).

10. Frank Kermode, 'What is Shakespeare's *Henry VIII* about?', *Durham University Journal*, n.s. IX (March 1948), 48–55, has usefully drawn attention to the 'falls' which constitute the play's action, though he seems to attach far too much authority to the person of the King: the fact that his "conscience has crept too near another lady" puts him firmly on the human level, as do most of his activities in the play and the comments of others upon them. Kermode, moreover, sees in the play a morality-significance which strains credulity. In *Henry VIII* virtue is recognized, but only Time and Fortune's wheel are operative.

SIX POINTS OF STAGE-CRAFT IN
THE WINTER'S TALE

BY

NEVILL COGHILL

It is a critical commonplace that *The Winter's Tale* is an ill-made play: its very editors deride it. A recent apologist, S. L. Bethell, after posing the question "Why is his dramatic technique crude and apparently incoherent?"[1] answers with the bold suggestion that Shakespeare was trying to be funny: instancing several examples in the Florizel-Perdita-Camillo-Autolycus-Shepherd-Clown sequences of iv, iv, he concludes: "...surely this is a deliberately comic underlining of a deliberately crude technique. Considering now the play as a whole, are we not justified in suspecting a quite conscious return to naïve and outmoded technique, a deliberate creaking of the dramatic machinery?"[2]

These conjectures may seem valid in the study, but have no force on the stage. Shakespeare's stage-craft in this play is as novel, subtle and revolutionary as it had been a few years before in *Antony and Cleopatra*, but in an entirely different way: just as he had then found the technical path to an actual and life-sized world—to the drums and tramplings of the Roman Empire—so, in *The Winter's Tale* he hit upon a means of entry into the fabulous world of a life standing (as Hermione says) in the level of dreams.[3]

Stage-craft is a word for the mechanics in the art of telling a story, through actors, on some sort of stage, *with a certain effect*. It must inventively use the facilities available to it. No one was more inventive than Shakespeare: deftness and dexterity of this kind mark all his work, and his surprises (so often, afterwards, felt to be 'inevitable') recall those in Beethoven, of whose last quartets the composer Balfour Gardiner said once to me, with a sigh of envy, "Ah, the desolating old monkey! Never without a fresh rabbit to pull out of his hat!"

Six main charges of creaking dramaturgy have been made against *The Winter's Tale*, severally, by Bethell and the Cambridge editors. Let us consider them one by one, with this thought in mind, that if Shakespeare has demonstrably told his story in certain rather unusual ways, he may well have had some special, and perhaps discernible, intention in doing so: the careful consideration of how a contrivance works may often guide us to an understanding of its purpose.

1. THE SUPPOSED SUDDENNESS OF THE JEALOUSY OF LEONTES

In *Pandosto* (we shall use Shakespeare's names) Leontes' jealousy is made slow and by increase plausible. Shakespeare weakens the plausibility of it as well by ennobling Hermione—after his way with good women—as by huddling up the jealousy in its motion so densely that it strikes us as merely frantic and—which is worse in drama—a piece of impossible improbability. This has always and rightly offended the critics.... (Sir Arthur Quiller-Couch).[4]

Then suddenly with no more hint of preparation—and no hint at all on the psychological plane—Leontes' jealousy comes full upon him (S. L. Bethell).[5]

In an appendix devoted to this subject Bethell adds the conjecture that if Shakespeare had intended Leontes to be jealous from the start he would have brought him on alone "to deliver an appropriate soliloquy".[6] This would indeed have been "a naïve and outmoded technique", one at least as old-fashioned as that which, long before, had so brilliantly opened *Richard III*. But in *The Winter's Tale* Shakespeare went about his business with new subtlety of dramatic invention. To understand it we must begin at the opening scene, a dialogue between Archidamus and Camillo, asking ourselves certain questions in dramaturgy.

What is the reason for this dialogue? What information does it convey? What is it supposed to do to an audience? At first sight it seems to resemble the opening scenes of *King Lear* and *Antony and Cleopatra*: just as Kent and Gloucester prepare us for the division of Lear's kingdom and introduce the Bastard, just as Philo and Demetrius announce Antony's dotage and prepare us to see him enter as a strumpet's fool, so Archidamus and Camillo prepare us to witness a kingly amity between Sicilia and Bohemia, his guest, and to introduce us to Mamillius. There is no other point in the little scene:

Cam. Sicilia cannot show himself over-kind to Bohemia. They were trained together in their child-hoods; and there rooted betwixt them then such an affection, which cannot choose but branch now... they have seemed to be together, though absent, shook hands, as over a vast, and embraced, as it were, from the ends of opposed winds. The heavens continue their loves!

Arch. I think there is not in the world either malice or matter to alter it. You have an unspeakable comfort of your young prince Mamillius.... (I, i, 23–38)

Now whereas Kent and Gloucester, Philo and Demetrius, prepare the audience for what it is about to see (technique of gratifying expectation raised), Camillo and Archidamus prepare it for what it is about *not* to see (technique of the prepared surprise): directed to expect a pair of happy and affectionate friends, the audience is startled by seeing exactly the opposite: the two monarchs enter separately, and one, perceived to be the other's host, wears a look of barely controlled hostility that may at any moment blacken into thundercloud. The proof of this is in the dialogue, which contains all the stage-directions necessary; Polixenes leads in with his elaborate lines:

> Nine changes of the watery star hath been
> The shepherd's note since we have left our throne
> Without a burthen: time as long again
> Would be fill'd up, my brother, with our thanks;
> And yet we should, for perpetuity,
> Go hence in debt: and therefore, like a cipher,
> Yet standing in rich place, I multiply
> With one 'We thank you' many thousands moe
> That go before it. (I, ii, 1–9)

Polixenes is an artist in the language of court compliment, at once flowery and formal, like Jacobean embroidery. All the flourish of his opening lines conveys no more information than this: "*I am visiting the King and have been here nine months.*" His closing lines, however, make it certain that he is standing beside Hermione (she is perhaps upon his arm?) and addressing her. With self-deprecating paronomasia, and a bow no doubt, he pays her compliment:

> And therefore, *like a cipher,*
> *Yet standing in rich place....*

To a visiting King there can be no richer place than next to the Queen. This Queen, however, has something specially remarkable about her: she is *visibly pregnant,*[7] and near her hour, for a day later we hear the First Lady tell Mamillius:

> The queen your mother rounds apace.   (II, i, 16)

This fact about her has been grasped by the audience at her first entry, because they can see it is so; they hear the visiting King say he has been there nine months; who can fail to wonder whether the man so amicably addressing this expectant mother may not be the father of her child? For what other possible reason can Shakespeare have contrived the conversation so as to make him specify nine changes of the inconstant moon? These things are not done by accident; Shakespeare has established a complex situation with the same inerrant economy, swiftness and originality that he used to open *Hamlet* or *Macbeth.*

How then is Leontes to bear himself? Again the clue lies in the dialogue, in the calculated contrast between the flowery language of Polixenes and the one-syllabled two-edged utterances of his host. To the airy conceits of his boyhood's friend, Leontes replies with ironic brevity, sprinkled with equivocation:

> Stay your thanks awhile;
> And pay them when you part.   (I, ii, 8)

To these lines Dover Wilson offers the illuminating note: "Though very gracious on the surface, this remark, Leontes' first, is ominous...'Praise in departing', a proverbial expression, meaning 'wait till the end before praising'."[8] The *équivoques* of Leontes continue to alternate with the flourishes of Polixenes, mannerly on the surface, menacing beneath:

> We are tougher, brother,
> Than you can put us to't.   (I, ii, 15)

> Tongue-tied, our queen? speak you.   (I, ii, 27)

"Our queen" are cold vocables for married love and "tongue-tied" is a familiar epithet for guilt. It is clear that Leontes, as in the source-story which Shakespeare was following, has long since been jealous and is angling now (as he admits later) with his sardonic amphibologies, to catch Polixenes in the trap of the invitation to prolong his stay, before he can escape to Bohemia and be safe. All this, as Dover Wilson's note points out, is easy for an actor to suggest, facially and vocally, and it is the shock we have been prepared to receive by the conversation of Archidamus and Camillo. We have witnessed a little miracle of stage-craft.

2. EXIT PURSUED BY A BEAR

The stagecraft is justifiably described as crude or naïve. We have the frequently remarked *Exit, pursued by a bear...* (S. L. Bethell).[9]

Now let us take Antigonus and the deep damnation of his taking off. The child Perdita is laid on the seashore.... All we have now to do as a matter of stage-workmanship is to efface Antigonus. But why introduce a bear? The ship that brought him is riding off the coast of Bohemia and is presently engulfed with all her crew. The clown sees it all happen. Then why, in the name of economy, not engulf Antigonus with the rest—or better still, as he tries to row aboard? If anyone asks this editor's private opinion, it is that the bear-pit in Southwark...had a tame animal to let out, and the management took the opportunity to make a popular hit (Sir Arthur Quiller-Couch).[10]

Let us note the mild self-contradiction contained in the above; if the appearance of a bear at this point would make "a popular hit" it would be a very good piece of stage-workmanship, supposing it to be consistent with the story to be told, as it demonstrably is.

...nor can it be disputed that tame bears (very tame) were seen upon the stage at this period. The popular *Mucedorus*, for example, was revived in 1610 or 1611, and a new scene was written...in which the clown, in attempting to escape from a white bear, is actually made to tumble over her on the stage.... After this it can hardly be doubted that Antigonus was pursued by a polar bear in full view of the audience at the Globe (J. Dover Wilson).[11]

Now the polar bear is an extremely dangerous beast, even if bred in captivity, and albino brown bears are of the utmost rarity, though it is true a pair was born at Berne in 1575. A brown bear could, of course, be painted white, but brown bears are cross and unreliable;[12] even if they were as mild as milk they could not be counted on for a well-timed knock-about routine such as is needed with Antigonus. On the other hand it is easy, even for a modest acrobat, to personate a bear, with an absolutely calculated degree of comic effect: he has only to be able to walk on all fours without flexing his knees and rise thence on to his "hind legs" for an embrace. There is of course no difficulty in making a bear-costume. Real bears are neither so reliable, so funny, nor so alarming as a man disguised as a bear can be; the practical aspects of production make it certain that no Harry Hunks or Sackerson was borrowed for *The Winter's Tale* from the bear-pit next door. We are back, then, at Q's question *"Why introduce a bear?"*

If we appreciate the problem in dramaturgy that faced Shakespeare at this turn in his story, the answer is clear enough: it was a *tour de force*, calculated to create a unique and particular effect, at that point demanded by the narrative mood and line of the play. It is at the moment when the tale, hitherto wholly and deeply tragic, turns suddenly and triumphantly to comedy. One may modulate in music from one key to another through a chord that is common to both; so, to pass from tragedy to comedy, it may not be unskilful to build the bridge out of material that is both tragic and comic at the same time.

Now it is terrifying and pitiful to see a bear grapple with and carry off an elderly man to a dreadful death, even on the stage; but (such is human nature) the unexpectedness of an ungainly animal in pursuit of an old gentleman (especially one so tedious as Antigonus) can also seem wildly comic; the terrible and the grotesque come near to each other in a *frisson* of horror instantly succeeded by a shout of laughter; and so this bear, this unique and perfect link between the two halves of the play, slips into place and holds.

There are those who will say this is a piece of far-fetched, subjective interpretation; but that is how the scene works on the stage, as Shakespeare foresaw that it would; he deliberately under-lined the juxtaposition of mood, achieved by the invention of the bear, in the speeches he put into the mouth of the Clown, grisly and ludicrous, mocking and condoling, from one sentence to another:

> O, the most piteous cry of the poor souls! Sometimes to see 'em, and not to see 'em; now the ship boring the moon with her main-mast, and anon swallowed with yeast and froth, as you'd thrust a cork into a hogshead. And then for the land-service, to see how the bear tore out his shoulder-bone; how he cried to me for help and said his name was Antigonus, a nobleman. But to make an end of the ship, to see how the sea flap-dragoned it: but, first, how the poor souls roared, and the sea mocked them; and how the poor gentleman roared and the bear mocked him, both roaring longer than the sea or weather....I have not winked since I saw these sights: the men are not yet cold under water, nor the bear half dined on the gentleman: he's at it now.   (III, iii, 88–110)

If Shakespeare did not mean it that way, why did he write it that way? So far from being crude or antiquated, stage-craft such as this is a dazzling piece of *avant-garde* work; no parallel can be found for what, at a stroke, it effects: it is the transformation of tragedy into comedy: it sym-bolizes the revenge of Nature on the servant of a corrupted court: it is a thundering surprise; and yet those Naturals that are always demanding naturalism cannot complain, for what could be more natural than a bear? That this scene is a kind of dramaturgical hinge, a moment of planned structural antithesis, is certain from the dialogue; we are passing from tears to laughter, from death to life:

> Now bless thyself: thou mettest with things dying,
> I with things new-born.   (III, iii, 115)

3. FATHER TIME

In this play of ours, having to skip sixteen years after Act 3, he desperately drags in Father Time with an hour-glass...which means on interpretation that Shakespeare, having proposed to himself a drama in which a wronged woman has to bear a child, who has to be lost for years and restored to her as a grown girl, simply did not know how to do it, save by invoking some such device (Sir Arthur Quiller-Couch).[13]

Time the Chorus is not central at all but a necessary mechanism of the plot... (S. L. Bethell).[14]

Both critics essentially regard Time as a mechanism for over-leaping sixteen years and therefore necessary to the plot. But in fact, if that is all he is there for, he is redundant. His choric soliloquy makes three plot-points: first, that we are to slide over sixteen years, second, that Leontes has shut himself away in penitence for his great sin, and, third, that we are about to hear of Florizel and Perdita. As all these points are clearly made in the scene immediately following (between Camillo and Polixenes, IV, ii), Time and his speech, so far as mere plot is concerned, could be cut without much loss; but the loss to the theme and quality of the play would be enormous, for Time is absolutely central to both and if he were not a character in the play, it would be necessary to invent him. His function is as follows: he shows us we are being taken beyond 'realism' into the region of parable and fable, adumbrated in the title of the play. Time stands at the turn of the tide of mood, from tragedy to comedy, and makes a kind of pause or poise at the play's centre; coming to us from an unexpected supernatural or mythological region, yet he encourages us (in spite of that solemnity) to enter with confidence, by the easy-going familiarity of his direct address, into that mood of comedy initiated by the no less unexpected bear. The same unique imagination envisaged both Time and bear for the great moment necessary to the narrative and to the theme it bears, when the hour-glass turns and the darkness passes. To take a further step in the defence of Time's presence in the play will perhaps lead me into the subjective interpretations I believe myself so far to have avoided; but the risk must be taken. Few will deny that the central theme is the sin of Leontes, which has its wages in the death, and seeming death or dispersion of all that he loves; but, under the guidance of Paulina, this sin is long and truly repented, and the self-inflicted wound, given, as Camillo says, by one who is "in rebellion with himself" is healed. But repentance and healing both take *time*; Time is the tester:

> I, that please some, try all. (IV, i, I)

Time is at the heart of the play's mystery; why should his visible presence offend? We do not take offence at Time with his hour-glass in a Bronzino or a Van Dyck; why then in Shakespeare? He who holds too tenaciously in the study of Shakespeare to 'realism' and the Unities, has left the punt and is clinging to the pole.

4. THE CRUDE SHIFTS TO CLEAR STAGE IN THE FLORIZEL-PERDITA-CAMILLO-AUTOLYCUS SEQUENCE

The stage-craft is justifiably described as crude or naïve...there is a patch of astonishingly awkward management towards the end of Act IV, Scene iv, beginning at the point where Camillo questions Florizel and learns he is determined to "put to sea" with Perdita (IV, iv, 509). Then we have:

> *Flo.*   Hark, Perdita (*drawing her aside*)
> (*To Camillo*) I'll hear you by and by.
> *Cam.*   He's irremovable,
> Resolved for flight. Now were I happy, if
> His going I could frame to serve my turn. (IV, iv, 514–17)

The conversation of Florizel and Perdita is required only to cover Camillo's explanation of his motives and this explanation is given to the audience in soliloquy, with more than a tinge of direct address (S. L. Bethell).[15]

There is nothing in the least awkward, crude or naïve about this stage-craft. As for direct address, its use has been among the chief glories of drama from Aeschylus to T. S. Eliot; let us, then, in considering Shakespeare, for a moment free ourselves of the limitations of the proscenium arch and its attendant fads, one of which is the denigration of soliloquy. It will be safer, too, to eliminate the stage-directions offered in the extract quoted, for they do not appear in Folio; we may have to replace them, but with a difference.

Next, let us consider the context. Perdita has said nothing for thirty lines; her last speech was one of sad resignation to fate:

> How often have I told you 'twould be thus!
> How often said, my dignity would last
> But till 'twere known! (IV, iv, 484–6)

Now she stands anxiously by, listening to her headstrong lover at odds with one who is (to her) an elderly stranger of grave authority, a friend and servant of the dreaded King himself; the Prince is wildly asserting that he is ready to be wiped out of the succession for her sake; she hears him end brusquely with a less than civil defiance of Camillo's kindly counsel:

> What course I mean to hold
> Shall nothing benefit your knowledge, nor
> Concern me the reporting. (IV, iv, 513–15)

Camillo replies with a mixture of rebuke and pleading:

> O my lord!
> I would your spirit were easier for advice,
> Or stronger for your need.

What if we suppose that Perdita, in sympathy with the caution of Camillo, makes some impulsive gesture towards him, at this point, to show her feelings? And why should not such a gesture be the cue for Florizel to swing round on her with his "Hark, Perdita" (as who should say, in a mood of bravado, "Now you listen to me, my girl!"), and take her a few steps upstage for a brief private colloquy, to divulge to her the plan he is keeping so secret from Camillo? To whom, over his shoulder, he throws:

> I'll hear you by and by.

This would lead very simply and convincingly to Camillo's

> He's irremovable,
> Resolved for flight....

Stage-directions such as these I have suggested are certainly no less authorized by the text than those in the extract quoted by Bethell; candid consideration may even judge them more in harmony with the line and feeling of the scene; and so, nearer to Shakespeare's intention. Be that as it may, no audience would be aware of any awkwardness or difficulty.

But Bethell does not base his case on a single instance:

A little later the device is repeated; Camillo has disclosed his plan and ends:

> For instance, sir,
> That you may know you shall not want, one word. (*They talk aside*)
> (*Re-enter Autolycus*)
> *Aut.* Ha, ha! what a fool Honesty is! etc. (IV, iv, 604)

At the end of his speech we have another stage-direction: *Camillo, Florizel, and Perdita come forward.* There is no natural occasion for this 'talk aside' since all three are engaged in it; its only purpose is to allow Autolycus his direct address to the audience on the gullibility of rustics. Worst of all is the device to allow Camillo a last explanation to the audience in an aside. Florizel exclaims:

> O Perdita, what have we twain forgot!
> Pray you a word. (*They converse apart*)

We never hear what they have forgot... (S. L. Bethell).[16]

Let us take these points one by one, first eliminating all the stage-directions quoted by Bethell, for they are the inventions of editors. We can invent our own if we need them. Folio reads (Camillo speaking):

> That you may know you shall not want: one word,
> *Enter Autolycus*
> *Aut.* Ha, ha, what a Foole Honestie is?

There is a colon in Camillo's line (transformed by Bethell into a comma). What is it there for? It is there to indicate a sudden pause; the cautious Camillo, in mid-sentence, has *heard* the approach of Autolycus, laughing, like a Jaques (*As You Like It*, II, vii). He stops, looks round behind him, sees the intruder, frowns, and draws his companions aside to conclude their highly secret colloquy in a corner, leaving the centre of the stage to the still laughing Autolycus. There is nothing very awkward or archaic in that.

Next comes the question what it is that Florizel and Perdita have forgotten; no doubt Bethell is right in supposing this a simple dodge to give Camillo a soliloquy, but no producer would find the smallest difficulty in masking that basic fact, and no audience would even be aware that he had done so; Shakespeare left many such stage-directions to our common sense. At this point upon common sense we must rely, for there are no pointers in Folio, which reads:

> *Flo.* O Perdita: what haue we twaine forgot?
> Pray you a word.

"Pray you a word" clearly must be addressed, not to Perdita, but to Autolycus, so as to draw him away as well, and leave Camillo isolated for his direct address. Therefore what they have forgotten concerns Autolycus too.

Now we have just witnessed a hasty exchange of garments between Florizel and Autolycus; nothing is easier than to suppose that Florizel, having left something that he and Perdita value in the garments he has given to Autolycus, and suddenly remembering, takes the rogue aside with Perdita to recover it. What could this 'something' be? Perhaps the betrothal flowers she had given her lover earlier in the scene, or some fairing bought from Autolycus—it does not matter what, *so long as the audience sees and recognizes it*; for if the audience can see what it is that the lovers have forgotten, there is no reason why they should be told what it is.

5. THE MESSENGER-SPEECHES IN V, ii

But the greatest fault of all, to our thinking—worse even than the huddling up in Act I—is the manner in which the play mishandles Leontes' recognition of Perdita.... If, having promised ourselves a mighty thrill in the great master's fashion, we really prefer two or three innominate gentlemen entering and saying "Have you heard?" "You don't tell me!" "No." "Then you have lost a sight"—why that is the sort of thing we prefer and there is no more to be said (Sir Arthur Quiller-Couch).[17]

It *is* the sort of thing we prefer; in practice this scene is among the most gripping and memorable of the entire play. Whoever saw the production of it by Peter Brook at the Phoenix Theatre in 1951–2 will remember the excitement it created. I know of at least two other productions of the play in which this scene had the same effect, and generated that mounting thrill of expectation needed to prepare us for the final scene. No doubt Shakespeare could have handled the matter just as rousingly in the way sighed for by Q, if he had so wished. Instead he decided on a messenger-speech scene for several voices (an unusual experiment) and made a masterpiece of it.

Bethell holds a different view from Q and believes that Shakespeare used this technique so as to have a last fling at court jargon. His comment on the scene runs thus: "This can only be burlesque; Shakespeare had always enjoyed a thrust at such affectation, and a straight line runs from Don Armado through Osric to these gentlemen in *The Winter's Tale*."[18] But there is no such "straight line". Don Armado is a fantastical foreigner and his language reflects it; Osric, the subtlest of Claudius' emissaries, emits a smoke-cloud of words with the intent to blind Hamlet (as he successfully does) into thinking him of no account; whereas he is the bearer of his death-warrant.[19] The Three Gentlemen of *The Winter's Tale* are neither Armados nor Osrics; they talk the same dialect of early seventeenth-century refinement and wit as is used by Archidamus and Camillo in Act I, scene i, and by Polixenes (though he speaks it in verse) in Act I, scene ii.

There may be a case to be made against the Metaphysicals and their wit, but I do not believe that Shakespeare was here making it; we, if we admire Donne and Crashaw, should not gird at the conceits of the Three Gentlemen. Let us consider their situation; never in the memory of court-gossip has there been so joyful and so astounding a piece of news to spread; they are over the edge of tears in the happy excitement and feel a noble, indeed a partly miraculous joy, for the oracle has been fulfilled; so far as they can, they temper their tears with their wit. What could be a more delightful mixture of drollery and tenderness, or more in the best 'Metaphysical' manner than

One of the prettiest touches of all and that which angled for mine eyes, caught the water though not the fish, was when, at the relation of the queen's death, with the manner how she came to't bravely confessed and lamented by the king, how attentiveness wounded his daughter; till, from one sign of dolour to another, she did, with an 'Alas,' I would fain say, bleed tears, for I am sure my heart wept blood....

(v, ii, 89)

Could Donne have found a better hyperbole than "wounded", or Crashaw a more felicitous conceit for eyes and tears?

6. THE STATUE SCENE

Of all Shakespeare's *coups de théâtre*, the descent of Hermione from her pedestal is perhaps the most spectacular and affecting; it is also one of the most carefully contrived and has indeed been indicted for its contrivance: "Hermione's is not a genuine resurrection...The very staginess of this 'statue' scene acknowledges the inadequacy of the dramatic means" (S. L. Bethell).[20] These dramatic means (Bethell seems to argue) are inadequate to certain religious ends he senses in the play. I had hoped in this essay to avoid those private, still more those metaphysical interpretations, to which even the best of us are liable; but since, by drawing attention to the fineness of Shakespeare's stage-craft in this scene, I may be aggravating the charge of staginess, let it be admitted certainly that Hermione is not a Lazarus, come from the dead, come back to tell us all; that she is *believed* dead is one of those errors which Time makes and unfolds.[21] The spiritual meaning of the play in no way depends on her being a Lazarus or an Alcestis. It is a play about a crisis in the life of Leontes, not of Hermione, and her restoration to him (it is not a 'resurrection') is something which happens not to her, but to *him*. He had thought her dead by his own hand ("She I kill'd")[22] and now finds her unexpectedly alive in the guardianship of Paulina. (So a man who believed himself to have destroyed his soul by some great sin might, after a long repentance under his Conscience, find that that very Conscience had unknown to him kept his soul in being and could at last restore it to him alive and whole.) That is the miracle, it seems to me, for which Shakespeare so carefully prepared.

It had to be a miracle not only for Leontes, but for the audience. His first dramaturgical job, then, was to ensure that the audience, like Leontes, should *believe her dead*. For this reason her death is repeatedly reasserted during the play by a number of characters, and accepted by all as a fact. Shakespeare's next care was to give credentials to the statue. The audience must accept it *as a statue*, not as a woman; so the Third Gentleman names its sculptor, an actual man, Giulio Romano; a novel trick to borrow a kind of authenticity from the 'real' world of the audience, to lend solidity to the imaginary world of the play; it seems to confer a special statueishness. For the same reason Paulina warns Leontes that the colour on it is not yet dry.

But above all Shakespeare stretched his art in creating for his 'statue' a long stillness. For eighty lines and more Hermione must stand, discovered on her pedestal, not seeming to breathe; that is, for some four long minutes. Those among the audience who may think her a living woman, encouraged by Paulina's promise to "make the statue move indeed", must be *reconvinced against hope that she is a statue* if the miracle is really to work excitingly for them. So when at last Hermione is bidden to descend Shakespeare does not allow her to budge; against all the invocations of Paulina, he piles up colons, twelve in five lines; it is the most heavily punctuated passage I have found in Folio. It can be no other than his deliberate contrivance for this special effect; only at the end of the long, pausing entreaty, when the suspense of her motionlessness has been continued until it must seem unendurable, is Hermione allowed to move:

> Musick; awake her: Strike:
> 'Tis time: descend: be Stone no more: approach:
> Strike all that looke vpon with meruaile: Come:
> Ile fill your Graue vp: stirre: nay, come away:
> Bequeath to Death your numnesse: (for from him,
> Deare Life redeemes you) you perceiue she stirres....

There is nothing antiquated or otiose in stage-craft such as this.

NOTES

1. S. L. Bethell, *The Winter's Tale: A Study* (1946), p. 47. This important work is a contribution to the imaginative and philosophical understanding of the play; although in my essay I have only quoted from it to disagree, the disagreements are largely of a technical kind on relatively minor matters.

2. *Ibid.* pp. 49–50.   3. III, ii, 78.

4. Sir Arthur Quiller-Couch and John Dover Wilson, *The Winter's Tale* (Cambridge, 1931, reprinted 1950, p. xvi). This work hereafter in these notes will be referred to as *W.T.* (Camb.).

5. Bethell, *op. cit.* p. 78.   6. *Ibid.* p. 122.

7. A point also noted by Miss M. M. Mahood in her *Shakespeare's Wordplay* (1957), p. 147, in discussing the first line spoken by Polixenes.

8. *W.T.* (Camb.), p. 131.   9. Bethell, *op. cit.* p. 48.

10. *W.T.* (Camb.), p. xx.   11. *Ibid.* pp. 156–7.

12. I am indebted to Mr R. B. Freeman, Reader in Taxonomy, University College, London, for reference to Marcel A. J. Couturier, *L'Ours brun, Ursus arctos L.* (1954), published by the author at 45 Rue Thiers, Grenoble, Isère, from which this information about bears is taken.

13. *W.T.* (Camb.), p. xix.   14. Bethell, *op. cit.* p. 89.

15. *Ibid.* pp. 48–9.   16. *Ibid.* pp. 48–9.

17. *W.T.* (Camb.), p. xxiii.   18. Bethell, *op. cit.* p. 42.

19. I accept the account of Osric's character put forward by Richard Flatter in his *Hamlet's Father* (1949), pp. 119–20.   20. Bethell, *op. cit.* p. 103.

21. IV, i, 2.   22. V, i, 17.

HISTORY AND HISTRIONICS IN
CYMBELINE

BY

J. P. BROCKBANK

The sources of *Cymbeline* are sufficiently known. What now are we to do with them? Source-hunting offers its own satisfactions and it is an acceptable mode of conspicuous leisure, but it should be possible still to bring it to bear more closely on the problems of literary criticism.[1] Its bearing, however, may differ from play to play. It is salutary, for instance, to recognize that striking debt owed by *The Tempest* to travel literature.[2] When we find that Shakespeare's contemporaries allegorized the historical event we may more readily discount E. E. Stoll's scepticism about allegory in the play. I think, too, that the play sheds a backward light upon its sources, making us more alive to their dramatic and poetic potential.

Cymbeline is a different problem. It is not so self-evident a masterpiece. There is the common passage and there is the strain of rareness. The sources and analogues could be used to explain away whatever fails to make an immediate, effacing impression. But they have too, I think, a more positive value. They can show that many of the play's uniquely impressive effects could have been won only out of that specific area of convention that Shakespeare chose to explore. Within this area we can distinguish something like a dramatic genre, and as a label we might take Polonius' infelicity 'historical-pastoral' or, in deference to received opinion, 'historical romance'. Such labels are useful because they tell us what sort of conventions to look out for, although each play is apt to define its own area, make its own map. My emphasis will be on the 'historical', for there is, I think, a way of reading the sources which lends support to Wilson Knight's claim that *Cymbeline* is to be regarded "mainly as an historical play".[3] Criticism may fault his quite remarkable 'interpretation' for trying to evoke a maximum pregnancy from conventions that are insufficiently transmuted from their chronicle and theatrical analogues; but it cannot fault him for recognizing that the fictions of *Cymbeline*, while owing nothing to the factual disciplines commonly called 'historical', seek nevertheless to express certain truths about the processes which have shaped the past of Britain. I shall argue that even the 'romantic significance'[4] of the play is worth mastering, and that we can best master it by way of the chronicle sources.

To initiate the appropriate dialogue between the play and its sources, we might say that *Cymbeline* is about a golden world delivered from a brazen by the agency of a miraculous providence. That archaic formulation would not have startled Shakespeare's contemporaries, and it might equally preface a discussion of the play's alleged transcendent meaning or of its manifest indebtedness to convention. I mean to use it first, however, as a clue to track Shakespeare's reading through the labyrinth of Holinshed.[5]

Holinshed's brief notice of the reign of Kymbeline reads like an old tale, and Shakespeare clearly felt no obligation to treat it as fact. He distinguished firmly between the Tudor material, whose documentary force he retained in the earlier histories, and the Brutan, with which he took the fullest liberties in *Lear* and *Cymbeline*.

There is, however, no obvious reason why he should have turned his attention unhesitatingly to Kymbeline, and since the names of the characters are scattered over a wide span of pages in the second edition of Holinshed, we may be confident that he was widely read in the Brutan phase of the history, that he began at the beginning, and that he read it quite early, culling the name "Iago" in its course. We may indeed regard *Cymbeline* and *Henry VIII* as the last fruits of the Brutan and Tudor chronicles in Shakespeare's dramatic art. They might be presented as complemental plays—a fantastical history and an historical fantasy, but the exercise would be premature without some excursion into the reading behind *Cymbeline*.

The First Chapter of the *Second Booke of the Historie of England* did most, I think, to determine the form and tenor of the play. It tells of the descent and early life of Brute, and includes this passage:[6]

To this opinion Giouan Villani a Florentine in his vniuersall historie, speaking of Aeneas and his ofspring kings in Italie, seemeth to agree, where he saith: "Siluis (the sonne of Aeneas by his wife Lauinia) fell in loue with a neece of his mother Lauinia, and by hir had a sonne, of whom she died in trauell, and therefore was called Brutus, who after as he grew in some stature, and hunting in a forrest slue his father vnwares, and therevpon for feare of his grandfather Siluius Posthumus he fled the countrie, and with a retinue of such as followed him, passing through diuers seas, at length he arriued in the Ile of Britaine."

Concerning therefore our Brute, whether his father Iulius was sonne to Ascanius the sonne of Aeneas by his wife Creusa, or sonne to Posthumus called also Ascanius, and sonne to Aeneas by his wife Lauinia, we will not further stand. But this, we find, that when he came to the age of 15. yeeres, so that he was now able to ride abrode with his father into the forrests and chases, he fortuned (either by mishap, or by God's prouidence) to strike his father with an arrow, in shooting at a deere, of which wound he also died. His grandfather (whether the same was Posthumus, or his elder brother) hearing of this great misfortune that had chanced to his sonne Siluius, liued not long after, but died for verie greefe and sorow (as is supposed) which he conceiued thereof. And the yoong gentleman, immediatlie after he had slaine his father (in maner before alledged) was banished his countrie, and therevpon got him into Grecia, where trauelling the countrie, he lighted by chance among some of the Troian ofspring, and associating himselfe with them, grew by meanes of the linage (whereof he was descended) in proces of time into great reputation among them: chieflie by reason there were yet diuers of the Troian race, and that of great authoritie in that countrie.

There is little here that would be admitted as a 'source' by the criteria of Boswell-Stone, but Shakespeare may well have recognized an opportunity to deploy the conventions of romance in a play made from one or other of the Brutan legends. His story of the lost princes as it has finally reached us is an invention not owed to, but consonant with the strange adventures of Brute. And *Cymbeline* touches, in a different order and to changed effect, the motifs of mysterious descent, hunting, murder (a boy killing a prince), banishment, and chance (or providential) encounter with offspring of the same lineage. There is a kind of obligation here, and in his choice of the names of Posthumus and Innogen (the wife of Brute) Shakespeare seems to offer a playful salute of acknowledgement.

The second chapter offers another piece of ready-made theatrical apparatus. Brute and In-nogen "arrive in Leogitia" and "aske counsell of an oracle where they shall inhabit". Brute kneels, "holding in his right hand a boll prepared for sacrifice full of wine, and the bloude of a white hinde", and after he has done his "praier and ceremonie...according to the pagane rite and custome", he falls asleep. The goddess Diana speaks Latin verses (which the chronicle translates) sending him to an isle "farre by-west beyond the Gallike land". "After he awaked out of sleepe", the chronicle goes on, "and had called his dreame to remembrance, he first doubted whether it were a verie dreame, or a true vision, the goddess hauing spoken to him with liuelie voice". Once again, the vision is not a source but an occasion. It may have licensed the vision of Posthumus—a stage theophany in a play which, like the myth, is concerned with the ancestral virtue and destiny of Britain. Shakespeare drew of course on his own experience of the theatre and perhaps on a memory of *The Rare Triumphs* for the specific form of the theophany, but whether by chance or design the verse form is oddly consonant with the chronicle.[7]

These early passages are important because they reveal most clearly the romantic, numinous aspect of Geoffrey's myth. But Geoffrey was also something of a tactical political moralist, and for him the high magical destiny of Britain was needlessly thwarted by emulation, "revenging" and "dividing". In the chapters between Brute and Kymbeline Shakespeare would have passed much material already exploited to serve a political moral by the authors of *Locrine*, *Leir*, *Gorboduc* and the pseudo-historical part of *Nobody and Somebody*—reigns which for the most part ask to be treated in the spirit of Richard Harvey's *Philadelphus*, as tracts for the times.[8]

The Third Booke opens with an account of Mulmucius Dunwallō, the law-giver, named in *Cymbeline* but evidently more fully celebrated in a lost play called after him.[9] Whether he took it from the old play or the chronicle, the name Cloten (given by Harrison to the father of Mulmucius[10]) may have had for Shakespeare a sly historical as well as articulatory propriety. The brassy Cloten and his mother are hypostatized versions of the arbitrary spleen and malevo-lence that Geoffrey often found antecedent to the rule of law.

Of the fifty or so rulers between Mulmucius and Cassibelane, Holinshed briefly describes a quarter and catalogues the rest. Only one (Elidure) seems to have been touched by the play-wrights, but Shakespeare ignored them and his interest was not quickened again until he reached the point where Geoffrey is confronted by Caesar, the old tale foiled by the modern history, fantasy by fact, romance by Rome. Shakespeare accepted the challenge to admit both, and I think J. M. Nosworthy mistaken in wishing he had done otherwise.[11] For had he done otherwise we might never have heard that "odd and distinctive music" which F. R. Leavis derives from *Cymbeline's* "interplay of contrasting themes and modes".

Kymbeline is named at the centre of a long section dealing with the Roman conquest and the tribute variously yielded and denied by the line from Cassibelane to Arviragus. Shakespeare's readiness to see the tribute as a momentous historical symbol is clear enough from the play, but before we begin to admire and analyse it is worth remarking that he was not alone in trying by supernatural stage machinery and symbolic verse to give something like apocalyptic scale to the tribute settlement. Jasper Fisher's academic play *The True Trojanes*, probably later than *Cymbeline* but apparently independent, testifies equally to a contemporary interest in the conflict and re-conciliation of the two "valorous races" represented by Cassibelane and Caesar.[12] But Shake-speare's treatment yields far more of the potential of Geoffrey's myth than Fisher's.

So far then, Shakespeare's reading offers a paradigm for an action which makes the reconciliation with Rome a high event in the magical movement of British history from the vision of Brute to the golden prospect of the vision of Cadwallader. But it is substance rather for a pageant or a masque than a play. To give it a richer content Shakespeare had to rely in the end on his own resources, but he had scope still to exercise his imagination on other elements in the chronicle. In pursuit of that "odd and distinctive music" he chose to modulate from the Brutan into the Roman key and from the Roman into the Renaissance Italian. The exercise is exquisitely playful, but what prompted him to attempt it?

Holinshed does not often chime well with Boccaccio; Geoffrey's 'romance' was not the sort which delighted sophisticated Italy. And yet it happens, oddly, that the chronicle can supply a gloss to Iachimo's confession in the last act: the dullness of Britain and the subtlety of Italy are Harrison's themes in chap. xx of his *Description of Britaine*. "For that we dwell northward", he says, "we are commonly taken...to be men of great strength and little policie, much courage and small shift"; and after entertaining and dismissing several versions of the same criticism he finishes by giving it a sharp twist to Britain's advantage.[13]

For if it be a vertue to deale vprightlie with singlenesse of mind, sincerelie and plainlie, without anie such suspicious fetches in all our dealings, as they commonlie practise in their affaires, then are our countrimen to be accompted wise and vertuous. But if it be a vice to colour craftinesse, subtile practises, doublenesse, and hollow behauiour, with a cloake of policie, amitie and wisedome: then are Comineus and his countrimen to be reputed vicious.

Harrison would have found Wilson Knight's emphasis on Posthumus as "the simple islander in danger of moral ruin" entirely congenial.[14] The conventional sentiment of the chronicle is concerned with the national character as well as the national destiny. Shakespeare may have seen in Boccaccio an opportunity to mediate the two.

There may have been a second little motive for calling *The Decameron* and *Frederick of Jennen* into the play. W. W. Lawrence compares Posthumus in Italy with "a young Englishman making the grand tour at the end of the sixteenth century", and the allegedly absurd anachronism might be lightly excused by a Chronicle passage used for one of Cymbeline's speeches:[15]

it is reported, that Kymbeline being brought vp in Rome, & knighted in the court of Augustus, euer shewed himselfe a friend to the Romans, & chieflie was loth to breake with them, because the youth of the Britaine nation should not be depriued of the benefit to be trained and brought vp among the Romans, whereby they might learne both to behaue themselues like ciuill men, and to atteine to the knowledge of feats of warre.

Within the spacious perspectives of *Cymbeline* the integrity of Britain is at once nourished and jeopardized by the 'civilizing' impact of ancient Rome and modern Italy upon its heroic and innocent but vulnerable youth.

The play's preoccupation with natural and sophisticated man is, however, something far more searching than anything the sources can suggest to jaded modern eyes. But we can get an inkling of how it might have struck Shakespeare from John Speed's *History* of 1611. Kymbeline himself was not much more for Speed than a name on a coin, but the period of his reign was a theme for rhapsody; it was the time that Christ was born and Augustus ruled in Rome. "Then were the times that great Kings and Prophets desired to see, but saw them not, when the Wolfe and the Lambe, the Leopard and the Kid, the Calfe and the Lyon fed together."[16] In a later passage Speed celebrates the marvellous correspondences between Virgilian and Messianic prophecy: "hee vseth the very words of the *Prophets* in speaking of *a Maid*, and *a Child of a new progenie borne and sent downe from heaven*, by whom the brassy and iron-like world should cease, and a pure *golden age* succeed." Even had it been published earlier, there would be no reason to suppose that Shakespeare read the *History*. The point is that the sceptical historian was a theologian still and could see fit to display these high conventional sentiments at this moment of his account of Britain. Holinshed's (or Fabyan's) brevities noticing the birth of Christ and the rule of Augustus may have stimulated in Shakespeare's imagination a comparable range of thought; hence what Wilson Knight calls the "theological impressionism" of *Cymbeline*.

The same part of Speed's *History* offers reflections on the "Originals of Particular Nations", comparing them on the one hand with "that first beginning of the universall prosemination of Mankind...simple and far from those artificiall fraudes, which some call *Wit* and *cunning*", and on the other to "that first neglective condition" to which men would revolve if "Lawes, discipline, and Customes" did not restrain them.[17] It is a polarity retained but greatly complicated in the play where the episodes of Cloten and the princes explore very nicely the possibilities of man exempt from the rule of law.

That fussy phrase 'historical-pastoral' invites in this context a theological exegesis, but Shakespeare tactfully subdues his material to honour the decorum of the theatre rather than that of theological history. Finding that within the span of Kymbeline's reign he could sustain the spell of Brute's, he undertook to charm Boccaccio and Caesar into the same "system of life".

It is one of the tasks of criticism to observe the poise of the dialogue, to adapt Derek Traversi's phrase, "between convention and analysis". But the poise registers, too, in the handling of stage conventions; the calculated anachronisms of the play as history are matched by a calculated naïvety in its theatrical technique: "the art that displays art", as Granville Barker has it. It seems possible that this springs from small beginnings in the chronicle too. An analysis of the peculiar use made of disguise and garments in *Cymbeline* might fairly open with Harrison's observation, "Oh how much cost is bestowed now adaies vpon our bodies and how little vpon our soules! how manie sutes of apparell hath the one and how little furniture hath the other?"[18] And it might pass to Holinshed's story of Hamo "apparelling himselfe like a Britaine" to kill Guiderius and of Arviragus who "caused himselfe to be adorned with the kings cote armour"; and then to the Scottish chronicle where Haie (Shakespeare's model for Belarius and his sons in the battle scene) refused the rich robes that the king offered him and "was contented to go with the king in his old garments".[19] Shakespeare could keep one eye here on the chronicle and the other on the fashionable theatre.

In turning from the history to the histrionics in the play, however, we must distinguish between that kind of theatrical virtuosity whose effects are merely startling and arbitrary, and that which serves a responsible purpose. The themes which the chronicle offered are portentous and had Shakespeare engaged with them too profoundly he would have tested the resources of the language and the responsiveness of the audience too severely. He would also have lost touch with the mood of the *Brut*, as he certainly does in *Lear*. He abstains therefore from using his giant's strength and allows certain points to be carried by a conventional gesture. His handling of disguise, soliloquy, stage situations, properties and even characters, secures in turn an apt "suspension of disbelief" and an equally apt "suspension of belief". Cloten and the Queen, for example, may be said to represent a range of complemental vices (roughly speaking, the boorish and sophisticated) which menace the natural integrity of the British court. But this is true only of the conventional configuration; they are never allowed to touch the audience deeply or urgently threaten their composure. "The euils she hatch'd, were not effected", it is said of the Queen; and they are not effected because Shakespeare uses soliloquies and asides to make her guile transparent, and allows even her gulls to see right through her. *Cymbeline* indeed lets us into all the secrets, even into the secrets of the playmaker's craft. The 'inconsistency' of Cloten and the Queen is not analysed, for example, but simply exhibited; with a faint but distinct irony and a touch of burlesque their vices are made compatible with that minimal virtue of defiant patriotism they display before the Roman ambassador.[20] The tension (such as it is) is kept on the surface, while in that earlier instance of Queen Margaret in *Henry VI* it has to be dug out. If the characters were defined and explored analytically the discordant potential of the material would fracture the play. It is indeed a tribute to the decorum of the piece that Posthumus cannot for long be compared with Othello, nor Iachimo with Iago, the Queen with Lady Macbeth or Margaret, Cymbeline with Lear, nor yet Cloten with Edmund or Faulconbridge. The stresses are less between good and evil characters than between the ingenuous and the disingenuous—the lighter way of putting it is the apter.

The play offers yet more daring sophistications of stage conventions than those deployed in the plots of the disarmed (and disarming) villains. The iteration, for instance, of the phrase "his meanest garment" leading up to that grotesque mock-recognition scene. In a play which makes so much of deceptive appearances and false judgments, there is sly irony in making the innocent Imogen a false judge and in allowing Cloten's indignation to be vindicated after death. The prevailing transparency of artifice makes one suspect that the 'clotpole' stage head was deliberately displayed as a hollow property to give bizarre point to the lines introducing it, "an empty purse, There was no money in't", and it refines or civilizes the violent pagan force of the symbolic justice administered to "That harsh, noble, simple, nothing" Cloten.

In detail as in large design the mode is self-confessedly artificial. The postulates are openly declared: "Howsoere, 'tis strange, Or that the negligence may well be laugh'd at: Yet is it true, sir"; "do not play in Wench-like words with that Which is so serious"; "This was strange chance"; "By accident I had a feigned Letter of my Masters Then in my pocket"; "Shall's have a play of this? Thou scornful page, there lye thy part"; "Let him shew his skill in the construction". Other touches recall *A Midsummer Night's Dream* rather than *Love's Labour's Lost*: "'Twas but a bolt of nothing, shot at nothing, Which the Braine makes of Fumes"; "What Fayeries haunt this ground?"; "mine's beyond, beyond". There are moments too of self-parody: when Cymbeline interrupts a more than usually mannered late-Shakespearian speech from Iachimo with "I stand on fire. Come to the matter"; and again (one suspects) when the gaoler's "fear no more Tauerne bils" might be Shakespeare's tongue-in-cheek backward glance at Imogen's obsequies. One needs to step lightly on these points; they are slender platforms for commentary. And much the same applies to the play's imagery; the patterns and iterations traced by Wilson Knight, Traversi and Nosworthy are undoubtedly there, but they are signs of opportunities lightly taken as occasion offers; they strike as sequences meant to be glimpsed rather than grasped.

All this does not mean that the entertainment is inconsequential. However conventional the frame of *Cymbeline*, it is still meaningful and it sets the more evocative and searching passages in the order of a significant design. But no matter how sharply-cut the stones in the filigree, we are reminded that the skilled craftsman has the strength to crush the fabric at will. "The best in this kind are but shadows."

It remains true, however, that *Cymbeline* is not organized from "a deep centre" like *The Winter's Tale*.[21] We are haunted by intimations of a profound significance, but it is constantly clear that the apocalyptic destiny of Britain cannot be reconciled with the form of pastoral-romance on any but the terms which Shakespeare offers.

We may sum up by taking a last glance at Imogen. Her votaries from Swinburne onwards may be allowed their extravagances and let pass with an "'Ods pittikins" if they will admit that perfection is not, after all, indivisible. Imogen's perfection is playfully extended to her cookery— "He cut our roots in characters". But she remains in some sense, still, the centre of the play. It is fitting that she should voice most memorably a version of the Virgil verse transmitted through the chronicle, "Et penitus toto diuisos orbe Britannos": "I'th'worlds Volume Our Britaine seemed as of it, but not in't: In a great Poole, a Swannes-nest."[22] She is a princess of Britain, yet theme for the praise of a Renaissance courtier; a pretty page for the Roman Lucius, yet aptly called a "heavenly angel". Her symbolic role is secured both by the dialogue (see the 2nd Lord's speech just before the bedchamber scene) and by the spectacle: "And be her Sense but as a Monument, Thus in a Chappell lying." When she lies 'dead' alongside the body of Cloten in the clothes of Posthumus, the spectacle is an evocative symbol of a triple sacrifice (though the word is too strong)—of an innocence that will revive, an animal barbarity which is properly exterminated and a duplicity (involving Posthumus) which has still to be purged.

Lucius is appropriately named after the first of the Christian kings of the British chronicle, and it happens that the political solution—the tribute allowed from sense of fitness and not won by force of arms—can endorse the ethical in a pageant finale announcing the Golden World with a touch of that "pagane rite and custome" which opens the *Brut*: "And let our crooked Smoakes climbe to their Nostrils From our blest Altars... And in the Temple of great Iupiter Our Peace wee'l ratifie."

My conclusion perhaps resembles too closely the "fierce abridgment" of the last act which "distinction should be rich in". But I would claim that substantially the same result could be reached through an inquiry into the theatrical analogues, from *The Rare Triumphs* through *Clyomon and Clamydes*, *James IV*, *Edward I*, *Common Conditions*, *The Wounds of Civil War*, *Tancred and Gismunda* and *The Dumb Knight* to the revived *Mucedorus*, the plays of Field and Beaumont and Fletcher to *The Second Maiden's Tragedy*. It might be shown, I think, that Shakespeare reconciled the conventions of primitive and sophisticated romantic drama to express similar reconciliations accomplished in the substance of the plot.

NOTES

1. I have in mind Hardin Craig's observations in 'Motivation in Shakespeare's Choice of Materials', *Shakespeare Survey*, 4 (1951). For the *Cymbeline* sources see J. M. Nosworthy's Arden edition (1955).

2. The material of *The Tempest* is reprinted in Frank Kermode's Arden edition (1954).

3. G. Wilson Knight, *The Crown of Life*, 2nd ed. (1948), p. 129.

4. Cf. F. R. Leavis, "Shakespeare...has taken over a romantic convention and has done little to give it anything other than a romantic significance." *The Common Pursuit* (1952), p. 177.

5. I have assumed that Shakespeare used the 1587 *Holinshed* and have ignored a few passages in lesser-known chronicles which might be faintly nearer to the play. My longer quotations are of material not reprinted by Nosworthy or by W. G. Boswell-Stone in *Shakespeare's Holinshed* (1896).

6. *Holinshed* (1587), vol. I, H.E., p. 7/B.

7. Cf. "An Ile which with the ocean seas
    inclosed is about,
  Where giants dwelt sometime,
    but now is desart ground." (*Holinshed* (1587), vol. I, H.E., p. 9/A.)

8. Richard Harvey, *Philadelphus, or a defence of Brutes and the Brutan history* (1593). It argues that the Brutans did exist as they show the qualities (mostly bad) that Aristotle leads us to expect from human nature. Harvey took from the history the cautionary politics Geoffrey put into it.

9. Other lost Brutan plays were the *Conquest of Brute* (*Brute Greenshield*) and *Uther Pendragon*. Had they survived we might have been better placed to recognize the conventions behind *Cymbeline*.

10. *Holinshed* (1587), vol. I, Description, p. 117/A. Boswell-Stone cites a later page where "Cloten" and "Clotenus" are named. But Harrison has "Cloten" with a "Morgan" nearby. Shakespeare may have known Chapter 22 of the 'Description of Britaine'; it gives an abstract of the whole history.

11. Arden *Cymbeline* (1955), p. l.

12. The play is printed in Hazlitt's *Dodsley*, 4th ed. (1875), vol. XII.

13. *Holinshed* (1587), vol. I, Description, p. 115/A.

14. *The Crown of Life* (1948), p. 147. Other points made there could be illustrated from the Description, Bk. ii, chap. 7.

15. W. W. Lawrence, *Shakespeare's Problem Comedies* (New York, 1931), p. 188. The *Holinshed* passage (vol. I, H.E., p. 33/A) is quoted by Boswell-Stone; cf. *Cymbeline*, III, i, 70.

16. John Speed, *The History of Great Britaine* (1611), p. 174. See also p. 189.

17. Speed, *History* (1611), p. 179.   18. *Holinshed* (1587), vol. I, Description, p. 172/A.

19. *Holinshed* (1587), vol. II, H.S., p. 155/B. See also M. C. Bradbrook, 'Shakespeare and the Use of Disguise in Elizabethan Drama', *Essays in Criticism* (2, 1952), 159–68.

20. I think Warren D. Smith (*Studies in Philology*, 49 (1952), 185–94) overstates his claim that Cloten is merely the "vulgar, ill-mannered villain" in this scene. Shakespeare writes perhaps with some memory of Holinshed's Voadicia (H.E., Bk. iv, chap. 11) as well as an eye on Jacobean courtly proprieties.

21. F. R. Leavis, *The Common Pursuit*, p. 174.

22. *Holinshed* (1587), vol. I, Description, p. 2/A.

SHAKESPEARE'S HAND
IN *THE TWO NOBLE KINSMEN*

BY

KENNETH MUIR

Littledale, in what is still the best edition of *The Two Noble Kinsmen*, made two preliminary assumptions: (1) that two authors are discernible in the play; (2) that Fletcher is one of them. Every modern critic would, no doubt, make the same assumptions. The difference of style in the two portions is apparent even to the casual reader; and general impressions are substantiated by more objective tests. Littledale, for example, applied four metrical tests to the scenes he supposed to be by two different dramatists, and arrived at the following conclusions:

	Fletcher	Non-Fletcher
Light endings	3	52
Weak endings	1	35
Light + weak	4	87
Percentage of feminine endings	52·9	28·6
Percentage of unstopt lines	24·6	56·1

The above table alone would establish the fact that the play was written by more than one dramatist. The following table (based on that of Chambers) shows that the figures for the non-Fletcherian parts of *The Two Noble Kinsmen* correspond roughly to the figures of Shakespeare's last plays. (Chambers' figures differ slightly from Littledale's because there is a doubt about the

Play	Percentage of feminine endings	Light endings	Weak endings	Light + weak	As percentage of blank verse
Cymbeline	32	78	52	130	4·9
The Winter's Tale	33	57	43	100	4·7
The Tempest	32	42	25	67	4·5
Henry VIII	47	52	38	90	3·4
Shakespearian part	32	45	37	82	7·1
Fletcherian part	59	7	1	8	0·5
Two Noble Kinsmen	30	50	34	84	8·0

authorship of one or two scenes.) These figures would clearly fit in with the theory that the non-Fletcherian scenes were written by Shakespeare. It will be observed that the percentage of feminine-endings remains approximately the same (30–33), much less than the Fletcher percentage, but that the percentage of light and weak endings rises after *The Tempest*. It will likewise be observed that the percentage of feminine endings in the scenes ascribed to Fletcher in *Henry VIII* is close to the percentage in the corresponding scenes of *The Two Noble Kinsmen*. This metrical argument therefore partly depends on the assumption that *Henry VIII* was written by Shakespeare and Fletcher, though even if Shakespeare wrote the whole play the argument from light and weak endings would still be valid.[1] Whether Shakespeare wrote them or not, there are some scenes in the play which from a metrical point of view might well be his, assuming he wrote a play soon after *The Tempest*.

Alfred Hart's vocabulary tests, which those who deny Shakespeare's hand in the play have conveniently ignored, are perhaps the most convincing proof so far adduced.[2] He divided the play into two parts—Act I, Act III, Scene i and Act V, Scenes i, iii, iv constituting the Shakespearian part—and he demonstrated not merely that the two sections of the play differed from each other, but that the Shakespearian section displayed the same characteristics as those of Shakespeare's last period. The following table, based on two of Hart's, shows the frequency of words not previously used by Shakespeare:

| | Previously unused words: | |
Play	1 word per *x* lines, where *x* =	Words new to our literature, where *x* =
Cymbeline	14	25
The Winter's Tale	13	28
The Tempest	10	18
Two Noble Kinsmen		
Shakespearian part	15	16
Fletcherian part	22	42

Hart goes on to show that the coinages by the part-author of *The Two Noble Kinsmen* were the sort of which Shakespeare was fond. If Hart's article were more widely known it is difficult to believe that Shakespeare's part-authorship of the play would not be universally accepted.

But it might be argued that there was some other dramatist, known or unknown, who was capable of writing these scenes and able to display by accident or design the same metrical characteristics as Shakespeare. H. D. Sykes claimed[3] that Massinger was the author of the scenes not by Fletcher; but as he also ascribed to Massinger the Shakespearian scenes of *Henry VIII* his methods would seem to be unreliable. He certainly offers a number of plausible parallels with Massinger's acknowledged work. He compares, for example, "widdoes to our woes" (I, i, 183) with "marriage of my sorrows" (*Thierry and Theodoret*, IV, ii); and, more strikingly, Emilia's line (V, i, 147)

Allow'st no more blood than will make a blush

with several lines by Massinger:

if impious acts
Have left thee blood enough to make a blush.

(*The Spanish Curate*, III, iii)

Thy intent
To be a whore, leaves thee not blood enough
To make an honest blush.

(*The Duke of Milan*, IV, iii)

the too much praise...
Could not but spring up blushes in my cheeks,
If grief had left me blood enough to speak
My humble modesty:

(*The Parliament of Love*, V, i)

Quite clearly these quotations are related to each other; yet Massinger was notoriously prone not merely to repeat himself, but also to echo other poets. It is significant that the two leading authorities on Massinger's work, A. K. McIlwraith and A. H. Cruickshank, did not believe that he had a hand in *The Two Noble Kinsmen*.

It is impossible to prove authorship by means of parallels. Many dramatists, including Fletcher and Massinger, are imitative; and they tend to echo their own previous work as well as that of other dramatists. But where there appear to be several echoes from Shakespeare's plays in a short passage, it seems more probable that Shakespeare was the author than that another poet combined echoes from a number of unpublished plays. Arcite's prayer is a case in point:

> Thou mighty one, that with thy power hast turnd
> Greene Neptune into purple, (whose Approach)
> Comets prewarne, whose havocke in vaste Feild
> Vnearthed skulls proclaime, whose breath blowes downe,
> The teeming Ceres foyzon...

The phrase "Greene Neptune" occurs in *The Winter's Tale* (IV, iv, 28) and the idea of its changing to purple—Senecan in origin—in Macbeth's "Making the green one red". The "vaste feild" recalls the "vasty fields" in *Henry V* (Prologue); "unearthed" recalls the use of "earth'd" in *The Tempest* to mean 'buried'; Ceres in the same play uses the word "foison", and Lucio in *Measure for Measure* (I, iv, 43) uses the phrase "teeming foison".

Another group of multiple echoes is to be found in III, i.

> This is a solemne Rite
> They owe bloomd May, and the Athenians pay it
> To th'heart of Ceremony. O Queene Emilia,
> Fresher then May, sweeter
> Then hir gold Buttons on the bowes, or all
> Th'enamelld knackes o'th'Meade or garden: yea,
> (We challenge too) the bancke of any Nymph
> That makes the streame seeme flowers: thou, O Iewell
> O'th'wood, o'th'world, hast likewise blest a place
> With thy sole presence: in thy rumination
> That I, poore man, might eftsoones come betweene
> And chop on some cold thought!

The masque in *The Tempest* affords a number of parallels:[4]

> ...And flat *meads* thatch'd with stover, them to keep;
> Thy *banks* with pioned and twilled brims,
> Which spongy April at thy hest betrims,
> To make *cold nymphs* chaste crowns;

There is a reference to *flowers* and bed-*rite* later in the masque. In *A Midsummer Night's Dream* (IV, i, 130–40) the month of May is linked, not unnaturally, with *rite*, *solemnity*, wood-*birds* and *world*; and in *The Merry Wives of Windsor* May is linked with *buttons* (III, ii, 70–1). Arcite's reference to Emilia as

Iewell
O'th'wood, o'th'world

recalls Imogen's description of her husband as "jewel in the world", Cerimon's comparison of Thaisa's eyes to "heavenly jewels" which "make the world twice rich", and the widespread jewel imagery in the plays of the last period.

But such echoes are not in themselves proof of Shakespeare's authorship. They might conceivably be by a clever anonymous imitator; or, since there is nothing surprising in the associations, the resemblances may be fortuitous. It is only when the associations are strange and unusual that they may be said to throw a convincing light on authorship.

Caroline Spurgeon discussed the possibility of determining authorship by a study of imagery; and the most enlightening study[5] of *The Two Noble Kinsmen* from this point of view is that by M. Mincoff. He shows that in the non-Fletcherian scenes much of the imagery is characteristic of Shakespeare, and that there is even an example of a running image (I, i, 77, 117, 167, 240). The author of these scenes shows another characteristic mark of Shakespeare's style, a rapid dissolving of one image into the next, as in the lines—

O my petition was
Set downe in yce, which by hot greefe uncandied
Melts into drops, so sorrow, wanting forme,
Is prest with deeper matter.

Here "the idea of melting drops of ice turns to drops of wax and the impression of a seal".

To these points may be added two others. Like Shakespeare, the author of these scenes sometimes links his images together by puns, as in the description of Palamon (V, iii, 55):

Palamon
Has a most menacing aspect: his brow
Is *grav'd*, and seemes to *bury* what it frownes on.

The other point reinforces the fact that the play was written by two dramatists, and fits in with the assumption that one of the authors was Shakespeare: the fields from which the imagery is drawn in the two parts of the play show some striking differences. There is less imagery drawn from nature in the Fletcher scenes, much less from business and wealth, and none at all from sickness and medicine. The other poet has no less than seventeen images derived from sickness and medicine: e.g.

cure their surfeit
That craves a present medcine...   (I, i, 211)

Thou purger of the earth...   (I, i, 51)

that peace might purge
For her repletion...   (I, ii, 24)

almost puts
Faith in a feavour...   (I, ii, 72)

that healst with blood
The earth when it is sicke, and cur'st the world
O' th pluresie of people...   (V, i, 70)

In spite, however, of the number of disease images, they do not seem to constitute iterative imagery, or at least they are not easily interpretable. Perhaps the iteration of Fortune—nine times in the non-Fletcherian scenes—and the thirty-six references to the gods have more significance. The sudden changes of fortune and the incomprehensible behaviour of the gods form the theme of the play.

Mincoff is right to maintain that

No author has been, or can be suggested whose style approaches that of the doubtful parts of *The Two Noble Kinsmen* even approximately as closely as Shakespeare's does. On the internal evidence alone Shakespeare remains the only possible candidate. The idea of an epigone, unschooled in philological analysis, imitating the minutiae of Shakespeare's style at a definite period down to the very metrical percentages, capable too of such splendid poetry, yet never, apparently, repeating the attempt, is too fanciful to need refutation.

Whether the evidence so far offered for the Shakespearian authorship of parts of *The Two Noble Kinsmen* amounts to positive proof is a matter of opinion. The case seems to me to be so strong that the onus of proof really rests on the sceptics; but I hope in the remainder of this article to bring forward some new and quite unanswerable evidence that Shakespeare wrote at least three scenes of the play.

E. A. Armstrong, in his imagistic study, *Shakespeare's Imagination* (1946), cautiously suggested[6] that image-clusters might be used as an aid to the authentication of Shakespeare's work: "Cluster criticism provides a powerful auxiliary weapon for the critic's armoury, but like every weapon it has to be used with discretion.... It would be deplorable if cluster criticism were to be regarded as in any way superseding other techniques or if its possibilities were to be so exaggerated as to bring its legitimate applications into discredit." Armstrong then refers to *The Two Noble Kinsmen*, and he says that examination of a few clusters in that play gives no "conclusive support" to the claim that Shakespeare was responsible for parts of it; on the contrary "it seems more probable that Shakespeare's influence rather than his handiwork is perceptible in it".[7] The purpose of this paper is to question the validity of this conclusion.

Some clusters, of course, are not peculiar to Shakespeare. Poets with approximately the same environment may be expected to have the same associations for particular words. It is not surprising even that the graduate Marlowe and the grammar-school product, Shakespeare, should have at least one cluster in common. Certain obvious clusters, therefore, can throw no light on authorship. Shakespeare, for example, associates *snow* with *chastity* and *Diana*, and indirectly with *heat*, *blood*, and *blush*.[8]

Look thou be true; do not give dalliance
Too much the rein: the strongest oaths are straw
To the fire i' the blood: be more abstemious,
Or else, good night your vow!

> I warrant you, sir;
> The white cold virgin snow upon my heart
> Abates the ardour of my liver.
>
> The moon of Rome, chaste as the icicle
> That's curdied by the frost from purest snow
> And hangs on Dian's temple: dear Valeria!
>
> Thou ever young, fresh, loved and delicate wooer,
> Whose blush doth thaw the consecrated snow
> That lies on Dian's lap!
>
>   ...my mother seem'd
> The Dian of that time: so doth my wife
> The nonpareil of this...
>
> Me of my lawful pleasure she restrain'd
> And pray'd me oft forbearance; did it with
> A pudency so rosy the sweet view on't
> Might well have warm'd old Saturn; that I thought her
> As chaste as unsunn'd snow.

The presence of the same associations in *The Two Noble Kinsmen* (v, i) cannot in itself be taken to prove that Shakespeare wrote this scene. Emilia prays to *Diana*:

> O sacred, shadowie, cold and constant Queene,
> Abandoner of Revells, mute, contemplative,
> Sweet, solitary, white as chaste, and pure
> As winde fand Snow, who to thy femall knights
> Alow'st no more blood than will make a blush,
> Which is their orders robe:

There is, however, a closer parallel to this passage in *The Winter's Tale* (IV, iv, 373–7), as Littledale pointed out:

> I take thy hand, this hand,
> As soft as dove's down and as *white* as it,
> Or Ethiopian's tooth, or the *fann'd snow* that's bolted
> By the northern *blasts* twice o'er.

It seems fairly certain that the lines in *The Two Noble Kinsmen* were written either by a conscious imitator of Shakespeare or by Shakespeare himself. None of the plays quoted above had appeared in print by the time *The Two Noble Kinsmen* was written, though a playgoer could have remembered and imitated the passages concerned.

Another cluster, for the discovery of which I am indebted to a former pupil, links the hind with dirt, smell, lust, disease, crime and death.[9] In the same scene of *The Two Noble Kinsmen* a silver hind is carried before Emilia, "in which is conveyd Incense and sweet *odours*"; and in the speech from which lines have been quoted above there are references to dirt (151 *maculate*), lust (153 *scurrill*, 154 *wanton*), crime (160 *guiltlesse*) and death (162 *doombe*). For the remaining link in the chain, disease, we have to go back to Palamon's speech, which has a nice selection of diseases (116 *crampe*, 118 *gout*, 119 *convulsions*). Unless it can be shown that some other dramatist shares these associations there is strong reason to believe that Shakespeare wrote this scene, and, of course, it is a scene which has been ascribed to him on quite other grounds.

Another scene which is thought by many critics to be Shakespearian is the first in the play. Here is to be found (115) the unusual word "uncandied"—a word which inevitably recalls "Discandying" and "discandy", both used by Shakespeare in *Antony and Cleopatra*. In one case (III, xiii) the word is associated with *cold, hail, dissolve*,[10] *drop, heart, moon, graveless* and *Nile* (153–66); and in the other case (IV, xii) with *melt, heart* and *sun* (18–28). In *The Two Noble Kinsmen* the Second Queen complains that her lord is unburied (cf. *graveless*):

> Showing the *Sun* his Teeth, grinning at the *Moone*...

Hippolyta uses the word "*heart*-deepe"; and the Third Queen says (114–23):

> O my petition was
> Set downe in *yce*, which by hot greefe *uncandied*
> *Melts* into *drops*...
> You cannot reade it there, there through my teares—
> Like wrinckled peobles in a glassie streame
> You may behold 'em!

The second of the passages from *Antony and Cleopatra* contains that most famous of image-clusters, flatterers–dogs–sweets; and it might perhaps be regarded as an argument against the authenticity of *The Two Noble Kinsmen* passage that there is no mention of either flatterers or sweets. But although other uses of *candied* (e.g. *Timon*, IV, iii, 226 and *Hamlet*, III, ii, 65) are linked with that cluster, there are no dogs—though there are flatterers—in the other *Antony and Cleopatra* passage, and neither dog nor flatterer in *The Tempest* context (II, i, 279). It is as though Shakespeare had worked the dogs and the flatterers out of his system in the great purge of *Timon of Athens*, the play in which this particular cluster is the iterative image.

The case of the osprey is perhaps even more significant. In *Coriolanus* (IV, vii), Aufidius describes the hero's march on Rome:

> I think he'll be to Rome
> As is the osprey to the fish, who takes it
> By sovereignty of nature.

So in *The Two Noble Kinsmen* (I, i, again) the First Queen tells Theseus:

> your actions,
> Soone as they mooves, as Asprayes doe the fish,
> Subdue before they touch.

It might be said that both authors derived their knowledge of the osprey from a common source were it not for the contexts of the two passages. In *Coriolanus* there are references to *war* (45), *breaking the neck* (25), *sword* (24), *lord* (41), and *sovereignty* (35); and more remotely to *tomb* (52), *darkened* (5), and *action* (5). In *The Two Noble Kinsmen* context there are references to *war* (145), *cords* (156), *knives*[11] (156), *lords* (154), *Kings* (152), *beds*=graves (152), *graves* (164), *shadows* (159), and *actions* (149). It might be argued that the author of the latter passage had consciously echoed the lines about the osprey from an unpublished play, and that he had unconsciously echoed some of the key words in the same context. But such an argument strains our credulity, and it is much more likely that the same poet wrote both passages.

This probability is raised to a certainty when we turn to yet another cluster in the same scene[12] —perhaps Armstrong's most impressive cluster. He detailed all the fourteen references to kites by Shakespeare and showed that in nearly every context there are references to death, food, spirits, bed and other birds, and that in every context there are references to three or more of these associations. There are the same associations with *hell-kite* in *Macbeth*, IV, iii, a passage to which Armstrong does not refer. As these associations are invariable with Shakespeare, their absence in a doubtful scene would almost be sufficient to prove that Shakespeare did not write it. But the mention of kites (44) in the first scene of *The Two Noble Kinsmen* is at the centre of the same cluster in its entirety—*ravens* (44), *crows* (45), *dead* (53), *slain* (50), *kings* (53), *bed* (31), *angel* (16), *pie* (21), and *devour* (74).

Another image-cluster analysed by Armstrong is that associated with the word 'hum'. When the word was first used by Shakespeare in *I Henry IV* (III, i, 158) it was linked with food (*cates*), music (*ballad-monger*), wealth (*mines of India*), and spirit (*devil*), but not with sleep or death. A year or two later, in *The Merry Wives of Windsor* (III, v, 141), Shakespeare used the word again, this time linked with *sleep, devil* and *cuckold*. He used it twice in *Henry V*: in one context linked with *drowsy* and *ghost* (IV, Prol.), in the other with *executors, honey, yawning, singing, flower-buds*, and *gold* (I, ii, 202). In *Hamlet* (V, i) the word is linked with *skull, tricks* and *inheritance*; in *Othello* (V, ii) with *kill, gnaw, bed, rose, spirit* and *adultery*—harking back to the *cuckold* of *The Merry Wives*. (The murder of Desdemona is, of course, the culmination of Iago's plot.) In *King Lear* the word is linked with Edgar's supposed plan to kill Gloucester, with *conspiracy, taste, relish, sleep, sounded, revenue*. Edmund, moreover, is the fruit of adultery. The word is used three times in *Macbeth*: in III, ii it is linked with *treason, meal, drowse, yawning, peal, note, Hecate* (for *spirit*) and *copy* (possibly standing for *wealth*). The killing of Banquo is being discussed in the context. In III, vi, the word is linked with *kill, feasts, meat, sleep* and *angel*, and the characters are virtually plotting against Macbeth. In IV, iii, the word is linked with *slaughter, deer, sound, tune, precious, ears* and *fiend*. In *Cymbeline* (III, v, 104) the word is linked only with *dead*, though Cloten hatches his plot soon afterwards. In *The Winter's Tale* (II, i, 71) it is linked with *bed*, with Hermione's supposed adultery ("not honest") and with the plot to kill Polixenes. In *The Tempest* (III, ii, 147) the word is linked with *kill, plot, sleep, sounds, airs, music, song, riches, ears, Ariel* (a spirit), and with the product of miscegenation, Caliban. By the end of Shakespeare's career, therefore, *hum* had picked up a whole cluster of associations—some of which are not mentioned by Armstrong—and any use of the word after 1610 might be expected to evoke some of the following associations: death, plot, food, sleep, music, song, flowers, wealth or value, ears, spirit, adultery or bastardy. Of these eleven associations all but one—

plot—duly make their appearance in the context of the sole use of the word in *The Two Noble Kinsmen* (I, iii, 76):

> the *flowre* that I would plucke
> And put betweene my breasts (then but beginning
> To swell about the *blossome*) oh, she would long
> Till shee had such another, and commit it
> To the like innocent Cradle, where Phenix-like
> They *dide* in perfume: on my head no toy
> But was her patterne; her affections (pretty,
> Though, happely, her careles we[ar]) I followed
> For my most serious decking; had mine *eare*
> Stolne some new *aire*, or at adventure *humd* on[e]
> From *musicall Coynadge*, why it was a *note*
> Whereon her *spirits* would sojourne (rather dwell on)
> And *sing* it in her *slumbers*. This rehearsall—
> (Which ev'ry innocent wots well comes in
> Like old importments *bastard*) has this end,
> That the true love tweene Mayde, and mayde, may be
> More then in sex dividuall.

A few lines later Hippolyta speaks of "a sickely appetite". (Perhaps the word immediately before this quotation, "arraignement", may serve as a substitute for *plot*: Shakespeare uses *arraign* on eight occasions, and on six of these in connexion with treason.[13]) Ten of these associations occur within fifteen lines, and the remaining one is only eight lines later. It is difficult to believe that Shakespeare was conscious of these associations, or that one of his imitators would have stumbled on so many of them. It can hardly be denied that Shakespeare wrote this scene too. It so happens that the word *hum* is used also in one of the Fletcher scenes (III, v), but here it is accompanied by none of the Shakespearian associations. Three other words which are the nodal points of Shakespearian clusters are to be found in Fletcher scenes—venison[14] (III, iii), hawk (II, v; III, v), bark (III, v)—but in none of these cases is there any sign of the accompanying clusters.

There appear to be no Shakespearian image-clusters in the remaining scenes of the play, but this does not necessarily mean that he had no hand in them. Only a few clusters have so far been isolated; and most of these, owing to the fact that Armstrong is an ornithologist, are connected with birds. In the plays of the last period—excluding *Pericles* and *Henry VIII*—only twelve clusters have been discovered. As no one pretends that Shakespeare wrote more than half of *The Two Noble Kinsmen*, it would be sanguine to expect more than one or two clusters in the authentic scenes. Yet, as we have seen, in addition to two of the Armstrong clusters (*kite* and *hum*) there are two or three others present in the first and third scenes of the first act and the first scene of the fifth. If the reader admits Shakespeare's hand in these scenes he is not likely to doubt that Shakespeare was responsible for other scenes as well. The various tests which have been applied (weak endings, light endings, scene endings, coinages) all receive reinforcement from a proof on imagistic grounds that Shakespeare wrote even part of a single scene. Since we have seen that Shakespeare wrote parts of three separate scenes, the evidence of other tests, together with the convictions of Coleridge, Bradley, Theodore Spencer and Middleton Murry, make it reasonably certain that Shakespeare wrote also the following scenes: I, ii; I, iv; III, i; v, iv. The play has as much right to be included in editions of Shakespeare as *Sir Thomas More* or *The Passionate Pilgrim*, and perhaps as much as *Titus Andronicus*, *Henry VI Part 1*, and *Pericles*.

NOTES

1. Metrical tests are no longer fashionable—it has become the fashion rather to sneer at them. This is doubtless due to the extravagant use made of them by some scholars. It would be absurd to argue that *The Tempest* was followed by *The Winter's Tale* and *Cymbeline* because of the percentages given above. But it would be equally absurd to pretend that there is no significance in the complete absence of light and weak endings in Shakespeare's early plays or in their frequency after 1608. Metrical tests, after all, merely express mathematically what every competent reader will recognize instinctively—that Shakespeare's later verse is very different from his earlier verse and different, too, from the verse of other known dramatists. This evidence is supported by Bradley's demonstration (*A Miscellany*, 1929, pp. 218–22) that six or seven of the nine non-Fletcherian blank-verse scenes end with a part line, and that this, frequent in the later plays of Shakespeare, was comparatively rare in the plays of Fletcher and Massinger.

2. *Shakespeare and the Homilies* (1934), pp. 242 ff.   3. *Studies in Shakespeare* (1919), pp. 1–17.

4. The presence of internal rhyme in the *T.N.K.* passage (*stream/seem*; *chop/drop*) suggests that it may originally have been, like *The Tempest* masque, in rhymed couplets:

> That I
> Poor man, might eftsoons come between and chop
> On some cold thought! thrice-blessed chance, to drop
> On such a mistress....

5. *English Studies* (1952), pp. 97 ff.   6. *Op. cit.* p. 188.

7. *Op. cit.* p. 188.

8. Cf. *Temp.* IV, i, 55; *Cor.* v, iii, 66; *Tim.* IV, iii, 386; *Cym.* II, v, 13.

9. Cf. F. D. Gibson, *Sport in Shakespeare* (Thesis in Library of University of Leeds). Cf. e.g. *R. III*, II, iv, 50–3; *C.E.* III, i, 74–88; *M.N.D.* II, i, 232–7; *A.Y.L.I.* III, ii, 102–14; *T.C.* III, ii, 190–203; *M.W.* III, v, 94–9; *A.W.* I, i, 102–4; *J.C.* I, iii, 106–111.

10. Littledale points out that the phrase "dissolve my life" appears both in this passage and in *T.N.K.* III, ii, 29 (apparently by Fletcher).

11. Littledale compares "cords, knives, drams, precipitance" with *Oth.* III, iii, 388:

> If there be cords, or knives,
> Poison, or fire, or suffocating streams.

12. Cf. K. Muir, *Notes and Queries* (1954), pp. 52–3.

13. Laertes' rebellion (*Ham.* IV, v, 93), Lear's arraignment of Goneril (*K.L.* III, vi, 48), Goneril's claim that the laws are hers (*K.L.* v, iii, 159), and the trial of Hermione for high treason (*W.T.* II, iii, 202).

14. Venison and hawk clusters have been analysed by Gibson, *op. cit.* I have searched in vain for image-clusters in Massinger's plays.

MUSIC AND ITS FUNCTION IN THE ROMANCES OF SHAKESPEARE

BY

J. M. NOSWORTHY

Most of the Elizabethan beliefs about music remain with us as familiar myths whose full implications are ignored. We know of the Platonic notion of the music of the spheres and of the Orpheus legend. We are aware, too, that for a Christian age there was literal truth in Job, xxxviii. 7: "When the morning stars sang together, and all the sons of God shouted for joy", and in the singing and playing of the angels before the throne of God in Revelation. The faculty which has tended to desert us with the passing of time is that of being permanently conscious of and responsive to the place of music in the Elizabethan scheme of things, of seeing it not simply as a diversion but as an act of faith, and as something no less essential to the overall pattern than the concepts of degree, the body politic, the elements and humours, and the like. Since, moreover, the dance was associated with music as a heavenly dispensation, Elizabethan attitudes are not easily borne in mind in an age like ours, when music in general is secular in intention, and that which accompanies the dance has little perceptible connexion with belief, religious or otherwise.

The Elizabethan triple pattern of creation comprised the great chain of being which stretched down from God, a series of correspondences, and the ordered movement, or dance, of all created matter. The clearest and most comprehensive exposition of this last figure is that given in Sir John Davies' *Orchestra*, a poem whose significance has been recently explored and illuminatingly discussed by Dr Tillyard,[1] and most of what Davies claims for the dance holds for the inseparable art of music. Davies relates the dance, in its normal physical manifestation, with the dance in the body politic, that in the earth and sea, and that of the spheres; and dancing is represented as the offspring of Love, which is the creator of the universal harmony, and directs man towards social unity and the recognition of the Beautiful. Creation, then, was an act of divine love, which wrested order from chaos, and established its creatures in a state of dancing whose perfection was impaired only by the Fall of Man, and the function of music in this process was precisely that defined by Dryden in his *Song for St Cecilia's Day*.

Music, therefore, took its place with other disciplines in the general scheme of education, whose purpose, according to Milton, was "to repair the ruins of our first parents by regaining to know God aright", and its practitioners, like the poets, sought to recapture the Golden Age and reveal the primal glory of Creation. Something of music's relevance to orthodox Christian belief can be inferred from the enthronement of St Cecilia as patron saint. For more than twelve hundred years she had been innocent of any musical attributes or attainments, but during the Italian Renaissance the familiar legend developed until she was ultimately credited with the invention of the organ. Though the English St Cecilia celebrations appear to be of post-Restoration origin, the saint and her alleged achievements were already familiar enough in Shakespeare's day.

The hard core of religious belief, as it applied to a dramatist of undeniably Protestant convictions, is excellently illustrated in a section of Samuel Rowley's *When you See me you Know me*. Here Prince Edward says of music:

> Truely I loue it yet there are a sort
> Seeming more pure than wise, that will vpbrayd at it,
> Calling it idle, vaine, and friuolous.

This provokes his tutor, the celebrated Dr Christopher Tye, to an eloquent defence:

> Your Grace hath sayd, indeed they doe vpbrayd
> That terme it so, and those that doe are such
> As in themselues no happie concords hold,
> All Musicke jars with them, but sounds of good,
> But would your Grace a while be patient,
> In Musickes praise, thus will I better it.
> Musicke is heauenly, for in Heauen is Musicke,
> For there the Seraphins doe sing continually,
> And when the best was borne, that euer was man,
> A Quire of Angels sang for joy of it,
> What of Celestiall was reueald to man,
> Was much of Musicke, tis sayd the beasts did worship
> And sang before the Deitie supernall,
> The kingly Prophet sang before the Arke,
> And with his Musicke charmd the heart of *Saule*,
> And if the Poet fayle vs not my Lord,
> The dulcet tongue of Musicke made the stones
> To mooue, irrational beast, and birds to daunce
> And last, the Trumpets Musicke shall awake the dead,
> And cloath their naked bones in coates of flesh,
> T'appeare in that high house of Parliament,
> When those that gnash their Teeth at Musicke sound,
> Shall make that place where Musicke nere was found.

To this the Prince then adds the appropriate microcosmic correspondence:

> As Musicke, so is man gouern'd by stops,
> Aw'd by diuiding notes, sometimes aloft,
> Sometime below, and when he hath attain'd,
> His high and loftie pitch, breathed his sharpest and most
> Shrillest ayre, yet at length tis gone,
> And fals downe flat to his conclusion, (*Soft Musicke.*)
> Another sweetnesse, and harmonious sound,
> A milder straine, another kinde agreement,

Yet mong'st these many stringes, be one vntun'd
Or jarreth low, or hyer than his course
Not keeping steddie meane among'st the rest,
Corrupts them all, so doth bad men the best.

This is essentially the musical outlook of Shakespeare, though revealed by him with greater variety of allusion and more flexibly applied to all human affairs. Thus, in *The Merchant of Venice*, there is assured faith in the music of the spheres and the divine origin and irresistible power of music over brute creation, while, in the famous exposition of Ulysses in *Troilus and Cressida*, the violation of degree is presented in terms of music:

Take but degree away, untune that string,
And, hark, what discord follows!

The by-dependances of such beliefs are often bewildering to the modern reader, who may occasionally find that there are in fact moments when music is quite as remote from present-day experience as mermaids or mandrakes.

Music in Shakespeare's Comedies and Tragedies

The Shakespeare canon as a whole admits the supposition that a consort of viols and recorders was always available when the need arose, but the songs are altogether more problematic. Any theories relating to the employment of singing-boys have to be received with the utmost caution, since such employment, judging from textual evidence, must have been very occasional. Many of the songs in the plays were intended for adult singers, and both Augustine Philips and Richard Cowley appear to have been employed primarily as musicians. It would, therefore, be tempting to surmise that, from 1598 onwards, one of these men was given an extended run as Balthasar, Amiens, Feste, the Clown in *Hamlet*, and Pandarus, but such a distribution, though musically satisfactory, does not inspire confidence dramatically. Considerations such as these necessarily render any hypothesis about Shakespeare's use of music and his conception of its dramatic functions highly tentative—at least up to about 1600. Nevertheless, certain reasonable conclusions can be drawn.

The earliest comedies are sparing in their use of music, and offer little that is not entirely conventional. A change of purpose is perceptible in *Love's Labour's Lost*, where two songs at the very end cut across the fantastic artificiality of the action and substitute the everyday realities of Dick, Tom, Marian and greasy Joan, with an effect that is almost didactic in such a context. In *A Midsummer Night's Dream*, the music appropriate to enchantments and nocturnal occasions is skilfully woven into the general pattern, yet it is, in the main, instrumental. The same holds for *The Merchant of Venice*, though this play does afford the fullest exposition of Shakespeare's musical faith, and *Much Ado about Nothing* makes no distinctive contribution. In *As You Like It*, however, there is a perceptible change. Here music and song are not only greater in quantity, but are also more carefully integrated, serving as they do to reinforce and illuminate the various themes of the play. Thus, the Arden setting, the holiday humour, man's ingratitude, the pre-occupation with the passing of time, and the resolve to take the present hour are all given musical expression. The flaw in presentation lies in the fact that Shakespeare has still to rely on the singing-man, for Amiens can scarcely be regarded as a character in his own right. No such objection applies to *Twelfth Night*, where musical and dramatic functions are admirably equated in Feste, and here, too, all the levels of meaning are reflected musically. The songs are now more poignant, and it is within the compass of the haunting phrases:

Youth's a stuff will not endure

and

For the rain it raineth every day

that the basic morality of the play lies. Another important feature of *Twelfth Night* is the clear-cut distinction it imposes between the higher order of song and the ballads and catches which make up Sir Toby's repertoire. Musical taste is thus made accordant with the Shakespearian concept of degree.

This musical symbolization of disorder occurs in two of the tragedies, *Othello* and *Antony and Cleopatra*, where traditional ballads serve as drinking-songs, but, with the notable exception of *Hamlet*, the tragedies as a whole make little use of music, and there is no reason to suppose that special settings were called for. The rich and expressive musical background of *Hamlet* rests upon the popular ballad, and principally upon the tune of "Walsingham" which Ophelia sings in IV, iv. There are few more beautiful melodies in the world of sound, and none more appropriate to the particular dramatic needs. The portrayal of madness must always have imposed a strain on the boy-actors, and the standard pattern of rhetorical lunacy deriving from *The Spanish Tragedy* and the Senecan tradition can hardly have seemed attractive to Shakespeare at this stage of his career. Ophelia's "snatches of old tunes" may therefore constitute a resolution of difficulties by evasion. The social distinctions that apply to the music of *Twelfth Night* are here presented in the contrast between Ophelia's songs and those of the Clown in the Graveyard scene.

The subsequent tragic period offers little of real musical interest, save for such isolated units as Desdemona's "Willow Song", which sustains the dramatic poignancy already achieved in the portrayal of the distracted Ophelia. *Timon of Athens* provides for a masque of Amazons, but whether this ever developed into anything more ambitious than a stage-direction is doubtful. The intention, however, reflects Shakespeare's eagerness to find occasion for music and its complements, and this in terms of the current popular form—the masque.

KING'S PLAYERS AND KING'S MUSICIAN

There is no evidence to suggest that any composer worked regularly for Shakespeare's company prior to 1607 or thereabouts. The musical contributions of the first decade seem, indeed, to have been extraordinarily diverse, but a closer linking of the arts was inevitable under James' patronage, since the masque now brought dramatist and composer into close collaboration. Several years ago, the present writer hazarded the conjecture that Robert Johnson, known as the composer of settings for *The Tempest* and of songs originally intended for *The Witch* but subsequently transferred to *Macbeth*, was regularly employed by the King's Company. This hypothesis was subsequently given shape by the researches of John Cutts, who has thrown a great deal of new light upon the use of music on the Jacobean stage.[2] Thanks to these, it now appears evident that Johnson, who, like Shakespeare and his fellows, had passed from the service of the Lord Chamberlain to that of the King, wrote incidental music for plays by Shakespeare, Jonson, Webster, May, Tourneur and Beaumont and Fletcher throughout a period extending from 1607 to 1616. If Cutts' attributions are correct, Johnson emerges as a person of no little importance to the student of Shakespeare's final romances.

MUSIC IN THE ROMANCES

The romances are, musically, the richest of Shakespeare's plays, and are of special interest precisely because a certain amount of what may reasonably be regarded as the original music has survived. Songs, comprising both special settings and traditional ballads, appear in greater profusion, and instrumental music serves not only for dances but also for theophanies and for various dramatic functions which may not, in the present state of knowledge, be dismissed as minor ones. The special settings, all presumably by Johnson, survive in various manuscripts, while the ballads still extant are, in the main, available in the extensive collections of Chappell[3] and Caulfield.[4] Certain of the original dances are probably preserved in a manuscript volume in the British Museum (Add. MS. 10444), a remarkable collection of masque and other music which has been unduly neglected, though its importance was pointed out long ago by W. J. Lawrence.[5] Since it is here convenient to tabulate these musical embellishments, notes are added relating to early settings, where these exist.

Pericles

    I, i, 11.   Music.

    II, iii, 98.   The Knights dance.

    II, iii, 107.   The Knights and Ladies dance.

    V, i, 80.   Marina sings.

    V, i, 234.   Music (for the theophany).

Cymbeline

    II, iii, 14.   Musicians.

    II, iii, 21.   Song: *Hark, hark! the lark.* A setting, possibly Johnson's, survives in Bodleian MS. Don. C. 57. Modernized transcript in the New Arden edition.

    IV, ii, 186.   Solemn music. (Belarius' "ingenious instrument".)

    IV, ii, 258.   Song: *Fear no more the heat o'the sun.* Caulfield gives an anonymous setting, but this may not be the original one. The text clearly implies that the lines were spoken, and not sung, in the initial performance, but the heading "Song" appears in the Folio, so that it is legitimate to conclude that music was supplied sometime between 1609 and 1623.[6]

    V, iv, 29.   Solemn Music and other music (for the theophany).

The Winter's Tale

    IV, iii, 1.   Song: *When daffodils begin to peer.*

    IV, iii, 15.   Song: *But shall I go mourn for that, my dear?* The anonymous setting given by Caulfield is perhaps the original one.

IV, iii, 132.   Song: *Jog on, jog on, the foot-path way*. Chappell prints the original setting. The tune appears under the title "Hanskin" in Queen Elizabeth's Virginal Book. Richard Farnaby wrote a set of variations on the tune, but whether he composed it is not clear. The tune first appears as "Jog on, jog on" in *The Dancing Master*. Another setting is given by Caulfield.

IV, iv, 165.   Music. Here a dance of Shepherds and Shepherdesses. A "Shepherds Masque" is preserved in B.M. Add. MS. 10444. Cutts thinks that this may have been written for *The Winter's Tale*.

IV, iv, 196.   Snatch: *Jump her and thump her*.

IV, iv, 199.   Snatch: *Whoop, do me no harm, good man*.

IV, iv, 220.   Song: *Lawn as white as driven snow*. A three-voiced form appears in John Wilson's *Cheerful Ayres* (1660). The original setting for solo voice was probably by Johnson.

IV, iv, 303.   Song: *Get you hence, for I must go*. The setting in New York MS. DX. 4175 was discovered by Cutts and was described by him, with transcript and facsimile, in *Shakespeare Survey*, 9.

IV, iv, 322.   Song: *Will you buy any tape*. An anonymous setting of uncertain date is given by Caulfield.

IV, iv, 352.   Here a dance of twelve Satyrs. A "Satyres Masque" is preserved in B.M. Add. MS. 10444, and the same music is printed in Thomas Simpson's *Taffel Consort* as Robert Johnson's. This music appears to have served for both *The Winter's Tale* and Jonson's *Oberon*.

V, iii, 98.   Music (for Hermione's descent).

The Tempest

I, ii, 376.   Song: *Come unto these yellow sands*.

I, ii, 396.   Song: *Full fathom five thy father lies*. Johnson's setting was first printed in John Wilson's *Cheerful Ayres*. Modernized transcript in the New Arden edition.

II, i, 184.   Enter Ariel, invisible, playing solemn music.

II, i, 300.   Song: *While you here do snoring lie*. The setting given by Caulfield is presumably Arne's.

II, ii, 44.   Snatch: *I shall no more to sea, to sea*.

II, ii, 48.   Song: *The master, the swabber, the boatswain and I*. Caulfield gives settings of this and the preceding snatch "as performed by Mr John Bannister". No doubt Banister (1630–79) composed these.

II, ii, 182.   Snatch: *Farewell, master; farewell, farewell!*

II, ii, 184.   Song: *No more dams I'll make for fish*.

III, ii, 130.   Song: *Flout 'em and scout 'em*. Ariel plays the tune on a tabor and pipe. The setting given by Caulfield is Purcell's.

III, iii, 7.   Solemn and strange music (for the dance of the strange Shapes). The dance entitled "The Tempest" in B.M. Add. MS. 10444 clearly belongs to the play. Cutts suggests that it belongs here, and that it is the work of Johnson. Modernized transcript in the New Arden edition.

III, iii, 82.   Soft music (for second dance of the strange Shapes). Possibly included in the foregoing.

IV, i, 44.   Song (?): *Before you can say 'come' and 'go'*.

IV, i, 60.   Soft music (for entrance of Iris). In B.M. Add. MS. 10444. "The Tempest" is followed by a short item simply called "A Masque". Cutts remarks that this is too short for a main dance or an antimasque, and conjectures that it may be music for an entry. If so, this would be an appropriate occasion.

ıv, i, 106.   Song: *Honour, riches, marriage-blessing.*

ıv, i, 138.   A graceful dance. This may be the "Haymakers' Dance" in B.M. Add. MS. 10444 as Cutts surmises.

v, i, 57.   Solemn music (for Prospero's spell).

v, i, 88.   Song: *Where the bee sucks, there suck I.* Johnson's setting was printed in Wilson's *Cheerful Ayres.* Modernized transcript in the New Arden edition.

The most obvious conclusion arising from this tabulation is that, as Shakespeare proceeded with the romances, he gave increasing prominence to music. *The Winter's Tale* is quantitatively far in advance of its predecessors, yet only a relatively small proportion of the play has musical embellishment, whereas music informs the action of *The Tempest* at all points. *Pericles* and *Cymbeline* do not, in fact, add greatly to the musical achievement of such plays as *Twelfth Night* or *Hamlet,* and their only distinctive feature lies in cognizance of the Court masque. *Pericles,* in its provision of music for the theophany, looks back to the 'Still Music' for Hymen in *As You Like It,* and, like *Timon of Athens,* utilizes certain merely formal elements of the masque. *Cymbeline* is more ambitious, but is uncertain in its treatment of music, as of so much else. The aubade is completely in accord with Shakespeare's earlier comic practice: the dirge is apparently spoken, and is thereby rendered the more perplexing. The vision, which employs the conventional music of a theophany, owes something to the masque, but the stage directions clearly show that it is not, in itself, a masque either in whole or part. Finally, there is something almost apologetic about the reference to "my ingenious instrument" to account for a consort of viols in a Welsh mountain retreat. The "solemn music" which it supplies seems to promise more than it actually performs. Both this play and *Pericles* are retrogressive in the sense that such music as they contain is a separable element whose total omission would make little or no essential difference.

Yet there is more to *Cymbeline* than this. It is, in general, a play which strives towards perfection and which, in its detailed account of Imogen's bed-chamber, discloses Shakespeare's own delight in what is perfect in the plastic arts. Music, quite irrespective of aubades, dirges and ingenious instruments, is ultimately woven into the pattern of the play as a regenerative, unifying and perfecting force. Hence, the Soothsayer, who resolves the final problems and who is appropriately named Philarmonus, envisages the new creative order in strictly musical terms:

> The fingers of the powers above do tune
> The harmony of this peace.

In such matters *Cymbeline* makes an almost complete break with the past. The new concern with painting, sculpture, music and the dance shows Shakespeare entering upon what might, if only the term were capacious enough, be called his "aesthetic period", while the notion of man in communion with God, and that a musical communion, marks an abrupt change from the previous tragic conception:

> Behold, the heavens do ope,
> The gods look down, and this unnatural scene
> They laugh at.

These intentions are more fully realized in *The Winter's Tale*, where the music is organic and where the fusion of the arts is closely related to the themes of Art and Nature, variously expounded, which are basic to the ethos of the play. Shakespeare's new conception of music as a re-creative or regenerative force is now quite evident. The division of the play into two parts relates, of course, to significances far more profound than the mere passage of sixteen years. The primary distinction is that between the period of chaos, dominated by Leontes, and that of regeneration, dominated by Perdita. In the first of these, music finds no place. Its first appearance in the play is, appropriately, at the precise point where the process of winning order out of chaos is begun, when the winter of the tale looks towards spring, and the future is seen in terms of "the sweet o' the year". Autolycus is concordant with the play's meaning less for what he is, "a snapper-up of unconsidered trifles", than for what his music symbolizes—the re-awakening of Nature, the sovereignty of the red blood and the hopeful travels of a merry heart. Regeneration is complete when the supposed statue comes to life at Paulina's command:

> Music, awake her; strike!

In IV, iv, the great debate between Perdita and Polixenes is amply supported by poetry, music and dancing, and the synthesis, which, save for comparable effects in *The Tempest*, is unique, defies analysis. The effect is, in some respects, comparable to the Sitwell-Walton *Façade*, where the sounds and rhythms of verse are barely distinguishable from those of music, and both are related to the motions of the dance. This may seem merely another way of saying that the Sheep-shearing scene is fundamentally a masque, but, although the formal elements, namely the dance of Shepherds and Shepherdesses and the antimasque of Satyrs, are straightforwardly presented, the total effect is of something more subtle, more unified and more meaningful than any masque.

That which serves for the part in *The Winter's Tale* serves for almost the whole in *The Tempest*, where these impalpable effects extend throughout the play. Shakespeare's unconstrained handling of the unity of time reduces the period of chaos to a single scene, so that Ariel and his music are able to operate almost at once. Decorum, which had perhaps been violated by the allocation of songs to Autolycus, is here preserved, since the higher flights of song are given to Ariel and his fellows, while the drunken characters, Autolycus' social equals, mouth ballads. Theophany and masque fall together, and, again, a new synthesis is achieved. Art and Nature are once more the philosophical theme, and music envelops them. Music is, in fact, ubiquitous:

> the isle is full of noises,
> Sounds and sweet airs, that give delight and hurt not.

and all characters are affected, even governed, by it. Caliban's brute nature is ennobled:

> Sometimes a thousand twangling instruments
> Will hum about mine ears, and sometimes voices
> That, if I then had waked after long sleep,
> Will make me sleep again: and then, in dreaming,
> The clouds methought would open and show riches
> Ready to drop upon me, that, when I waked,
> I cried to dream again.

and Ariel relates, in terms reminiscent of *The Merchant of Venice*, how the grotesques were charmed and rendered powerless by music:

> Then I beat my tabor;
> At which, like unback'd colts, they prick'd their ears,
> Advanced their eyelids, lifted up their noses
> As they smelt music: so I charm'd their ears
> That calf-like they my lowing follow'd through
> Tooth'd briers, sharp furzes, pricking goss and thorns,
> Which enter'd their frail shins.

So, too, music affects the nobler characters. Thus Ferdinand:

> This music crept by me upon the waters,
> Allaying both their fury and my passion
> With its sweet air; thence I have follow'd it,
> Or it hath drawn me rather.

And finally "some heavenly music" is the concomitant to Prospero's abjuration of his rough magic, and is accounted by him

> the best comforter
> To an unsettled fancy.

Each of the romances is an advance upon its immediate predecessor, philosophically as well as technically, and music comes to occupy a conspicuous and effective position in the moral and metaphysical fabric. These plays are basically a mirror of the Creation in human terms, with love shaping a new world out of chaos to the sound of music and the motions of the dance, and this pattern is most fully achieved in *The Tempest*, which is, in the highest sense, an educational document—a consistent picture of man regaining to know God aright, in which the experience and understanding of all the main characters, virtuous and erring, are enriched, and the ruins of our first parents are repaired. The progress of the romances, then, is towards a dramatic action which is surrounded and shaped by music and its companion, the dance, and this is the product of an attitude to life, and not merely of the professional dramatist's desire to utilize the new and fashionable resources of the masque. The enormous popularity of the Court masque at this period may, it is true, have planted ideas in Shakespeare's mind, but the conduct of those ideas is entirely his own. Had he found the formal masque congenial, he would, no doubt, have made contributions no less distinguished than those of Ben Jonson. But the fact is that he did nothing of the kind, and it is legitimate to surmise that he regarded this species of entertainment as something ephemeral which did not, at this late stage, accord with his accumulated dramatic wisdom and the gravity of his thought. The impetus behind music and the dance as utilized in these final plays is, at root, a neo-Platonic one, and the intention is that they should reflect that concept of divine order which informs the dramatic pattern at all points. Music is there, in the last analysis, to direct thought and action "beyond beyond" to a "brave new world" in which the Golden Age is restored.

NOTES

1. E. M. W. Tillyard, *Five Poems*, pp. 30–48.

2. I am much indebted to his thesis, *The Contribution of Robert Johnson, King's Musician, to Court and Theatrical Entertainments*.

3. William Chappell, *Popular Music of the Olden Time* (1855–99).

4. J. Caulfield, *A Collection of the Vocal Music in Shakespeare's Plays*. This valuable, though uncritical, collection was published in 1864, but must, on the evidence of the author's preface, have been compiled round about 1800.

5. W. J. Lawrence, 'Notes on a Collection of Masque Music' (*Music and Letters*, III (1922), 49–58).

6. *Cymbeline*, ed. J. M. Nosworthy (New Arden Shakespeare), pp. 223–4.

THE MAGIC OF PROSPERO

BY

C. J. SISSON

There is magic enough in Shakespeare, of one kind or another, from his very first play onwards. We may be inclined to reject Talbot's conception of the Pucelle, in *1 Henry VI*, as a witch, a servant of the Devil, and a sorceress, as inconsistent with her characterization and speeches, until we reach Act V, Scene iii, when we unexpectedly find her busy with spells and conjuration of fiends who appear only to indicate the end of their intervention on her behalf. In comedy, Puck's first entry in *A Midsummer Night's Dream* introduces the theme of magic fairy power which is the motive force in the geometrical plot of four lovers of changing allegiance. It may well be doubted whether in either play the possible relation of the fictional magic to current beliefs and superstitions was of any consequence to the dramatist or to the audience. It was not so in some of Shakespeare's later plays, in *Macbeth* or in *The Tempest*, for example. In them it is a matter of importance that the magic which lies at the dramatic heart of the play should find a response in the serious attention of the audience.

It is noteworthy that the element of the supernatural should play an increasing part in the plays of Shakespeare's last period. In *The Tempest*, of course, it is all-pervasive. In *Cymbeline* an elaborate and spectacular vision embodies a dream of the sleeping Posthumus in prison. A soothsayer reports a private vision portending success to the Roman wars in Britain, and at the end of the play expounds the oracular message discussed by Posthumus upon his awakening. Both prophetic visions are accomplished in the event. In *The Winter's Tale* the oracle of Apollo speaks and is reported at the trial of Hermione who has put herself upon his judgement. The oracle convinces Leontes of his injustice and he accepts the divine punishment inflicted upon him in the death of Mamillius and the apparent death of Hermione. The dénouement involves a piece of apparent magic by Paulina, who is careful to disclaim the aid of wicked powers. "If this be magic," says Leontes, "let it be an art lawful as eating." In *Pericles*, among many wonders, we have the magic music of the spheres, heard only by Pericles and the audience, heralding the vision of Diana appearing to Pericles in a sleep induced by the music. A similar masque-like vision appears to Queen Katharine asleep at Kimbolton in *Henry VIII*, heralded here and accompanied throughout by mortal music. But the Queen in her sleep takes part in the action, "as it were by inspiration", holding up her hands to heaven in response to the vision. The element of magic, significantly enough, is absent in *Timon of Athens*, though the play has its share of other spectacular features.

For the most part it is clear that in these plays Shakespeare is following the fashion of these later days for elaborate spectacle on the stage, which was fed by the development of the Masque at Court, the most sought-after of all forms of entertainment. The stage in effect made the Court Masque available to the wider audience of the professional theatre. The masque-element proper presents additional spectacle in these plays, as even in the severely designed *Timon of Athens* with its Masque of Cupid and Amazon Ladies. And with all this goes a multiplication of

70

song and instrumental music interspersed in the dramatic action. It is not to be doubted that Ben Jonson, the Master of the Masque, drew a line between masque and play as forms of art, and that this profusion of spectacle is aimed at in the Address to the Reader prefaced to *The Alchemist*:

thou wert never more fair in the way to be cozened than in this age, in poetry, especially in plays, wherein now the concupiscence of dances and antics so reigneth as to run away from nature and be afraid of her, is the only point of art that tickles the spectators.

It is the more significant, therefore, in this wealth of conventional spectacle, that *The Tempest*, like *Macbeth*, requires of the audience as of the reader some belief in the bases of its magic. In both plays the existence in real life of the forms of magic represented is a necessary condition of their dramatic effect. The treatment throughout is literal and serious. To approach *The Tempest* as pure fantasy, as a superior pantomime, is to rob it of its true significance. It is well to compare the treatment of this play with that of Ben Jonson's *The Devil is an Ass* in order to realize the different worlds in which they move. Ben Jonson deliberately injects medieval dramatic allegory in Iniquity the Vice into the grotesque absurdity of his mocking demonology, in which Pug is diminished into a mere caricature of a human serving-man. Indeed, Pug confesses that "the name of devil is discredited in me". In *The Alchemist* no quarter is given to any form of claim to exceptional powers or gifts. All is fraud, deceit, and mere folly and greed. There, as in the *Masque of Queens* and *The Sad Shepherd*, alchemy, witchcraft, sorcery, demonology, and fairy-lore are all the product of hard reading in books. Maudlin the Witch in *The Sad Shepherd* quotes Theocritus upon Hecate. Her son Lorel claims Pan for father. And Puck is her serviceable devil. It would be difficult to conceive of more literary magic. His authorities even for the appearance and dress of witches are Horace, or Lucan, or Apuleius. All this was, of course, deliberate on Jonson's part. He is aware enough of current practices and beliefs of his own day in England, as we may see in casual observations buried in the elaborate scholarly commentary upon *The Masque of Queens*. Certain practices "are yet in use with our modern witchcraft". He recalls from his own childhood stories of sorcery by images of wax at Islington under Elizabeth. He refers to magic potions "familiar with our popular witchcraft", and to the strange claims to power so common in the confessions of witches.

Topical allusions in his plays to notorious dealings in magic of his own day, to Simon Read, to Kelly, to Forman, to Abraham Savory and others, stretch even the learning of Percy Simpson for adequate comment. The episode of Dapper and the Queen of Fairies in *The Alchemist* is a reflection of the actual adventures of Thomas Rogers, a Dorsetshire gentleman and an Oxford graduate, as I have shown.[1] And a few years later Thomas Moore and his wife, as Simpson records, fell into a similar trap with the notorious Wests. In 1607 Simon Read deluded Toby Mathew into the belief that he had familiar spirits to help in the finding of stolen money. The spirits' names are given: Heawelon, Faternon, Cleveton. The statute of Henry VIII referred to in *The Alchemist*, against "multiplication" of gold by alchemy, presumes the possibility of such powers, or at least general belief in such powers. A statute against witchcraft and the conjuration of evil spirits was enacted by Parliament under Elizabeth in 1563 and it was confirmed in 1604 under James I. Yet nowhere does Ben Jonson depart from his resolutely satirical, destructive approach to magic of all forms.[2]

There is some foundation in law for the order of the accusations made by Face to Subtle in the magnificent quarrel with which *The Alchemist* opens, from bawd to conjurer and on to witch and sorcerer. Conjuration and witchcraft are carefully distinguished in law, as in Cowel's *Law Dictionary* of 1607. Conjuration is the exercise of command over evil spirits. The source of this power may be prayer or the invocation of God's holy name, compelling the Devil to obey the conjurer. Witchcraft, on the other hand, is a friendly and voluntary conference and agreement between the wizard or the witch and the Devil or a familiar spirit, in which the fulfilment of desires is obtained at the cost of gifts, perhaps of blood, more generally of the soul thus surrendered to the enemy of man. Both properly differ from enchantments or sorceries, being personal conferences with evil spirits, whereas sorceries use spells and charms, without apparitions. But generally all forms of magic are apt to be practised together by its exponents, and the law forbids them all, common law and ecclesiastical alike. Here most plainly of all we find the universal basis of felony in both Church and State as it is expressed in the formula of indictment which attributes it to the instigation of the Devil, an explanation accepted and indeed confessed again and again by Elizabethan offenders, even in civil cases in the Court of Chancery.

There were Subtles in plenty in England when Shakespeare was busy with his latest plays, and more sinister figures too. Certainly the career of Abraham Savory, mentioned in *The Devil is an Ass*, offers a progression of crime parallel to Face's denunciation of Subtle. And he too, like Subtle, like Faustus, bore the title of Doctor, and not solely for his practice of physic. The magician, in the popular view, wore the robes of learning. The spell of power, the magic book, the book of secrets, was his instrument and the source of his wonderful gifts. It was an age when even reputable physicians rested their claims upon books of secret skills handed down to them, or bought by them, as we see exemplified by Helena's use of Gerard de Narbon's book of receipts in *All's Well That Ends Well*, or in the secret remedy that even the great Dr William Harvey reserved for a wealthy patient suffering from the stone. And Savory, upon a visit to Rome, having bought from a Jew there a book of medical recipes, set up as a physician in Sussex with no training or other qualification.

This, and other new information about Savory, is derived from proceedings in the Court of Chancery. A very unpromising set of pleadings[3] merely refers to an alleged debt of 1611 of Thomas Windsor to Savory of £100. But Savory and Windsor alike sought in the legal debate to injure the opponent's credit, and catastrophic revelations about Savory ensued when depositions were taken.[4] He was the son of a poor hat-maker in London, and lived by shifts, including occupation as an actor with the Duke of Richmond's company, as a dramatist, and a teacher of fencing. He professed physic at Rye in Sussex, and when driven thence set up brothels in Thames Street, in Westminster, and near the Red Bull Theatre in Clerkenwell, successively. He practised magic and conjuration, calling up spirits and devils, and came before the Court of High Commission for conjuration and witchcraft. This was a revival of earlier ventures in Sussex, when he cast horoscopes, and had a familiar spirit who helped him to find lost and stolen goods for the losers. It appeared to him in the night-time in the shape of a naked arm. In the notorious case of the bewitching of the Earl of Essex and the poisoning of Overbury, Savory succeeded Simon Forman, upon Forman's death, as sorcerer used by the Countess to disable the Earl. For these activities he was arrested upon the orders of the Archbishop of Canterbury, came before the Lord Chief Justice several times, and was imprisoned. Unlike Mrs Turner and others involved, he escaped with his life, and survived certainly until 1623, the date of these proceedings in Chancery.

Thomas Andrews of Thames Ditton, who was Windsor's legal adviser, giving evidence in Chancery, relates how he was present in November 1615 at the arraignment of Mrs Turner before the Lord Chief Justice, Sir Edward Coke, and reports upon the nature of Simon Forman's sorceries used in this matter. After Forman's death she found in his house two "leaden pictures of a man and a woman about half a foot long, and certain moulds of brasse by which he conjured." She found also "a cloth of silke wherein were certain words tending to sorcerie As wycrosse bycrosse dycrosse highcrosse recrosse &c together with names of certain spirits and devils". And these instruments of sorcery were used by Savory upon Essex after the death of Forman. Here we have the full panoply of black magic at work with images, figures, and spells, with the conjuration of devils. The spells reported here are apparently perversions of the holy word, the Cross, and were presumably embroidered in the silken cloth.

A certain sympathy may be felt for Forman, especially upon knowledge of new facts concerning his life for which I have not space here. He was the victim of the most merciless persecution by the College of Physicians, possibly because of his serious qualities as an unlicensed practitioner of medicine, and he may seem to have been in some measure driven into more perilous means of livelihood in his later years. But the activities of men like Forman and Savory were a sinister and notorious feature of English life, especially in the increasingly dangerous underworld of London, during the first two decades of the seventeenth century. The stage was bound to have a care in its representation of magic to confine itself to its less offensive forms, the more so when the magic practised in real life came to impinge upon affairs of state, as in the Essex-Overbury affair, or in Elizabeth's reign when the Privy Council dealt with "pictures of wax" at Windsor as threats against the Queen's life. Even Ben Jonson's satire observed limits in subject-matter and in treatment which permitted his plays to satisfy the censorship. There is evidence of caution and tact in Chapman's introduction of a spectacular scene of conjuration into *Bussy d'Ambois*, in which Comolet, clad in magic robes, utters an elaborate magical invocation to Behemoth, emperor of the legion of spirits of the West, bidding him appear with Ashtaroth, shining, splendid, and helpful. Behemoth appears upon the call, with a guard of torchbearing spirits under his command, and speaks and acts at Comolet's bidding, on behalf of Bussy.[5] Bussy is thus employing a conjurer, and successfully, to raise spirits and to serve his purposes. Nothing could well seem more dangerous, unless the outcome were the dreadful retribution that fell upon Faustus.

But Chapman handles the matter with marked care. The conjurer Comolet is a "holy friar". His conjuration is couched in Latin. And the substance of his conjuration is strictly confined to such classical content as might have satisfied Horace, with Styx, Avernus, Hecate and Night its themes. Bussy, in addressing the Friar, his "most honoured father", entreats his "deep skill In the command of good aerial spirits, To assume these magic rites". The Friar consents, since "it concerns so nearly The faith and reverence of my name and order", and explains how

> I have put on these exorcising rites,
> And by my power of learned holiness
> Vouchsafed me from above, I will command
> Our resolution of a raised spirit.

Behemoth accepts this view of the matter, and he also addresses Comolet as "holy Friar". The ground seems to be fully covered. The conjurer is a holy man, using sacred learning. The spirits are "good aerial spirits", obedient to divine powers. And their intervention is salutary, discovering hidden truths.

It may be observed that in 1611, the probable date of *The Tempest*, both Forman and Savory were in full practice in London, and Jonson's recent *Alchemist* of 1610 was still occupying the stage and people's thoughts. If Jonson was careful, and Chapman was careful, both careless on occasion and punished for their carelessness, we might be sure that Shakespeare would avoid all possible offence in his introduction of magic into these late plays. There is clearly no cause of offence in dream-visions, oracles, soothsayers, or magic music of the spheres, in *Cymbeline*, *Pericles*, *The Winter's Tale*, and *Henry VIII*. These are theatrical commonplaces and have no origin in those dangerous and current forms of magic of which the law and the Privy Council took cognizance. But *The Tempest* lives and moves throughout in magic. Prospero is a magician and a conjurer, with all the implements of the professional practitioner, a book of secret magic learning, a magic staff, and a magic robe like that donned by Subtle in his dealings with his victims. He has spirits at his command, with power over the elements, the wind and the seas. Like Oberon in Greene's *James the Fourth* he can spell-bind men from moving, a known power of witchcraft. And magic music waits upon him.

The effectiveness of *The Tempest* as a play requires that some measure of assent should be given by the audience to this portrait of a magician. Otherwise it is a pure fantasy, on the level of modern pantomime. Certainly Dryden had no doubts upon the subject when he came to translate *The Tempest* into the idiom of his own day;

> I must confess 'twas bold, nor would you now
> That liberty to vulgar wits allow,
> Which works by magic supernatural things.
> But Shakespeare's power is sacred as a king's.
> Those legends from old priesthood were received,
> And he then writ, as people then believed.
>
> (Davenant-Dryden, *The Tempest*, Prologue.)

Certainly under Charles II men were not so completely enlightened in comparison with Shakespeare's England. In Charles' General Pardon sorcery was specifically excluded from its benefits. And there is ample further evidence in legal proceedings, as in writings of the time. But Dryden's point is clear enough. The submissive assent of an audience for dramatic effect which was required for Shakespeare's play is no longer available in Dryden's theatre and audience, which were more sceptical about magic.

Given this basis of popular belief for Prospero's powers in *The Tempest*, provided for in the laws of England, and paralleled in the life of the time, it was a matter of importance that Prospero as a magician should be disassociated from the evil manifestations of such powers, the more so as he is a rightful sovereign Duke.

There is a famous passage in *1 Henry IV*, Act III, Scene i, Hotspur's baiting of Owen Glendower's claims to magical powers, following upon his claims to supernatural signs and portents marking him off from other men. King Henry has already acknowledged those very claims, referring to him as "that great magician, damned Glendower", "damned" because of his secret alliance with the powers of evil. There is no doubt concerning Hotspur's real respect for Glendower. Why, then, does he go out of his way to make a mock of Glendower's magical art? The conflict, of course, has dramatic effect, and emerges naturally enough from Hotspur's character. A modern audience rejoices in it. Certainly, some of Glendower's talk to Hotspur may have seemed to be "skimble-skamble stuff", but his main claims had to be taken seriously enough. Conjuration was a felony on the statute-book, and Savory among others was tried for it in Shakespeare's time. Two of Elizabeth's Northern Earls were widely believed to practise these arts, Henry Clifford, Earl of Cumberland, commonly spoken of as the Wizard Earl, and Henry Percy, Earl of Northumberland. In *Henry IV*, Glendower is a rebel against the reigning King. There was surely need on grounds of policy to have doubts cast on his magical powers. It was a dangerous matter to suggest any notion that rebellion against a lawful sovereign, or plots against his person, might have the effectual support of supernatural powers. And certainly there was need to distinguish between a wizard sovereign, Prospero, and "damned Glendower", in the exercise of magical arts.

A full account is given by Prospero himself of the origin and nature of his powers. He neglected his duties as Duke, his study being all in "the liberal arts", "transported and rapt in secret studies". Deposed and exiled, the especial favour and protection of Providence rescued him from a sinking, unseaworthy ship. His studies included astrology, and he recognizes the auspicious star guiding him to the restoration of his dukedom. He controls the elements, he can raise storms at sea, and aerial spirits come at his call. His powers are superior to those of Sycorax, a damned witch guilty of terrible sorceries, and therefore banished from Argier, and even could command Setebos, her god, according to Caliban. Ariel, once under her magic mastery, and bound, for refusal to do evil, to a punishment which her powers could not undo, was freed by Prospero's higher powers. Sycorax deals in evil spells and charms, and her spirits take the ill-omened shape of toads, bats and beetles, as with other witches. (The distinction is sharply made between the powers of Sycorax derived from evil communion with the devil, the father of her son Caliban, and the powers of Prospero, derived from deep study of the secrets of nature.) This is made plainly evident in the instruments of his power, his mantle, his staff, and his book, in which alone his magic resides. His spirits are good spirits, and Ariel's nature is opposed to evil-doing, whereas Caliban is the poisonous child of a wicked dam. Like the master of Rosalind in *As You Like It* in her light-hearted claims to magic, Prospero is "a magician most profound in his art and yet not damnable". He has no dealings whatever with the powers of evil. His spirits are of the air or of the upper world of the elements, not infernal spirits of the underworld of hell. His magic, in fact, is philosophy, in its higher reaches. It is White Magic both in origin and in purpose and effect.

It is very significant, therefore, that we cannot trace in Prospero's exercise of his magic art any parallel to the powers and feats claimed by the professional magicians in contemporary practice, as far as I have found them recorded. Prospero does not 'cast figures', and he does not work with incantations. He does not draw circles or utter spells. He charms Ferdinand from moving by the power of his 'stick'. This power, even if it belonged to Merlin of old in the *Morte d'Arthur*, finds no place in the practice of Savory or of Forman. Nor does Prospero's power to induce sleep in Miranda which, be it observed, is put in action after he has put on his magic mantle at I, ii, 169 ("Now I arise").

The only obvious approach to the known evil powers of witchcraft is, of course, the raising of a tempest to affect the fate of ships at sea, a more particular form of the association of witches with elemental disturbances such as we see in *Macbeth*. King James had reason to recall the manifestation of this power exercised against him and his bride Anne of Denmark, an incident reflected in *Macbeth* in the Witches' persecution of the *Tiger* and its master. It was perhaps sailing pretty near the wind for Shakespeare to introduce this power, though it was necessary to his plot. But it is Ariel who creates the storm: it is the element of air in turmoil, and not the work of devils. And "There's no harm done" in the wreck, as Prospero assures the pitiful Miranda, and not a soul on the ship suffers from his action. All is done to good and desirable ends.

There is a strong classical element in the dramatic picture of Prospero's magic, which tends to remove it further from that contemporary realism which Shakespeare was desirous to avoid as far as he could without denying to his play the necessary response in his audience. There is, for example, evidence enough of his reading of Ovid's *Metamorphoses* in the reflection, both in general ideas and in verbal borrowings, of Ovid's Medea in Book VII. This is particularly marked in Prospero's "Ye elves of hills" speech in v, i, which owes much to Ovid. The episode of the banquet, again, in III, iii, with its spectacular vanishing, is plainly derived from Virgil, where the Harpies devour the food laid before Aeneas and his company in Book III of the *Aeneid*. In this masque-like device a stage-direction runs "Enter Ariel, like a harpy", and presently Prospero praises Ariel for his performance of "the figure of this harpy".

There are disconcerting phrases, indeed, in Prospero's invocation in v, i, which seem inconsistent with the general picture of his white magic and import an element of what he himself calls "rough magic", the violence and chaos of black art. It is difficult to reconcile ourselves, for example, to his claim to have opened graves and to have resurrected the dead. But the fact is that Shakespeare has been unwary in his borrowing from Ovid, and has read too much of Medea into Prospero's speech. For this was one of Medea's especial powers.[6] Here, indeed, and not for the first time, we may truly say that Shakespeare had too much education, not too little. The invocation, in fact, conflicts with his conception of Prospero as a white magician.

We may be tempted to read into *The Tempest* a symbolical representation of a world in which God, or Providence, exercises direct rule by constant intervention in the person of Prospero. The island is a restricted area, fitted for such a rule, and it is an island of beauty. It is indeed the Utopia of Gonzalo's imagination and desires, free from the complexities of human society in civilized countries, save that it has a sovereign. But that sovereign, Prospero, if all-powerful and all-knowing, is moved by benevolence in his sovereignty, like the love of God. He is capable of anger, even as the wrath of God may turn to the punishment of evil. Justice lies in his hands alone, the image of divine justice in direct operation, free from all the uncertainties of human justice even in delegation from God to King and from King to magistrates and judges.

Tempting as this may be, we should perhaps be better advised to see *The Tempest* as in some degree a companion-piece to *Measure for Measure* in Shakespeare's notable concern in his later plays with problems of justice. There we see the image of divine justice in the Duke delegating his justice to human instruments, and of the imperfections of that human justice exemplified in Angelo. Here we see perhaps in Prospero the learned and philosophical ruler, working justice, righting wrongs, defeating rebellion, in his own right as the Vicar of God in his own country, a visible Providence— a conception that would be grateful to the learned and philosophical King James the First.

NOTES

1. 'A Topical Reference in *The Alchemist*', in *Adams Memorial Studies*, 1948.
2. The fullest and most authoritative account of the subject is G. L. Kittredge's *Witchcraft in Old and New England* (1929).
3. P.R.O. C3/392/5.   4. P.R.O. C24/501/. Windsor *v.* Savory.
5. Act IV, Scene I. In the copy of Shepherd's *Chapman* in my possession, formerly R. Warwick Bond's copy and bearing his annotations, he concludes upon this scene in the brief words, "Awful stuff".
6. *Metam.* VII, 206: "*manesque exire sepulchris*".

THE NEW WAY
WITH SHAKESPEARE'S TEXTS:
AN INTRODUCTION FOR LAY READERS
IV. TOWARDS THE HIGH ROAD

BY

J. DOVER WILSON

By the beginning of the War of 1914–18 it was becoming clear, thanks to the work of Pollard and Greg, that the study of Shakespeare's texts was making a fresh start, the right start at last, because leading to the true high road, from which there would be no turning back. It was, as I shall now show, some years yet before we actually found it. But round about 1920 many of us already felt confident that we were close upon it. To what extent Greg shared this premature optimism I do not know. But his intimate friend and fellow bibliographer Ronald McKerrow, a man almost morbidly cautious by temperament, was contemplating an edition of Shakespeare as early as 1910,[1] so that I suppose both men must have considered this a not impossible task even then. As for their senior, and my intimate friend, Alfred Pollard, he was certainly an optimist, for I possess a typescript copy of the Textual Introduction to the *New Cambridge Shakespeare* (published in *The Tempest* volume, 1921) which he had read with approval and in the margins of which he had pencilled suggestions, some of which found their way into the published version. Yet that Introduction, though I still think it well-planned, seems a generation later almost ludicrously optimistic in tone.

This optimism was in large measure due to an accident, namely that hard on the heels of the publication of Pollard's convincing thesis that the original editions of Shakespeare's plays were much closer to his autograph manuscripts than had hitherto been assumed, three important discoveries were made each of which seemed to give us glimpses of those manuscripts. One was the determination by Maunde Thompson of the kind of hand Shakespeare wrote and the consequent discovery or re-discovery of a scene by him in the manuscript *Book of Sir Thomas More* at the British Museum, which helped to show us how he spelt. But, this being the subject of my previous article, nothing need be said about it here.

Nor need I say much either about the other two since I shall have to discuss them in a later article. Suffice it to note here, first, that in 1911 Percy Simpson, then a classics master in a London grammar school, published a little book called *Shakespearian Punctuation* which seemed to revolutionize our ideas of Elizabethan punctuation in general and of Shakespeare's in particular; ideas which Pollard immediately turned to admirable purpose in the edition of *Richard II* which he produced in 1916; and, second, that somewhere about 1916 Pollard and I were examining together a facsimile of the 1600 quarto of *A Midsummer Night's Dream* when we stumbled upon a succession of brief passages of irregularly divided verse in the opening sixty-two lines of Act V which convinced us, and a number of other scholars, that behind the print lay a page or two of manuscript drastically revised by Shakespeare; that he had touched up the original throughout by writing brief additions in the margin, which left him no room for the proper verse-division, and so left the compositor no clue to where each line should end. We felt we had almost caught Shakespeare in the act of composition.

These discoveries seemed to give good ground for a fair measure of optimism. It looked as if editors had only to decide, in regard to any particular original text, whether it was printed from Shakespeare's manuscript or from a prompt-book, and then proceed to edit it in the light of the newly acquired knowledge of how Shakespeare wrote, how he spelt, how he punctuated, and how at times he revised portions of the dialogue by making additions in the margin. But the situation turned out to be far more complicated than was, or could be, realized at that stage. The development indeed of Shakespearian textual research in the twentieth century has followed the lines of every other scientific enquiry: theory continually modified or reformulated as fresh facts come to light and new questions come into men's minds. And A. N. Whitehead's aphorism, "Seek simplicity and distrust it", which Greg set in the front of one of his more speculative monographs, may be taken as the moral of the whole story. One cardinal over-simplification at the outset was due to a natural reaction against the extreme pessimism of earlier views, which as I pointed out in my first article had found dogmatic expression in an essay on the First Folio published in 1902 by Sidney Lee. Here is a typical passage which perhaps did more than anything else to provoke Greg and Pollard to frame a sounder hypothesis and a passage they clearly continued to have in mind as a kind of counter-irritant for another thirty years. In Shakespeare's theatre, Lee wrote,

No genuine respect was paid to a dramatic author's original drafts after they reached the playhouse. Scenes and passages were freely erased by the managers, who became the owners, and other alterations were made for stage purposes. Ultimately the dramatist's corrected autograph was copied by the play-house scrivener; this transcript became the official 'prompt-copy', and the original was set aside and destroyed, its uses being exhausted. The copyist was not always happy in deciphering his original, especially when the dramatist wrote so illegibly as Shakespeare, and, since no better authority than the 'prompt-copy' survived for the author's words, the copyist's misreadings encouraged crude emendations on the actor's part. Whenever a piece was revived, a new revision was undertaken by the dramatist in concert with the manager or by an independent author, and in course of time the official playhouse copy of a popular piece might come to bear a long series of new interlineations. Thus stock-pieces were preserved, not in the author's autograph, but in the playhouse scrivener's interlineated transcript, which varied in authenticity according to the calligraphy of the author's original draft, the copyist's intelligence, and the extent of the recensions on successive occasions of the piece's revival.[2]

What amazes the modern scholar most about these statements is not so much their wrong-headedness—in point of fact we shall presently see that Lee had ground for some of them, and even today it would be difficult to disprove every one—as the complete and enviable confidence with which they are put forward. In 1909 Pollard replied by defending the Folio text and exposing Lee's ignorance of the conditions of publishing and printing at that period. In a series of lectures he called rather fancifully *Shakespeare's Fight with the Pirates* and delivered at Cambridge in 1915 he went a step further and erected, in place of Lee's now discredited theory of a congeries of corrupt transcripts, a counter-theory which may roughly be described as 'one play, one manuscript'. In other words, he pointed out that the theatre was unlikely to have possessed more than one or at most two manuscripts of any given play—generally, he thought, only one—and that it was from such manuscripts that the bulk of the original editions of Shakespeare were printed.

There seemed indeed several excellent reasons for believing that the acting companies kept down their copies of a play to a minimum. To multiply copies would have increased the chances of theft by pirates on the look-out for texts they could sell to publishers. Transcription too would mean paying a scrivener, an expense it is legitimate to assume the company might well avoid if the author's manuscript was straightforward enough to serve as prompt-copy. And Pollard pointed to what looked like positive evidence that authors' manuscripts could be and were so used. For example Greg, reviewing Lee's Introduction to the Oxford facsimile in 1903, had disposed of his statement that "stock pieces were preserved [at the theatre], not in the author's autograph but in the playhouse scrivener's interlineated manuscript"[3] by referring him to the British Museum manuscript copy of Massinger's *Believe as you List* which was indisputably a prompt-book in the author's handwriting. To this Pollard added in 1915 two other manuscripts, namely *Sir Thomas More*, described in my article of two years back, and a queer sort of play called the *Launching of the Mary* (1633), both also at the British Museum.

Furthermore, coming closer to Shakespeare, he observed that some of the Quarto and Folio texts bore evident traces of the playhouse which he could only call "prompter's notes", and among these texts were the Quartos of *Romeo and Juliet* (1599), of *A Midsummer Night's Dream* (1600), and of *Much Ado* (1600), all of which he then strongly suspected were printed directly from Shakespeare's manuscripts; a suspicion that soon deepened into certainty. Of such "notes" the most conspicuous examples were stage-directions or speech-headings in which the name of an actor appeared instead of the character he impersonated. Thus we have "Enter Will Kemp" (i.e. the comic actor in Shakespeare's company) instead of "Enter Peter" at IV, v, 102 of *Romeo and Juliet* (1599), and "Kemp" and "Cowley" (another comic actor) in place of "Dogberry" and "Verges" as speech-headings in IV, ii of *Much Ado* (1600). Other instances quoted in 1915 were stage-directions referring directly to the theatre, such as "Enter the King of Fairies at one doore with his traine; and the Queene, at another, with hers" (*Midsummer Night's Dream*, II, i, 55)—this in the wood near Athens; or "Enter Romeo and Juliet aloft" (*Romeo and Juliet*, III, v); and stage-directions in the imperative mood, such as "Whistle Boy" (*Romeo and Juliet*, V, iii, 17); "Ly downe" (*Midsummer Night's Dream*, III, ii, 85); "Shoute within: they all start up, Winde hornes" (*Midsummer Night's Dream*, IV, i, 138), where "within" as always in Quarto and Folio texts means "within the tiring-house" or in modern phrase "behind the scenes".

Stage-directions like these, Pollard nevertheless admitted, might have been penned by Shakespeare himself,[4] since they would come naturally to a dramatist writing for the theatre and with performances in mind. In view of later developments this admission is a notable instance of Pollard's cautious perspicacity; as also is the following summing up of the matter, in his edition of *Richard II* published a few months afterwards:

When a new play was accepted by a company of players it is evident that copies must have been made of the different parts, so that each actor could learn his own.... A clean copy may have been made at the same time for the use of the Prompter, or (as appears to have been the case with...Massinger's *Believe as you List* of 1631) the author's own manuscript may have been taken for this purpose. To copy a play of this length [*Richard II*] would have occupied a scrivener some three or four days, and although the cost would not have been great, probably about five shillings, it is by no means certain that the Company incurred it, as with a single complete text and the actors' 'parts' they would be fairly secured against accident. Even if this cost were incurred, it seems probable...that the clean copy made by the scrivener would have been considered better worth keeping than the author's draft, and that thus, whether there was one complete copy or two, it was probably the one in Shakespeare's handwriting which...reached the printer.[5]

This, in effect, anticipated the full-blown doctrine of the relation between prompt-book and author's manuscript as stated by McKerrow fifteen years later. But Pollard, rightly at this date, was chiefly concerned with killing the old false doctrine that Shakespeare's printed texts were separated from his manuscripts by an unknown series of more or less corrupt transcripts, and he therefore insisted that prompt-book and author's manuscript might be the same 'book' and pointed out that as far as the available evidence went they sometimes were. And if he misinterpreted, as we shall find he did, what he called the "prompter's notes" in the Shakespearian Quartos he was not alone in that: the misinterpretation was to govern textual theory for many years yet. Even as late as 1930 no less an authority than E. K. Chambers was still declaring that the occurrence of actors' names in dramatic texts "must be due to the book-holder", i.e. the prompter, and he furnished a complete list of such names in Shakespeare's texts to illustrate the point.[6] Nor were the ideas of Chambers on the subject of theatrical manuscripts any further advanced at this time than Pollard's had been, since he wrote:

While they are sometimes in the hand of the author, and sometimes in that of the book-keeper or another scribe, it is clear that the same copy might serve both as the official "book" endorsed by the Master of the Revels [i.e. the censor], and as a working stage-copy, probably an actual "prompt-copy", for the ordering of performances. And in *Believe as you List* and *Launching of the Mary*, at least, we have evidence that this copy might be the author's own original.[7]

—which was only repeating Pollard's statement of 1916 in other words.

The truth is that of the forty-five manuscript playbooks belonging to the popular theatre which have come down to us from before the Puritan Revolution only those happening to contain the hands of both author and prompter had so far, for one reason or another, attracted the serious attention of scholars. And it is perhaps significant in this connexion that only two had been printed for the Malone Society[8] before Pollard wrote in 1916; and though another eight were added before 1930 none of these, with one exception, exhibited features which might have led Chambers to question or develop Pollard's view. Yet Greg had already described the exception in an article published in 1925, though it may be doubted whether even he recognized its full significance and certainly Chambers did not. Nevertheless this article marks a considerable advance, and I must now, therefore, give some account of it.

Its title, 'Prompt Copies, Private Transcripts, and the Playhouse Scrivener,'[9] suggests an echo of the passage from Lee quoted above, and the suggestion seems borne out by Greg's reference at the outset to the publisher's preface to the Folio of Beaumont and Fletcher, 1647, from which Lee drew most of his inferences regarding the copy for the Folio of Shakespeare. In any case

Greg was clearly to some extent still preoccupied with Lee's theory; his purpose being to discover, by examining certain late Jacobean and early Caroline manuscript playbooks belonging to the King's Men, what at that date was the function of the playhouse scrivener and the prevalence of transcripts for private patrons in the Company that had been Shakespeare's until his death in 1616. With the help of Sisson, who was just then editing Massinger's autograph *Believe as you List* (1631) for the Malone Society, he was able to identify the hand of the 'book-holder' who prepared that text for the stage with the hand of the man who transcribed two other manuscript playbooks; one Beaumont and Fletcher's *Honest Man's Fortune*, bearing the censor's allowance dated 1624 and probably a prompt-book, and the other a specially elaborate private transcript of Fletcher's *Bonduca* obviously commissioned by or for a wealthy collector seemingly many years later than the play's first appearance on the stage somewhere between 1609 and 1614. That this scribe was a playhouse scrivener who acted as 'book-holder' or at any rate could prepare prompt-books we have *Believe as you List* to show. In two other playhouse manuscripts, however, both again belonging to the King's Men and both transcripts, Greg found the hand of a different scribe altogether, and a scribe that F. P. Wilson was able, in an article following Greg's a year later,[10] to prove belonged to a certain Ralph Crane, a professional scrivener, who found occasional employment as a copyist for the King's Men, and whose dramatic manuscripts exhibit certain peculiarities which persuaded Wilson, and have since persuaded Shakespearian scholars generally, that Crane was in some way connected with the preparation of the copy of the First Folio of Shakespeare for the printers.

Of this exciting conjecture, which incidentally put out of court a minor conjecture of my own entertained for some ten years, I must once again postpone discussion to a later stage. But to anticipate a little, it fitted in with the even more interesting results that followed from Greg's discovery that the other scribe was actually the King's Men's book-holder. For from documentary evidence to which his attention was drawn later it turned out that this scribe was a certain Edward Knight, who had been book-holder for Shakespeare's company since 1624, if not before; and may well, as Greg came to believe by 1955, have been the virtual editor of the First Folio on behalf of Heminge and Condell.[11] Thirty years lie between those conclusions and Sisson's discovery in 1925 that the book-holder whose hand is evident in Massinger's autograph *Believe as you List* was also the transcriber of Fletcher's *Honest Man's Fortune*. But the chain of evidence, which includes links I have not been able to touch upon here, is complete and affords a very pretty example of the new way with Shakespeare's texts.

Of even greater relevance to our immediate purpose however was still a third discovery in this pregnant article of 1925. As he read through the private transcript of Fletcher's *Bonduca* above mentioned Greg found that the scrivener, later identified with Knight, had omitted two or three scenes at the beginning of Act v, because they were missing from the manuscript he was copying, and had attempted to cover the gap by giving, probably from memory, a very brief indication of their contents, and by adding a note in explanation. From this note it appears that looking for the play, then fifteen or twenty years old, Knight discovered that the prompt-book, which he calls "the booke where by it was first Acted from", had disappeared, so that the copy he was making "hath beene transcribed from the fowle papers of the Authors, which were found". He does not say where he found these "fowle papers"; but Greg, jumping to a natural conclusion, assumed that it was at the theatre, i.e. "in the archives of the King's Company".

Here Greg was less cautious than E. K. Chambers who tacitly demurred and suggested alternatively that the "fowle papers" may have been preserved by the author himself or his representatives.[12] But Greg's guess was correct, and his discovery of Knight's reference to "fowle papers" marks the entry of that term, now accepted as the regular Elizabethan term for an author's rough draft, into the vocabulary of Shakespearian textual critics, with whom moreover it is also now an axiom that the foul papers and the prompt-book based upon them were generally kept together at the Globe. Yet neither Greg nor Chambers seems at that time to have appreciated the precise meaning of foul papers and when Greg spoke of "fair copy" the expression did not necessarily connote the 'book' or prompt-book. He was getting very 'warm', as the children say, but was not yet quite 'there'. The progress of the investigation up to this point is, however, a good illustration of the following observation in the Introduction which he wrote for the magnificent volumes entitled *Elizabethan Dramatic Documents* published in 1931:

> Every item of historical evidence performs a two-fold function: positively it enlarges the basis we have to build on, and enables us to extend the structure of valid inference; negatively it is often of even greater service in limiting the field of admissible conjecture.[13]

And another passage, relating more particularly to the manuscript material which he here made accessible to his fellow scholars, may be quoted from the same Introduction:

> It is hardly too much to say that the Plots and the Part reproduced in this collection, and the Books [i.e. MS. playbooks] of which specimens are given, form an indispensable background to all useful thought and a framework to which must conform all valid conjecture, concerning the textual phenomena and history of the Elizabethan drama.[14]

Yet the 'documents' were not enough by themselves. What brought us finally on to the editorial highway was a closer study of the printed texts as only an editor, who was also an expert bibliographer, could study them. Pollard's work on *Richard II* had involved something of the kind; for he did everything an editor should do with that play except publish a critical text and write explanatory notes. But as we have seen he lacked in 1916 sufficient knowledge of the manuscript documents. By 1931, however, another bibliographer, with a knowledge of the documents probably equal to Greg's and with an unrivalled knowledge also of late sixteenth and early seventeenth century printing and printed books, was deeply engrossed in the problems facing an editor of Shakespeare. I mean Ronald McKerrow, who in 1929 reverted to the project he had laid aside in 1910 by accepting an invitation from the Clarendon Press to produce *The Oxford Shakespeare*. The first question confronting him was one that, well acquainted as he was with the books printed at that period, must often have occurred to him, namely why is it that the original texts of Shakespeare are so much worse printed than the ordinary run of other Elizabethan and Jacobean books? And the solution he found to this problem and expounded in a couple of articles dated 1931 and 1935 respectively, opened another chapter in the history of textual criticism.

In the famous passage I quoted earlier from Dr Johnson's *Proposals for printing the Dramatick Works of William Shakespeare* (1756) he crowned, you may remember, his imaginary account of the progressive corruption which the said works endured at the hands of actors, copyists, the piratical compilers of stolen players' parts, and so on, by declaring that "they suffered another depravation from the ignorance and negligence of the printers, as every man who knows the state of the press in that age will readily conceive".[15] This abuse of Shakespeare's printers was echoed by critics and editors for another hundred and fifty years until there arose bibliographers in the land, Pollard, Greg, McKerrow, who did indeed know "the state of the press in that age" and therefore refused to believe that the bulk of errors and eccentricities of the quarto and folio texts were due to the drunken aberrations of compositors. Yet there the ill-printed texts were, the 'good quartos' of *Love's Labour's Lost*, *Romeo and Juliet*, and *Hamlet* being the worst of the lot; and Pollard, obviously puzzled, was driven to plead as follows, "in extenuation of the inaccuracy of Elizabethan printers in their dealings with plays".[16]

Let us remember that they worked in wooden houses in which the windows were very small and glazed with imperfectly transparent glass; that they worked long hours, probably at least eleven or twelve a day, which means not only that their powers of attention were often overstrained, but that much of their work must have been done by rushlight; that they had to deal with a text which even when there is no suspicion of corruption often puzzles professors; and finally that, when they could get it, they drank ale for breakfast and ale for dinner and ale for supper. No doubt the ale was small, but its effect may have been cumulative.... Surely a generation which drinks tea and coffee and has workshops with large windows and electric light, and an eight-hour day, and has never to deal with any copy in the least resembling the plays of Shakespeare, should not be too forward in despising these poor men. Nevertheless the fact remains that they did make mistakes and made them in quantities.

This eloquent apology may not be without interest to the craftsmen of a press which is printing this article and has been printing manuscripts from my pen over a period of fifty years. They may even have a greater fellow feeling for their predecessors than Pollard imagined, since some years ago a page of my foul papers came back to me, no doubt inadvertently, with the words "Bloody Copy" scribbled across it in red ink by the Cambridge master-printer of that date.

In McKerrow's eyes, however, the excuses Pollard offered were beside the point, or rather his reference to the difficulties of Shakespearian copy was enough to explain everything, or almost everything, odd or bad in the printed texts, once these were considered in the light of what was now known about playhouse manuscripts in general and were compared with other books produced by the London printing-house of that age. He began by proving that "Elizabethan printers reproduced with reasonable accuracy the manuscripts before them" and cited as evidence three books of the period, chosen at random. To quote his argument in a convenient summary by Greg:

In the 5,391 lines of Book IV of *The Faery Queene* the Oxford Press editor finds less than two dozen errors, mostly trifling, and only two passages in which there could be any doubt of the correct reading, both open to easy emendation. In *Greene's News from Heaven and Hell*, a pamphlet of 62 pages, there is again the usual sprinkling of misprints, but says McKerrow "not, I think, a single error which could cause a moment's difficulty in reading". And in ten folio pages of *The Treasury of Ancient and Modern Times*, printed by Jaggard in 1619, "I noted eighteen errors of which only one is at all serious". Why then does the Folio text of *Coriolanus* "in some 3,400 lines contain, apart from many errors or irregularities in punctuation and line arrangement, at least twenty-one passages in which conservative modern editors have had either to emend the text or admit their inability to do so? Why does the second quarto of *Hamlet*...contain at least a dozen passages of similar incorrectness?"[17]

The Jaggard folio of 1619 was an example of special relevance since of course he was printing Shakespeare's First Folio at about the same date. There must then, McKerrow continues, have been "something peculiar about the manuscripts of dramatic works sent to the printer". Not all such works, however, for we have *The Workes of Beniamin Jonson* quite respectably printed in 1616; but they, to be sure, were seen through the press by the author himself as Shakespeare's never were. One can assume too that prompt-books, that is to say manuscripts so clearly written and set out that the prompter could find his way about them with ease and rapidity, would not have presented any difficulty to a printer.

Thus by a long and elaborate train of reasoning, most of the steps in which I must omit, McKerrow led us to a conclusion from which there is no escape, namely that the copy for a badly printed quarto or folio text was not the prompt-book but the dramatist's foul papers of which the prompt-book was a fair copy thoroughly tidied up for performance. As for those actors' names and theatrical stage-directions which Pollard had called "prompter's notes" and pointed to as evidence that the texts containing them were derived from prompt-copy, an instance here and there, McKerrow admits, might have been jotted down by the prompter as he first read through the foul papers; but the bulk of them came undoubtedly from Shakespeare's pen. "What could be more natural", he asks,

than that a skilled dramatist closely connected with the theatre and writing, not with any thought of print, but with his eye solely on a stage production, should give stage directions in the form of directions to the actors (as they might appear in a prompt-book), rather than as descriptions of action viewed from the front of the theatre? Probably he would use either type of direction as it happened to occur to him, just as we find them mixed in the manuscript of the *Two Noble Ladies*[18] which is held to be in the hand of its author.... Even the occasional mention of the name of an actor seems to me far from unnatural in the manuscript of such a dramatist as Shakespeare, who was writing for a particular company with which he was closely connected. Psychologically it is, I think, just what we should expect. To a man with a good power of visualization such as every successful dramatist must have, and who knows in advance what actor will fill each of the more important roles, the actors themselves must have been more or less constantly present in his mind as he wrote. I suspect, indeed, that this fact was responsible for the extraordinary vitality and vividness of some of Shakespeare's minor characters. Dogberry and Verges were so life-like because they were not merely a constable and a watchman in the abstract, but actually the Kemp and Cowley whose every accent and gesture Shakespeare must have known, *playing* a constable and a watchman. And if this is so, what more natural than that Shakespeare, who was notoriously careless about the names of his minor characters, just because they were, I think, to him his friends and fellow-actors playing such parts, should momentarily forget the names which he had assigned to the characters and put down instead the much more familiar names of the actors themselves?[19]

I make no apology for quoting this at length since nothing more illuminating had been written up to that time about Shakespeare's original texts. And what a fine piece of imaginative criticism it is ! If I know my McKerrow, he hesitated not a little before committing himself to it in print. And yet anyone familiar with the Quartos in the original has only to read what he says to be instantly convinced of its truth to fact. The article was a landmark in bibliographical research, and became immediately of the greatest possible value to Shakespearian editors.[20]

Moreover it completed the work of Alfred Pollard; for though McKerrow disproved Pollard's theory of "prompter's notes" and showed that contrary to Pollard's reading of the situation prompt-book and author's copy were seldom identical,[21] he provided much stronger reasons for Pollard's optimism, converted indeed a belief that many Quarto and Folio texts were printed from Shakespeare's own manuscripts, into a certainty. Furthermore, not only did the article "bring the author's draft into the fore-front of the critical picture", to quote Greg again,[22] but by inference it gave a pretty clear pointer to which Quarto or Folio texts were most closely associated with Shakespeare's manuscripts. In other words, it reversed the assumptions or scepticisms of earlier editors. In their eyes a text full of misprints, irregularities in line-arrangement, and signs of theatrical influence was assumed without question to have been corrupted by actors or copyists; whereas they approached with confidence a clean straightforward text. The modern editor, on the other hand, regards the clean text with suspicion since he feels fairly sure that some scrivener or other, to say nothing of a magisterial prompter, stands between him and what Shakespeare wrote. But his heart leaps up when he finds himself dealing with a badly printed text since he has hopes that it may bring him within sight of the master's foul papers. Yet to assume that a clean text was printed from the prompt-book direct is dangerous to say the least of it; for, as McKerrow also notes, while the players would not have hesitated to release the foul papers for publication, since these, having been transcribed, had done their work, they would certainly have been very reluctant to part with their legible acting copy, all ready for performance, and endorsed with the censor's allowance.

Four years after this first article McKerrow published a second in which he supplemented the first by explaining another striking difference between Shakespearian texts, long since observed but never before understood. In the stage-directions and speech-headings of some the names of characters are consistently rendered throughout; in others character-names thus employed may vary in form. As an example of the latter he cited the folio text of *The Comedy of Errors*. In this, he remarks, the names

frequently depend, much as they do in a novel, on the progress of the story or on the person with whom the character is conversing. Thus the father of the two brothers Antipholus, whom we know from the text to be named Egeon, is in the opening stage-direction described as *"Merchant of Siracusa"* and throughout the first scene is, as a speaker, simply *Merchant*. In the next scene, however, a different merchant (of Ephesus) appears, and later, in IV, i, another. Both these characters are called as speakers simply "Merchant" (*Mar., E.Mar., Mer.*). In V, i, however, while this last Merchant is on the stage Egeon enters and recognizes his sons. As his original designation of "Merchant" is now in use for someone else, Egeon becomes first "Merchant Father" (*Mar. Fat.*) and later simply "Father".[23]

As for the two pairs of twins, the similarity of their names and the necessity of distinguishing one twin from the other put the scribe responsible for the script to all sorts of shifts leading to strange abbreviated forms. And McKerrow went on to show that similar variations in character-names are to be found in *Romeo and Juliet* (Q2), *Midsummer Night's Dream* (Q1), *Love's Labour's Lost* (Q1), *All's Well that Ends Well* (F), *The Merchant of Venice* (Q1) and *Titus Andronicus* (Q2) and, contrasted with these seven, seven others in which such variations are not found, namely *The Two Gentlemen, Taming of the Shrew, Measure for Measure, Twelfth Night, King John,* and *Macbeth.* The conclusion he drew from all this was much what it had been in the earlier article: that is, that irregularity points to Shakespearian foul papers, regularity to some sort of fair copy, perhaps made by a professional scribe. Indeed, so closely associated are the two sets of phenomena and so similar the conclusions arrived at that it looks as if in the second article McKerrow was working out a detail he had overlooked when writing the first. In other words, we shall probably not be far wrong if we assume that the significance of the whole thing only gradually dawned upon him.

It should be noted, for example, that he did not remark upon the importance of the distinction between regular and irregular texts for an editor until the very end of the second article. What he wrote as a conclusion to his article of 1935 may well stand as a conclusion to mine, since it shows that the editorial highway had been reached at last.

If there is anything in this view...if we can with some confidence assert that a play showing, in the character names, irregularity of the kind which I have described, was printed directly from the author's MS., the fact seems to be of considerable importance, for such plays must necessarily be regarded for purposes of textual criticism very differently from those which we can suppose to derive from a fair copy made by someone else. In the one case we must allow for confused corrections and careless writing, but can take it for granted that the compositor had before him something which, though perhaps difficult to decipher, embodied the intention of the author, and that the text as we have it must represent fairly closely what the MS. *looked like* to the compositor. In the other case the compositor would presumably be working from a MS. which would in itself be easily legible, but the text of which might already have been tampered with by someone who had views as to what the author ought to have written, and who placed the construction of a readable text above the duty of following closely the *ductus litterarum* of his original. The kinds of error which we should expect to find in prints from MSS. of the two groups may evidently be very different.[24]

NOTES

1. See R. B. McKerrow, *Prolegomena for the Oxford Shakespeare* (1939), p. ix.
2. *Facsimile of the First Folio*, Oxford (1902), p. xviii.
3. *The Library*, 2nd ser., IV, 258–85, 'The bibliographical history of the First Folio'.
4. A. W. Pollard, *Shakespeare's Fight with the Pirates*, 2nd ed. (1920), pp. 64–5. The *Midsummer Night's Dream* references are to Grigg's facsimile of the Fisher Quarto.
5. *Idem, King Richard II: a new quarto* (1916), pp. 96–7. A dramatic manuscript, *A Second Mayden's Tragedy*, is also described as "author's own manuscript" by Pollard, but in error. Cf. Greg's ed. of it for the Malone Society.
6. E. K. Chambers, *William Shakespeare* (1930), I, 164, 237; cf. also I, 50, 122, 181.
7. E. K. Chambers, *ibid.* I, 124–5.
8. I.e. the *Second Mayden's Tragedy* and *Sir Thomas More*. For the Malone Society see *Shakespeare Survey*, 9, p. 78.
9. *The Library*, 4th ser., VI, 148–56.
10. F. P. Wilson, 'Ralph Crane, Scrivener to the King's Players', *The Library*, 4th ser., VII, 194–215.

11. W. W. Greg, Introduction to *Bonduca* (Malone Soc. 1951), and *The Shakespeare First Folio* (1955), pp. 78–9 and note C on p. 100.

12. E. K. Chambers, *William Shakespeare*, I, 125.

13. W. W. Greg, *Elizabethan Dramatic Documents* (1931), p. x.

14. *Ibid.* p. xi.

15. Raleigh, *Johnson on Shakespeare* (1908), p. 2; *Shakespeare Survey*, 7, p. 52.

16. A. W. Pollard, *Richard II: a new quarto* (1916), pp. 20–1.

17. W. W. Greg, *The Shakespeare First Folio* (1955), p. 104.

18. Edited for the Malone Society, 1930.

19. R. B. McKerrow, 'The Elizabethan Printer and Dramatic Manuscripts', *The Library*, 4th ser., XII, 273–5.

20. Soon after it appeared I began editing *Hamlet* and found in the passage just quoted the key to its main textual problem. See my *Manuscript of Shakespeare's Hamlet* (1934), p. 90.

21. In point of fact all three examples Pollard cited and relied upon turned out to be abnormal in one way or another, and so not to the point. Cf. Greg, *The Shakespeare First Folio*, pp. 93–5.

22. Greg, *ibid.* p. 96.

23. R. B. McKerrow, 'A suggestion regarding Shakespeare's Manuscripts', *Review of English Studies*, XI (Oct. 1935), pp. 460–1.

24. *Ibid.* p. 465.

A PORTRAIT OF A MOOR

BY

BERNARD HARRIS

Recently, the Shakespeare Institute acquired a portrait of the Moorish ambassador to Elizabeth in 1600—a portrait which is of considerable interest to students of history, of art and of the theatre (Plate I). For the historian it gives character to an episode, nowhere fully recorded, in the diplomatic relations between England and Barbary. It forms, too, a handsome and out-of-the-common addition to the gallery of Tudor portraits. For those concerned with the theatre its interest is twofold. First, although it lacks the direct relevance to stage-history attaching to Peacham's sketch of Aaron, it may well assist a producer of *The Merchant of Venice* when he comes to the stage-direction, "Enter Morochus, a tawny Moore all in white". The second point of theatrical interest is at once more speculative and much more significant. The picture presents "ocular proof" of what the Elizabethans saw as a Moor of rank, one whose presence with his companions in London a year or so before the usually agreed date of *Othello* caused much contemporary comment. Idle speculation, of course, must be curbed; but at least we are entitled to wonder whether an audience alert for the topical would not look for a true Barbarian on their stage. This ambassador from Mauretania, we have to remember, was Othello's countryman. Iago refers to his master as a "Barbary horse" and elsewhere uses the term "barbarian"; after the dismissal from Cyprus, he tells Roderigo that Othello is going to Mauretania, a lie designed to imply the general's final disgrace—his loss of high office among Christians and his ignominious return to his own people.

Obviously Othello's character is the invention of Shakespeare's imagination; obviously, too, the account of his general life and crime, with details concerning his rank and race, come from Cinthio's *Il Moro*. Yet we still argue about Othello's features, on which the source is silent and the play confusing. We know that he is black and a Moor; that the Elizabethans were inexact in their use of the terms "Moor" and "negro"; that in glossing "Moor" as "negro" Onions seems to cut this knot, but really leaves us with two loose ends which an inconsistent stage practice has never tied up. Through all this ambiguity of terminology and stage tradition the portrait of the Moorish ambassador reminds us of the common acquaintance of the Elizabethans with real, as distinct from fictional, Moors; and here interest in the picture goes beyond speculation.

To recount the story of the embassy in some detail is to take us nearer to Shakespeare's England, perhaps even, in a sense, to Shakespeare's Moor. Cinthio's is not the whole tale after all; the fundamental dramatic contrast of racial difference is Shakespeare's first departure from his source. Primarily this derived from the mind which had conceived Shylock, yet it was a contrast in contemporary reality, not in cosmopolitan Venice but in insular England; an incompatibility illustrated in 1600 by the reception and behaviour of the Moorish visitors.

Relations between England and Barbary, of which Morocco was part, had been characterized by commercial ambition and diplomatic expediency from the time of the first voyage made by

The Lion in 1551. James Alday, who had apparently inspired the traffic, complained bitterly that while the great sweat kept him from the ship at Portsmouth, "Windam had her away from thence, before I was able to stand upon my legges, by whom I lost at that instant fourescore pound" The prize was indeed great, but the race was for the strong, and many notable merchant families were soon embarked on it. The trade, much of it in imported sugar and exported cloth, was contested by Spain and Portugal, whose spheres of influence it transgressed; it was further complicated by merchant rivalry, by changes in foreign policy, and endangered by pirates of all nations.

In the fifty years since *The Lion* had first sailed, many problems of mutual concern for England and Barbary remained unresolved. The Barbary Company of 1585, headed by the Earls of Leicester and Warwick, achieved little regulation of affairs and was never incorporated, its first charter expiring in 1597. Many of its members were naturally also trading for the dominant Levant Company, whose success perhaps implied the commercial defeat of the Barbary Company. Certainly the trend of political opinion in the last decade of the sixteenth century was against an overt alliance of arms for further assault on Spain. By 1600, when the Barbarian ambassador came to suggest joint aggression, Elizabeth was already wary of the dangers presented by a weakened Spain and an ascendant France. She had not invited the embassy, but welcomed it no doubt as offering a means of insurance, although one for which the policy was unlikely to mature.

Diplomatic relations between England and Barbary had always been a compromise, in a sense compromising. The questionable alliance was put in terms of the advice offered Elizabeth in 1586, that "Her Majesty in using the King of Fez, doth not arm a barbarian against a Christian, but a barbarian against a heretic". But the heathen hand, though welcomed against Spain, was rarely taken in public. The military prowess of the Moors, typified in the Battle of Alcazar, coloured the drama of the day. But diplomatic exchange waited upon emergencies. The Armada brought a Moroccan emissary to England, and Essex's raid on Cadiz in 1597 inspired eventually the embassy of 1600. For two years later, emboldened by England's success, and hopeful of her active support, Muley Hamet, King of Barbary, proposed the grand design of the total conquest of Spain.

Elizabeth was then corresponding with him upon more mundane affairs; one, of long standing, was the release of some captives from the Low Countries; another concerned a dispute over the estate of a merchant Southern, about whose goods his partner Richard Tomson and the official agent John Waring were wrangling.

The Tomson brothers, Richard, George and Arnold, with their kinsman Jasper, were merchant adventurers. Richard, a servant of Cecil and holder of monopolies in almonds, dates, capers and molasses, had been accused of bringing into the trade as many interlopers as there were members of the Barbary Company. Doubtless the Tomsons' service to Cecil gave them safety at home, and gun-running made them popular with the Moors.

It was to Jasper that the King of Barbary confided his ambition. Jasper had been in the campaign of Mahomet III against the Emperor in 1596, and Muley Hamet was naturally interested to learn details of this encounter between heathen and Christian arms. In a letter of June 1599 Jasper relates to Richard Tomson how the King, his chief adviser Azzuz, his principal secretary (the future ambassador) and an interpreter between them kept him up all night in conversation. He did not share the Moors' enthusiasm for an armed alliance, protesting that the Cadiz raid had been a reprisal for the Armada, not an attempted invasion. Talk of an army of 20,000 Englishmen and 20,000 men and horses from Barbary put Jasper out of his depth. When he suggested that such matters ought to be discussed at a higher level he was asked if he had friends close to the Queen—and hence he requests Richard, presumably through Cecil, to canvass the idea at Court, if only for amusement's sake.

Rumour of alliance soon arose. In October 1599 the Venetian ambassador in Germany reported that Elizabeth had use of a port in Barbary from which to harass Spanish shipping. This probably met Elizabeth's needs. She continued to write to Muley Hamet about Southern's estate, the return of prisoners, and the restitution of money robbed from two Englishmen in Morocco.

The King countered with proposals for an embassy, to be disguised as a trade mission to Aleppo, calling at England for the sake of mutual regard. Letters of recommendation, assurance of safe-conduct, and transport for the whole party—including nine returning prisoners—were requested. Merchants were desired to ship them to England, to Aleppo, and home again. The real business of the embassy was too secret for correspondence, and a formal letter of June 1600 explains that the ambassador in person would treat of proposals for an alliance. The Ambassador was the King's secretary, Abd el-Ouahed ben Messaoud ben Mohammed Anoun, supported by al Hage Messa and al Hage Bahanet, and accompanied by an interpreter Abd el-Dodar, by birth Andalusian.

George Tomson, writing to his brother Richard for Cecil's information, gives an informal description of these principal members of the embassy. He did not think the Ambassador a very good choice. Although "a naturall Moore borne" he was a Fessian, which "the natural Moore houldeth baseness". Azzuz was his superior in council. Sharp-witted and literate, el-Ouahed flattered for advantage and was conceited. He had solicited letters from Moroccan agents to their masters in England on his behalf, and George's letter is partly to counterbalance his own composition in this kind.

In fact, the old man Messa "was thowt should have gone for principall", but after many such employments had recently disgraced himself by hiding from the King two *balas* rubies purchased abroad. Messa and Bahanet were to conduct the business in Aleppo, and were also authorized to deal with English merchants who had precious stones to sell.

Of the real business of the embassy George had no idea, "Here yt is so secreat that none knoweth the grounde of their goinge", but in view of Jasper's foreknowledge such profession of ignorance was probably diplomatic.

The interpreter, described as being "of more sense than all the rest and a verie honest man", had soldiered in Italy, according to Juan de Marchena, and would speak Italian to the Queen, though ordinarily using his native Spanish. The Ambassador knew a little Spanish, too, but scorned to speak it except with inferiors. His King lacked even this accomplishment.

A higher opinion is held by Thomas Bernhere in recommending el-Ouahed to the famous Edward Wright, though we must bear in mind that his letter was probably one of those solicited. El-Ouahed here is described as being capable of understanding Wright's navigational inventions; Bernhere declares that he had been instructed to select certain instruments for his own and the King's use. These might be brought back to Morocco for engraving, or completed in England, since the Ambassador "being a perfect penman can set the Arabique letters figures and words down very faire". He was also likely to be interested in "the experiments mathematical of the load stone". Bernhere's letter in general emphasizes the enduring Arab learning in scientific navigation, essential to their journeying "over a Sandy sea".

The letters of both Tomson and Bernhere show that the purpose of the embassy was more than diplomatic, and that its contact, as much as at Court, would be with such merchants as Alderman Edward Holmedon, Grocer, of the Levant and Barbary Companies.

At the end of June 1600 the sixteen members of the embassy, together with the prisoners, sailed from Morocco in *The Eagle*, under Robert Kitchen. The news that Spanish ships had cruised to intercept them in the Straits brought Muley Hamet home in consternation from the field. But the danger was avoided, and the embassy reached Dover harbour on 8 August.

There was some embarrassment at their coming. Sir Thomas Gerard, who in April 1600 had overcome problems set by the eighty members of the French Ambassador's train and a shortage of horses, now found greater social difficulties in receiving the small party of Barbarians. By 11 August the preparations were incomplete, when he wrote to Cecil, "I have moved the merchants for the Ambassador's diet, but they all plead poverty, and except her Majesty discharge it, it will rest upon himself. My Lord Mayor has taken Alderman Radclyffe's house for him." Anthony Radcliff had been Sheriff in 1585–6. The fact that in 1601 the Privy Council considered his house in the Strand, near the Royal Exchange, a suitable residence for Count de Beaumont, the French Ambassador, upon its vacation by the Duke of Lennox, the Scots Ambassador, must be weighed against the allegation of a contemporary letter-writer, probably Winwood, that the Moors were to be entertained "without scandall, and for that purpose they are lodged in a house apart, where they feed alone". The relationship between domestic privacy and segregation was probably close, but the usual diplomatic hospitality was offered to the Moors. Gerard and a group of merchants met them at Gravesend on 14 August, and brought them into London on the following evening tide. Rowland White commented to Sir Robert Sidney, "no Tyme yet appointed for their Audience; they are very strangely attired and behauiored".

Five days later they had their first audience of Elizabeth at Nonsuch, and White gives a detailed account:

The Embassador of *Barbary* had Audience vpon Wednesday last; here was a roiall Preparacion, in the Manner of his receuing; rich Hangings and Furnitures sent for from *Hampton* Court; the Gard very strong, in their rich Coatees; the Pentioners with their Axes; the Lords of the Order with their Collars; a full Court of Lords and Ladies. He passed thorough a Gard of Albards to the Cownsell Chamber, where he rested; he was brought to the Presence, soe to the Priuy Chamber, and soe to the Gallery; where her Majestie satt at the further End in very great State, and gaue them Audience.

The 'Winwood' letter quoted above adds the detail that "At the end of his Audience, her Majesty for a further grace to the States Agent, caused him to be present, and soe she receaved [the nine captives] of the Barbarian with one hand, she gave them to him with an other."

Although the interview was conducted in Spanish through Lewkenor, White remarks that before departing "the Interpreter of the Embassy spoke *Italian*, and desired to deliuer some

Thing in priuate, which her Majestie granted. On which Mr *Lewknor* and the Lords removed further of. Yt is giuen out, that they come for her Majestys Letters to the *Turke*, to whom a brother of this King of *Barbaries* is fled, to complaine against him."

On 31 August the ambassadors requested another audience and seemed anxious to arrange for their eventual departure. Still surrounded by mystery, they were received at Oatlands on 10 September. Admitting that the business of the Moors "hath bene very secretly handled, which is not yet come to Light", White offers a new version in which

yt is sipposed, that he makes good Offers to hir Majestie, yf she will be pleased to Ayde hym with Shipping, fitt for his Portes, to conduct in safety some Treasure he hath by Mines, in Part of the *Indies* conquered by hym, which now he is forced to carry by Land, and to maintain an Army to safconduct yt, and sometyme yt is taken from hym by Force.

This information of White's is nearer the true business of the embassy as set out in a memorandum of el-Ouahed's, of which a translation is endorsed by Cecil "15 Sep. 1600 The Barbarie Embassadors proposition to the Queen, delivered to Mr Secretarie Harbart and me". The main proposal was for an alliance between England and Barbary against Spain. Muley Hamet declared that he possessed a great army of proven quality, all manner of munitions, materials for shipbuilding, and iron. If an English fleet could be provided, he would take the war to Spain. England and Morocco, once united in arms, could seize from Spain both the East and West Indies and divide the spoils. The whole memorandum is exploratory and tentative. Elizabeth is invited either to send her own ambassador to Morocco to discuss a treaty further, or to conclude one in England with a different envoy from Barbary, while el-Ouahed continues his pretext of a journey to Aleppo. But the latter is at Elizabeth's disposal if she prefers him to escort an English envoy to Morocco. In any event, Muley Hamet cautions that el-Ouahed's route should be by Aleppo. A later note of the Ambassador's, when Elizabeth had decided to employ her own negotiator to the King, seeks a reassurance that the other members of the embassy will be shipped to Aleppo if the Queen requires el-Ouahed to return direct to Morocco.

This insistence upon preserving a useless pretext, and the Moors' need of transport, became a great embarrassment to the Privy Council. On 22 September they requested the help of the Levant Company, and were refused. Captain Edward Prynne, a pensioned seaman in Cecil's service, who was in charge of the arrangements for the Moors' hospitality, offered passage on a friend's ship. But the Council had instructed him to arrange for a warship under Captain King to be got ready. This scheme had the approval of the Lord Admiral, the Earl of Nottingham, who pointed out to Cecil that it was not fit for the Queen's honour that the embassy should return in other than a man-of-war, that the proposed salt ship was inadequately armed, and that the warship could do useful service on the return journey by spying out Spanish preparations. But the Moors shrank from such a bellicose leave-taking, and the Council had to instruct Lord Buckhurst, the Lord High Treasurer, to reimburse Captain King for his preparation of the warship, and cancelled the whole plan on 8 October.

New complications soon arose. The Russian Embassy from Boris Godunov arrived the next week, and may have extinguished some of the interest in the Barbarian visitors. White reported that the Moors would take their leave of the Queen on either 15 or 16 October, and on 15 October in fact John Chamberlain assured Dudley Carleton

The Barbarians take theyre leave sometime this week, to goe homeward, for our merchants nor mariners will not carry them into Turkie, because they thinck it a matter odious and scandalous to the world to be friendlie or familiar with Infidells but yet yt is no small honour to us that nations so far removed and every way different shold meet here to admire the glory and magnificence of our Queene of Saba.

On 21 October Chamberlain wrote again that "The Barbarians were yesterday at Court to take theyre leave and wil be gon shortly; but the eldest of them, which was a kind of priest or prophet, hath taken his leave of the world and is gon to prophecie *apud infernos* and to seeke out Mahound theyre mediator."

Messa's death, uncharitably referred to here, must have delayed the Moors' going, though this was clearly awaited on 1 November, when Nicholas Mosley, the Lord Mayor of London, wrote to Cecil in the following terms:

I have thought good, before the departinge of the Barbarie Imbassador, to let your Honour understande that, upon your Honours letters for repaiment, I have caused to be delivered unto Captain Primme, at sundrie times, the some of 230^{li} toward the defraying of the Imbassador his charges, which will not discharge all that is owinge. And Mr Ratlefe, in whose howse he is lodged, expecteth some consideracon for the use of his howse, and spoile made by them.

By this date the Ambassador would seem to have outstayed his welcome in official quarters, and certainly with Alderman Ratcliff; and Philip Honyman had already noted that "The merchants took little pleasure in his being here". Honyman alleged, indeed, that the commercial purpose of the embassy was more serious than the diplomatic, and that the Ambassador's "dryft was, under colour of thir formall voyadge, to lerne here how merchandize went, and what gaine we made of their sugors, that he might raise the prices accordingly". Stow repeated this charge of the merchants, with the embellishment that the Moors,

during their half yeares abode in London, . . . used all subtilities and diliggence to know the prises wayghts measures and kindes of differences in such commodities as eyther there country sent hither or England transported thither. They carried with them all sorts of English wayghts measures and samples of commodities.

It seems likely that the persistence of the Moors resulted in the warning issued by the Privy Council, during the period of the embassy, to Alderman Edward Holmedon and other merchants, about the manipulation of sugar prices.

However, unpopular on all sides, the Barbarians stayed on to the end of the year, and courtesy was somehow maintained. Stow records that on "the 17th November being the Queen's day the Queene being then at Whitehall, a speciale place was builded only for them neere to the parke doore to behold that day's triumph". Of the same occasion, using new-style dating, de Boissise, the French Ambassador, informed his king that on "le 23 de ce mois la Royne est arrivée en ceste ville avec la cérémonie et pompe accoustumée voire avec plus grande à l'occasion des Ambassadeurs de Moscovie et de Marroc, ausquelz elle a voulu monstrer sa magnificence". With consummate timing, dating his preface "At London this three and fortieth most ioifull Coronation-day of her sacred Maiestie", the young John Pory brought out *A Geographical Historie of Africa*, a translation of the fifty-year-old work "Written in Arabicke and Italian by John Leo a More, borne in Granada and brought vp in Barbarie". In his dedication of these "first fruits" to Cecil, Pory declares that "at this time especially I thought they would prooue the more acceptable: in that the Marocan ambassadour (whose Kings dominions are heere most amplie and particularly described) hath so lately treated with your Honour concerning matters of that estate." A lost book, entered on 4 September as "the widow of England and her seven sons strangly tormented to Death by the Turkes in Barbary", may represent a less cultured attempt to make capital out of the Moors' presence.

By all accounts they were difficult guests. The "speciale place" accorded them at the triumph in Whitehall was doubtless again a courtesy and a convenience. Stow, the chronicler nearest in time to the embassy, is also the fullest and most hostile, claiming that

Notwithstanding all this kindness shown them together with their dyet and all other provisions for six moneths space wholly at the Queenes charges, yet such was their inveterate hate unto our Christian religion and estate as they could not endure to give any manner of alms, charitie, or relief, either in money or broken meat, unto any English poore, but reserved theire fragments and sold the same unto such poore as would give most for them.

Such behaviour was no doubt unfavourably regarded in London, and other personal customs excited curiosity, such as that "They killed all their own meat within their house, as sheep lambs poultry and such like, and they turned their face eastward when they killed anything."

Stow's final conjectures, first, that "being returned it was supposed they poysned their interpreter, being born in Granado, because he commended the estate and bounty of England", and second, that "the like violence was thought to be done unto their reverend aged pilgrime least he should manifest England's honour to their disgrace", are careful to acknowledge their basis in unsympathetic rumour. But common opinion probably endorsed his conclusion that "It was generally judged by their demeanors that they were rather espials than honourable ambassadors for they omitted nothing that might damnifie the English Merchants".

Stow's reference to their six months' stay is our best indication of the date of their departure, probably at the beginning of February 1601. A warrant of the Privy Council in May 1601 declares that "the Ambassadour doth by her Majesty's leave and permission take with him one John Rolliffe, a mann of learning, and Richard Edwards, an apothecary, to serve the Emperour his master", and further orders "every of you to whom it shall or may appertaine to suffer the foresaid John Rolliffe and Richard Edwards to go forth of the realme and attend on the said Ambassadour with such apparrell, bookes and other necessaryes as they do carry with them for their use. Whereof wee require you not to faile."

The warrant is unlikely to have been issued retrospectively, so that Rolliffe and Edwards must have followed the Ambassador to Morocco, for on 27 February 1601 Muley Hamet wrote to tell Elizabeth of the embassy's safe arrival home, and of their favourable report upon her reception of them. The King accepted her excuse of inconvenience to merchants for her failure to ship the Moors to Aleppo. Elizabeth, in a letter of 20 October 1600, had instructed Henry Prannell, an agent resident in Morocco, to continue discussions about an alliance, and some idea of the nature of her diplomatic handling of the King of Barbary is to be gained from the memorandum in response, which he attached to his letter of 27 February. She first stipulated that England's help should be kept secret from Spain, an implausible but sensible necessity since she was simultaneously negotiating for peace with the King of Spain; she set the cost of equipping a fleet at £100,000, to be provided in advance, against her credit, out of prize money taken by the Moors from Spanish possessions; she needed the treasure immediately.

Muley Hamet was equal to the bluff; the money, he said, was at hand, only it was difficult to transport it safely. Elizabeth was asked to send a tall ship, under some person of responsibility, and in secret. Meanwhile, he requested the Queen to think further about the military aspect of the proposed treaty, and reminded her that the purpose should not be to sack Spain and her territories, but to take and hold them for ever. His final request was for her special ambassador, to carry into being the prospect of an omnipotent alliance of England and Barbary.

The unreal vision soon faded. When Elizabeth resumed the correspondence after the settlement of the Essex affair, it was only to write of such matters as the release of prisoners and the difficulties of some English merchants in Morocco. Even in these simple matters her ambiguous diplomacy continued. After the embassy had gone home an Act of the Privy Council had arranged the deporting of "negars and blackamoores", whose great numbers in England irritated Spain, and fostered trouble against her. Elizabeth's release of Moorish captives later had the double advantage of conciliating both Spain and Barbary.

Within two years of the embassy both Elizabeth and Muley Hamet were dead, and Barbary was engulfed in civil wars. George Tomson came home penniless to recover debts from the merchants in London, and George Wilkins began his account of *The Three Miseries of Barbary*.

Officially, the embassy of 1600 was forgotten. Camden recorded it with formal resonance, in the hollow phrases "*Ab austro enim Hamettus Rex Mauretania Tingitanae, a Septentrione Boris Pheodorici Imperator Russiae, omni studio amicitiam ejus ambierunt*". Thomas Gainsford put both embassies in his list of such distinguished foreign tributes in *The Glory of England* of 1618, though noting of Barbarians and Russians alike that they "from a stubborn bestialitie seemed to vilipend the managing of many affaires by outward forme; yet were driven to applaude our generall happines."

Informally, among the merchants, the Barbary Embassy was remembered for a precedent when argument arose concerning the payment for the Turkish Ambassador's entertainment in 1607. Then Richard Stapers, of the Levant Company, reminded Salisbury that "in the late Queen's time there came an Ambassador from the King of Barbary, to whom she gave maintenance all the time he was here, and 100 *l.* at his departure, and yet he gave nothing here".

It seems impossible that the Moors should have come empty-handed, yet it may be true. Rowland White's description of their audiences has no mention of such customary gifts as those presented by the Russian Ambassador, who, White tells us, gave Elizabeth "in open Sort, a Timber of Sables, and one sengle Paire of excellent goodnes". We remember that the presents sent by the Great Turk in 1583 had included "4 lyons roiall, 12 turkish swords, 4 cases of knives, 12 unicorns horns, 20 hangings of cloth, A Bed for a Galley all of cristal and gold, 1 chest of Chrystal, 2 Horses", and that Stow accused the Moors of neglecting the poor. Along with their "stubborn bestialitie" went considerable naïvety, as is shown by White's account of their visit

PLATE I

THE MOORISH AMBASSADOR TO QUEEN ELIZABETH, 1600

PLATE II

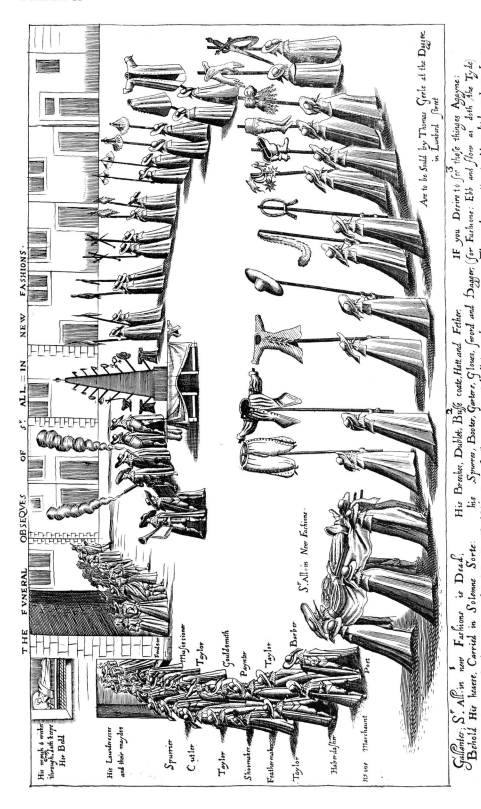

THE FUNERAL OBSEQUIES OF SIR ALL-IN-NEW-FASHIONS

to Hampton Court, "where they saw and admired the richnes of the Furniture; and they demanded how many Kings had built yt, and how long it was a Doing". Certainly behind the bombastic diplomatic mission, lay only shrewdness and commercial cunning; and behind that, if the rumours had any truth, was insensitivity and cruelness, even murder.

To Elizabethan Londoners the appearance and conduct of the Moors was a spectacle and an outrage, emphasizing the nature of the deep difference between themselves and their visitors, between their Queen and this "erring Barbarian". When Shakespeare chose, for this audience, to present a Moor as his hero, he was not perhaps confused in his racial knowledge, simply more aware than his contemporaries of the complex pattern made by white and black.

NOTES

The portrait in oils of the Ambassador appeared as Lot 65, "Portrait of Abdul Guahid, Moroccan Ambassador to the Court of Queen Elizabeth I", when it was sold at Christie's on 11 November 1955. The purchaser, Mr George Higgins, after having it completely cleaned and restored, exhibited it at the Ruskin Galleries in Stratford-upon-Avon during the autumn of 1956, when, through the co-operation of Mr Higgins and Mrs Constance Thomson, it was acquired by the Shakespeare Institute. The earlier provenance of the picture is still being investigated.

The portrait is on a panel 45 in. × 31 in. To the left of the head is inscribed "1600", "Abdvl Gvahid", and "Aetatis 42": to the right is the description "Legatvs Regis Barbariae in Angliam". The artist is unknown, but the giving of the Ambassador's age, not known from other documents, suggests an authoritative portrait, rather than a casual painting.

The sources from which the account of the embassy is taken have been listed here, rather than in the numerous and repetitive footnotes otherwise needed:

Les Sources Inédites de L'Histoire du Maroc, Angleterre, 3 vols., ed. de Castries (Paris, 1918–35); P.R.O., State Papers, Domestic, Elizabeth, vol. CCLXXV; State Papers, Foreign, Barbary States, vols. XII and XIII; Cal. of S.P., Spanish, vol. VII; Venetian, vol. X; Acts of the Privy Council, ed. Dasent, vol. XXX; H.M.C. Cal. Cecil MSS., Parts IX, X, XI; The Sidney Papers, ed. Collins, 2 vols.; John Chamberlain's Letters (Camden Society), LXXIX; J. Nichols, Progresses and Public Processions of Queen Elizabeth, 3 vols.; A. B. Beaven, The Aldermen of the City of London, 2 vols.

STC 4496 Camden, Annales; STC 11517 Gainsford, The Glory of England; STC 15481 Johannes Leo, 'Africanus', A geographical historie of Africa; and STC 23337 Stow, Annales.

The writer wishes to acknowledge the kindness of the Earl of Leicester who gave permission to consult MS. 678 in the Library of Holkham Hall; of Dr W. O. Hassall, of the Bodleian Library, librarian at Holkham Hall; of Professor Leslie Hotson, who supplied references and comment, and of Mr David Lockie, who gave further assistance and provided a quotation from the forthcoming edition of the Calendar of the Cecil MSS. at Hatfield House for the year 1607.

THE FUNERAL OBSEQUIES OF
SIR ALL-IN-NEW-FASHIONS

BY

F. P. WILSON

This engraving is in the collection of prints bequeathed to the Bodleian Library by the antiquary, Francis Douce. The press-mark is Douce Prints, Portfolio 138, no. 89. No other copy is known, and it is shown here, in reduced facsimile, for the first time. The original measures some $11\frac{7}{8} \times 8\frac{3}{8}$ inches. Of the printseller, Thomas Geele, little is known. His name appears in the imprint of the 1630 reprint of *Baziliωlogia*, a series of engravings of English monarchs. In the first issue the imprint reads: "Printed for H: Holland, and are to be sold by Comp: Holland ouer against th'exchange 1618": in 1630 this becomes "Are to be sould by Thomas Geele at the dagger in Lumbard street 1630". His name is not found on the title of the reprints of 1628, 1638, and 1662.[1] For information about another set of prints published by Geele I am indebted to Professor W. A. Jackson. He issued *c.* 1626 and from the same address a set of twelve plates illustrating the Months, with verses signed on the last plate "A[braham]. H[olland]." (Abraham Holland, who died in 1626, Henry Holland, and possibly Compton Holland were sons of Philemon Holland of Coventry, the "translator-general in his age".) The only copy traced is in the Huth (now Harvard) copy of Nicholas Breton's *Fantasticks* (1626). There they are bound up at the appropriate places, but as they are found only in this copy and as they illustrate Breton's text only in the most general way, the probability is that they were not made for the book. Geele's name has disappeared from a later issue, also undated, which bears the imprint of Thomas Booth at the Glove in Cornhill: of this issue there are copies in the British Museum Print Room and in the Huntington Library. These two bits of evidence suggest that Geele flourished *c.* 1625–30, and we shall not go far wrong if we assign "Sir All-in-New-Fashions" to about the same date.

While the plate may invite much detailed comment from a historian of costume, little general comment is necessary in view of the explanatory verses. It will be observed that among the debtors who follow the knight to his grave are one poet, one painter, one "Musissioner", and no less than four tailors. "Fendsor" for fencer is a notable example of an engraver's spelling. The knight's boots give point to the attack on "the manner of cutting boots out with huge, slovenly, unmannerly, and immoderate tops", so that "one pair of boots eats up the leather of six pair of reasonable men's shoes".[2] His beard is in the 'stiletto' fashion of the early sixteen-twenties. The verses refer to his ruffs and falling bands, but the engraving seems to show only the unstarched falling bands. As late as 1616, however, both were being worn: "Will you wear your ruff or your band?" asks a servant in an Italian-English dialogue. "The weather is warm," answers the master, "give me my band."

English satirical engravings of this period are very rare, and the merit of this one will seem the more striking when it is put beside the crude woodcuts with which we are familiar in the popular books and plays of the period. Such accomplishment did not spring out of nothing, but I have not been successful in discovering whether the inspiration was native, Dutch, German, or French. The theme, of course, was native. The artist was doing in his own medium what the dramatists, pamphleteers, and character-writers had long been doing. His knight is the man who "wears a whole lordship on his back", an old proverbial saying of which Shakespeare makes use in *King John* (II, i, 70). He is Jonson's Fastidius Brisk. And as a social pest he does not escape the notice of the character-writers: he is Overbury's "Fine Gentleman", and like Earle's "Idle Gallant" he "is one that was born and shaped for his clothes; and, if Adam had not fallen, had lived to no purpose".

NOTES

1. See A. M. Hind's *Engraving in England in the Sixteenth and Seventeenth Centuries,* pt. II, pp. 115–39. The title-page of 1618 is reproduced in A. F. Johnson's *Catalogue of Engraved English Title-Pages* (1934), Elstrack no. 15.

2. *Leather* (1629) in *Social England,* ed. A. Lang, pp. 326–7.

MARTIN PEERSON AND THE BLACKFRIARS

BY

MARK ECCLES

Since the Blackfriars playhouse was famous for its music, it is interesting to find a musician among the sharers in the Revels company early in the reign of James I. Martin Peerson wrote music for the voice, and it is possible—though this is conjecture—that he may have helped train the boys' voices and may have composed or arranged songs for the Blackfriars, as Marston, another sharer, wrote plays. The Children of the Chapel began to act at the Blackfriars in 1600, when Richard Burbage leased the theatre to Henry Evans. On Twelfth Night, 1600/1, the boys presented before Queen Elizabeth "a showe with musycke and speciall songes".[1] Songs star their plays, from *Cynthia's Revels* and *Poetaster* to *The Knight of the Burning Pestle*. Their patent of 1610, after the boys had left the Blackfriars to the King's Men, includes the name of another musician, Philip Rosseter.

Peerson is first heard of as the composer of music for the song, "See, see, ô see, who here is come a Maying!", in Jonson's *Highgate Entertainment* of 1604. The *Dictionary of National Biography* implies that he wrote it when he was only fourteen, since the year of his birth is given as about 1590; but Miss Wailes has shown in Grove's *Dictionary of Music and Musicians* (1954 edition) that he was probably born between 1570 and 1574 at March, Cambridgeshire. In 1604 or 1605 "Martin Pierson" was "presented for a Recusant Papiste and denyeth the doctrine of the Church to be apostolical".[2] "Martin*us* Pierson de *p*arochia Sancti Olavi in Silverstrete in warda de Creplegate London", musician, was indicted for recusancy, with Jonson and others, on 9 January 1605/6.[3] As this record shows, Peerson was then living not far from where Shakespeare lodged at the house of Christopher Mountjoy in Silver Street.

In 1606 Peerson held a share in the company of the Children of the Queen's Revels at the Blackfriars. This information comes from a suit, Kendall *versus* Peerson, in the uncalendared proceedings of the Court of Requests at the Public Record Office.[4] Edward Kirkham, William Rastell, and Thomas Kendall, citizen and haberdasher, had in 1602 bought a half-interest in the Blackfriars company from Henry Evans and Alexander Hawkins.[5] Evans and Hawkins disposed of other shares, since John Marston later sold to Robert Keysar for one hundred pounds his one-sixth share in the Blackfriars apparel, properties, and playbooks.[6] Peerson in December 1606 sold his interest for forty-five pounds to Thomas Kendall. Kendall died in 1608 and was buried on 11 June at St Andrew's, Holborn. His will, dated 8 June, named as overseers Edward Kirkham of the Strand, gentleman, and Thomas Leedam of Southwark, yeoman. He made bequests amounting to seventy-three pounds, and left the rest of his estate to his wife Anne.[7]

Peerson was described as "Martin Pierson of Newington, Middlesex, gentleman", when he was sued on 31 January 1608/9 by Edmund Kendall and Anne Kendall, widow and executrix of Thomas Kendall. Edmund declared that he had been bound with his brother Thomas in eighty pounds to pay Peerson forty-five pounds, and that Thomas had paid to Peerson, or to his use, amounts of five, eight, and fourteen pounds, "allthoughe happily not at the stricte dayes" nor "full soe muche as he should haue donne", so that he forfeited his bond. In 1608 "Thomas Kendall sickned and then made his last wyll...and then videlicet some fewe dayes before midd-sommer nowe last past he dyed of very weake and poore estate. and yet unadvisedly" his widow Anne took upon her the probate of his will. Peerson sued Edmund and Anne separately in King's Bench, whereupon Edmund threatened to sue Anne on his counterbond from Thomas. Anne stated that she was willing to pay in reasonable time the eighteen pounds still due, though "very hardly able to paye", and asked that Peerson be ordered to show cause why he should not accept this amount instead of suing on the bond for eighty pounds.

Peerson answered on 11 February, by his counsel Thomas Foster, that

He this defendant and one Edwarde Kîrkham and some others were partners and sharers of Certayne sommes of money proffittes and Emolumentes made had growinge and arysinge by Reason of certayne playes and enterludes then vsuallye acted and performed by the Children of the Queenes maiesties Revelles within the parishe of St Anne in the blacke ffryers London and also were severallye possessed of Certayne apparrell occasionallye to be vsed by the said Children in their saide playes and enterludes.

On 11 December 1606 he had speech and communication with Thomas Kendall about selling to Kendall his share and his part of the apparel. They agreed that Kendall should have

all suche arrerages as att the makinge of the saide Obligacion wear due to this defendant for or by Reason of his part or share of and in the premisses or his partnershippe aforesaide and likewise that he the said Thomas Kendall should paye or acquyte and discharge this defendant of all suche arrerages and charges as were then or from thenceforth should bee due or payable by this defendant or Justlye challenged att this defendantes handes by or in respecte of his partenershippe aforesaide (exceptinge that this defendant was to paye for the dyet of one which was then his boye or servante and one of the actors of the saide playes or enterludes).

Peerson assigned to Kendall all his estate in the "premises" and Kendall gave bond to pay forty-five pounds for his part and partnership. Kendall paid the first five pounds, and at other times, although not at the days specified, twenty-two pounds more. Since Peerson was willing to give Kendall time to pay the remaining eighteen pounds, Kendall undertook to pay twenty-seven shillings due for part of the charges for the diet of Peerson's boy, but he never paid this sum, nor nine pounds which Kirkham claimed that Peerson as a partner owed at the time of the transfer to Kendall. Peerson, therefore,

is nowe sued att the Guildhall in London for the said twentye & seaven shillinges parcell therof and is threatened and in danger att the pleasure of the saide Edwarde Kirkham by him to be sued for the residue amountinge with the said twentye and seaven shillinges to the some of nyne poundes.

Peerson said that he did not intend to take the penalty of the bond, provided the plaintiffs would satisfy Kirkham for the arrears and pay the rest of Kendall's debt, with interest and costs of suit. The Court of Requests ordered Peerson to cease his actions on the bond and instructed Anne

Kendall to bring in the eighteen pounds she owed. Peerson agreed to accept this amount and received it on 1 June 1609.[8]

The Coram Rege Rolls of King's Bench record Peerson's suits against the two Kendalls. "Martinus Peirson generosus", by his attorney William Langhorne, on 28 October 1608 sued Anne Kendall for the penalty of the bond, eighty pounds, and twenty pounds damages.[9] Anne replied in Hilary term, the following January, that she had administered all her husband's estate and had nothing of his left. Peerson declared that she had, and a jury was called to try the case in Easter term. Peerson also sued Edmund Kendall, citizen and haberdasher, for eighty pounds, and ten pounds damages.[10] The record quotes the condition of the bond made on 11 December 1606: that Thomas and Edmund Kendall should pay Peerson, "at the nowe shopp or writinge place of Augustyne Browne scrivener" in St Clement Danes, forty-five pounds, of which five pounds were due on 6 January 1606/7, twenty on 24 June, and twenty on 25 January 1607/8. Edmund answered that he had paid all these sums, but Peerson's denial is supported by Edmund's own statement in the Requests suit. A jury of twelve men from St Clement Danes was summoned for Easter term, but both suits in King's Bench were stayed by injunction from the Court of Requests, where the matter was settled.

The purchaser of Peerson's share was evidently the Thomas Kendall who was paid in 1604 "for furnishing the Children wth apparrell and other things needfull for the shewe" and for making caparisons and bases for the horses that drew the chariot in the triumph honouring the new Lord Mayor, Sir Thomas Lowe, haberdasher. Jonson made the "device, and speech for the Children" and a book was printed, but the pageant is now known only from accounts of the Haberdashers' Company.[11]

Kendall played a larger part than has been recognized in managing the affairs of the boys at the Blackfriars. He began by buying his share in the company in 1602. When the Children of the Chapel became the Children of the Queen's Revels in 1603/4, the patent named as managers Edward Kirkham, Alexander Hawkins, Thomas Kendall, and Robert Payne. Henry Evans had secured a bond by which Kirkham, Kendall, and William Rastell promised to pay him eight shillings every week when plays were acted. Claiming forfeiture of the bond because Kendall had not paid this sum on 16 June 1604, Evans sued Kendall that summer in King's Bench. The poet Samuel Daniel, licenser of plays for the company, brought a similar suit against Kirkham after Kendall's death for not paying sums specified in a bond which Kirkham and Kendall had made to Daniel on 28 April 1604.[12]

Kendall and his partners replied to Evans by petitioning Chancery to issue an injunction to stay the action at common law.[13] Three witnesses gave interesting evidence about "the house in the blackfriers where the Queenes Ma[ties] children of the Reuells vse to plaie". David Yeomans, a tailor who could not sign his name, testified that Kirkham, Kendall, Hawkins, and "one Gibbyns" had made an inventory of the playhouse apparel and goods when Yeomans was "taken in by the masters of the said plaie house to be tyreman in the roome of one Robert Rutson and one Goffe". Another inventory had been made about April 1606 by Kirkham, "one Nowell" as assignee to Kendall, Hawkins, and "one Woodford" (whose dealings with Chapman and the Paul's Boys have been disclosed by Sisson, *Lost Plays of Shakespeare's Age*). This inventory was made after Evans offered to Kirkham, Nowell, and Gibbyns "to haue their playe bookes apparell and *properties* belonging to their plaies to be praised and lotted that eu*ery* one should haue his share deliuered to him", six or eight weeks before 3 June 1606, when Yeomans was examined. Thomas Hedgeman, gentleman, deposed that Kendall had not paid his share for repairs, though he had agreed to pay at a conference with Kirkham, Hawkins, Gibbins, Woodford, and Mrs Evans. At the request of Evans, Hedgeman had also dealt with Kendall to pay the arrears of the eight shillings a week which Evans claimed were owing him for sixty-one weeks, and now for eight weeks more "of latter tyme". William Strachey testified on 7 July 1606 that two years since he had heard the plaintiffs or their assigns refuse to pay the eight shillings a week, and that "they haue still refused, and doe yet refuse" an offer, which he had often made on behalf of Evans and Hawkins, "that the plaie bookes goodes apparell and properties" should be "praysed and valewed by indifferent men, that euery party might haue that wch of right belongeth to him". Strachey held a sixth share, for he recalled that about two years past he had paid Evans three pounds and a mark as his sixth part for repairs (which must have cost in all, therefore, twenty-two pounds). He said that he had seen "a bill of the particular reparacons of the said howse wch hath bene delyvered by or from one Burbidg who ys brother to him that ys Landlord of the sayd howse wherby Henry Evans one of the defendantes hath bene required to doe those reparacons" and that "the said Burbidg for aught this deponent hath yet knowne or herd to the Contrary doth howld him self satisfyed wth such reparacons as hath bene done in and abowte the said howse". Cuthbert Burbage evidently looked after the property for Richard. Strachey "thinketh he hath herd" the defendants say that Kirkham and Rastell or their assigns paid their sixth parts, "but they saye they cannot gett the other Complainant Kendall to paye his sixth parte of the said Charges".

When King James visited Oxford in 1605, Kirkham and Kendall sent up costumes and properties for the college plays; and the producers of Christmas plays at Westminster School in 1606/7 "paid Mr Kendall for ye apparrell and beards".[14] Kendall took an apprentice, Abel Cooke, on 14 November 1606, and his suit in 1607 preserves the only known record of the terms on which a boy player was apprenticed (Hillebrand, pp. 197-8). Kendall agreed with the boy's mother to take Abel for three years as one of the Children of the Queen's Revels, to "abide with and searve" Kendall and act "to the vttermost of his power and habilitye". The boy left the company after six months, but his mother declared that he had Kendall's written consent. The fact that Kendall increased his investment by buying Peerson's share in December 1606 shows that he still had faith in the venture even after the company's many troubles over *Philotas*, *Eastward Ho*, and *The Isle of Gulls*. Early in 1608 one of Chapman's plays on Biron and a lost play laughing at the King himself made James vow "they should never play more", yet they did, though Marston was sent to Newgate. After Evans threatened to bring Kendall to trial on the action begun in 1604, Kirkham and Kendall signed a new bond to Hawkins on 4 June 1608, promising to pay fifty-four pounds on "hallomas day" at the "Common dyning hall of Greyes Inne" (Hawkins v. Kirkham, mentioned by Hillebrand, p. 189 n.). Within a week of signing Kendall was dead, leaving it to his widow and Kirkham to meet the claims by Peerson and by Daniel or an assign suing in his name.

Kirkham and Anne Kendall engaged in two Chancery suits in 1609, one against Daniel and the other against Evans and Hawkins. Since the second suit has not been known before, I shall cite evidence given on oath by two witnesses. The first, testifying on 22 May, was Percival Golding of St Clement Danes, gentleman, aged twenty-nine, a son of Arthur Golding, the translator of Ovid.[15] Kendall had bequeathed a gold ring to his friend Mr Percival Golding, who signed the will as a witness.

One problem in understanding the history of the Blackfriars has been to find the reason why Kirkham and his partners signed a bond in 1602 agreeing to pay eight shillings a week to Evans. Wallace assumed that it was "evidently as salary for managing the theatre".[16] Just the opposite was true, according to Golding: the payment was agreed on because the partners were desirous that Evans "should no further intermedle wth the affayres of the Playe house of Blackfryers, but should leave them to be managed by the *said* Alexander Hawkins". Golding also gave two reasons for the replacing of the bond to Evans by a new bond to Hawkins in 1608. By the new bond, under penalty of eighty pounds, Kendall and Kirkham promised to pay fifty-four pounds to Hawkins to refer their disputes to arbiters, because, Golding said, they hoped by arbitrament to receive from Hawkins and Evans more than fifty-four pounds, and because it was promised that Evans "should forbeare to haue any further dealing*es* or intermedlinge in the affayres of the sáyde Playhouse" and that Hawkins "should take vppon him the managinge of the buisnies there as in former tymes he had don". The witnesses were not examined on Kirkham's inter-rogatories asking whether Evans or Hawkins had taken any apparel or instruments from the "Joynct stock" out of a room which adjoined the great hall and which had a door with two locks and two keys, one key to be kept by Hawkins and Evans and the other by Kirkham and his partners.

The second witness for Kirkham, "Henry Outlawe of Carbuncle streete in the *parishe* of Cheston" (Cheshunt), Herts, gentleman, aged forty-three, testified on 22 June 1609. He said that, when appointed by Kendall and Kirkham divers times to go into the "Scoolehouse" and the room over it, he "was resisted and kepte out" by Evans (in 1604 according to evidence quoted by Hillebrand, p. 185). He made one particularly interesting statement: "That by the space of aboute fyftene wekes together in the first yere of the King*es* M[tyes] Raigne in Englande" (24 March 1603 to 23 March 1604) Evans, or others by his appointment, had received to the value of thirty shillings a week or thereabouts "for the vse of the stooles standinge vppon the Stage at Blackfryers", for which he had never given any account to the sharers of the house. This testimony provides clues, though not answers, to several problems in stage history. For one thing, it shows that Evans as lessee kept the money collected for seats on the stage. A stool could be hired for sixpence, according to *Cynthia's Revels* and *The Gull's Hornbook*, or sometimes for twelvepence, according to *The Roaring Girl* (1611).[17] If Evans hired out from thirty to sixty stools a week, the Blackfriars stage seems to have had room to hold quite a large number of seated spectators. Clearly there must have been more than one performance a week. Although Hillebrand held the view that "the boys played only once, or at most twice, a week", it would seem more likely that at this time they were acting several times a week, as Chambers and Wallace believed.[18] The epilogue to *Eastward Ho* ends, "May this attract you hither once a week", but other plays may have been acted at other times during the week. I suggest that the Black-friars company gave three performances a week, since William Strachey testified that he used to come to the Blackfriars and receive his part of the profit from plays "sometymes once, twyce, and thrice in a weeke".[19]

Outlawe also said that plays were being acted at the Blackfriars for fifteen weeks together in the first year of King James. On the evidence available when he wrote, Chambers concluded that the London playhouses were closed from March 1603 to February or April 1604,[20] but it appears that they may have reopened earlier. The Blackfriars company could have begun playing again in December 1603 and continued for fifteen weeks before the first year of James' reign ended on 23 March 1603/4. Richard Burbage recalled that Evans spoke with him about giving up his lease during the first year of the reign, because of the great plague and the lack of profit; yet Wallace found evidence that by 8 December 1603 Evans had spent eleven pounds on repairing the Blackfriars property.[21] The suggestions here made are only tentative, since they depend on the memory of a single witness. It should be possible to find further evidence.

We should also be able to learn more about Martin Peerson. He became master of the singing boys of St Paul's and lived in Paul's Churchyard, where Humphrey Moseley, the publisher of plays, witnessed his will in 1650.[22] Of his two printed books, *Private Musicke* (1620) contains his setting for Jonson's song in the 1604 entertainment and *Mottects or Grave Chamber Musique* (1630) includes songs set to words by his patron Fulke Greville. A MS. volume of "Madrigals, etc. by John Milton (father of the poet), Martin Pearson" and others is described in a Quaritch catalogue of 1877.[23] During 1956 most of Peerson's extant music was sung on the Third Programme of the B.B.C., and his songs and madrigals were a delight to hear.

NOTES

1. Chambers, *The Elizabethan Stage* (1923), II, 42–3.

2. Consistory Court of London Correction Book, 1604–1605, quoted by F. W. X. Fincham in *Transactions of the Royal Historical Soc.*, 4 ser., IV (1921), 132.

3. Dom Hugh Bowler, *London Sessions Records 1605–1685*, Catholic Record Soc. XXXIV (1934), 7–8; Eccles, 'Jonson and the Spies', *Review of English Studies*, XIII (1937), 385–97.

4. Requests 2/462, part 1.

5. F. G. Fleay, *A Chronicle History of the London Stage* (1890), pp. 208–51; H. N. Hillebrand, *The Child Actors*, Univ. of Illinois Studies in Language and Literature (1926), pp. 175–205.

6. C. W. Wallace, *Nebraska Univ. Studies*, X (1910), 336–60.

7. Wills in the Archdeaconry Court of London, Guildhall MS. 9052/box 3.

8. Requests Decrees and Orders, 5–7 Jas. I, pp. 585, 628, 684, 717.

9. K.B. 27/1413, part 2, membrane 1167.

10. K.B. 27/1413, part 2, membrane 1167 dorso.

11. *Malone Soc. Collections*, III (1954), 63; *Ben Jonson*, ed. Herford and Simpson, XI (1952), 586.

12. The best account of the Revels company is by H. N. Hillebrand in *The Child Actors*, where he first printed records of three suits: Evans v. Kendall, Kirkham and Anne Kendall v. Daniel, and Kendall v. Cooke. The suit against Daniel is also discussed by R. E. Brettle in *Review of English Studies*, III (1927), 162–8.

13. C. 33/107, f. 600, court order of 5 April 1605; C. 24/327/22, depositions in 1606 by witnesses for Evans and Hawkins, defendants, v. Rastell, Kirkham, and Kendall, plaintiffs. For these references I am indebted to C. J. Sisson, *New Readings in Shakespeare*, I (1956), 188–91, and to S. G. Culliford, 'William Strachey, 1572–1621', unpublished thesis at the University of London.

14. *Malone Soc. Collections*, I (1911), 247; J. T. Murray, *English Dramatic Companies*, II (1910), 169.

15. C. 24/351/48. Louis T. Golding, *An Elizabethan Puritan* (1937), describes Percival's MS. history of the Veres, his kinsmen.

16. *Nebraska Univ. Studies*, VIII (1908), 202; cf. *The Elizabethan Stage*, II, 46.

17. Allusions to sitting on the stage are collected in *The Elizabethan Stage*, II, 535–7.

18. *The Child Actors*, p. 178; *The Elizabethan Stage*, II, 556; *Nebraska Univ. Studies*, VIII, 239.

19. C. 24/327/22. See also L. B. Wright and V. Freund, introduction to Strachey, *The Historie of Travell into Virginia Britania*, Hakluyt Soc. (1953), p. xix.

20. *The Elizabethan Stage*, IV, 349–50. Chambers noted that Lent began on 22 February 1603/4, but the orders against playing in Lent were not always enforced (I, 315–16). In 1603 the theatres may have been open for two or three weeks in April and May: F. P. Wilson, *The Plague in Shakespeare's London* (1927), p. 110.

21. Fleay, *Chronicle History*, p. 235; *Nebraska Univ. Studies*, VIII, 203.

22. Jeffrey Pulver, *A Biographical Dictionary of Old English Music* (1927); C. S. Emden, 'Lives of Elizabethan Song Composers', *Review of English Studies*, II (1926), 421–2.

23. J. M. French, *The Life Records of John Milton*, I (1949), 215. Cf. A. Hughes-Hughes, *Catalogue of Manuscript Music in the British Museum*, I (1906), 6.

DRAMATIC REFERENCES FROM THE SCUDAMORE PAPERS

BY

J. P. FEIL

The Scudamore family, from whose papers the following excerpts are drawn, was an ancient one, with its seat at Holme-Lacy in the county of Hereford.[1] Sir John Scudamore, who received the first letter quoted, was Gentleman Usher to Queen Elizabeth, Standard-bearer to the Band of Gentlemen Pensioners and one of the Council for the Marches of Wales. He sat in five Parliaments for the County of Hereford, was Custos Rotulorum and High Sheriff in 1581, a close friend of Sir Thomas Bodley, and a contributor to his Library.[2] His son, Sir James, was the prototype of Sir Scudamore in the *Faerie Queene*.

The remainder of the following letters were addressed to Sir James's son, Sir John. Born in 1601, he was made a baronet on 1 June 1620, and became a follower of Buckingham. After being created Baron Dromore and Viscount Scudamore of Sligo on 1 July 1628, he retired to his seat, but kept informed of events by means of weekly newsletters from London. At the close of 1634 Charles appointed him Ambassador to France, a post which he filled from June 1635 until January 1639. While in Paris he kept in touch with his old friend Laud, and entertained Hobbes, Sir Kenelm Digby and Milton when they were there. He introduced Milton to Grotius in May 1638.

The first Viscount was succeeded in 1671 by his grandson, John Scudamore (1650–97), on the death of whose son, James, in 1716, the peerage became extinct. James's only daughter and heiress, Frances (d. 1750) was divorced by the 3rd Duke of Beaufort for incontinence, and in 1746 married Charles Fitzroy (afterwards Scudamore), natural son of the 1st Duke of Grafton. Their daughter, another Frances, conveyed the estates of the Scudamores to Charles Howard, 11th Duke of Norfolk, whom she married in 1771. She became a lunatic several years before her death in 1820, and a Chancery action was instituted to determine her rightful heir. Her deeds and family papers became a Chancery Master's Exhibit, and were later deposited in the Public Record Office (Class C115, "The Dowager Duchess of Norfolk's Deeds, etc."). H. R. Trevor-Roper printed the Laud as well as the Bodley letters in the collection, but the other letters seem to have remained unnoticed.[3] (The bulk of the class consists of early deeds and manor rolls.) I discovered them only through the kindness of the incomparably helpful E. K. Timings of the Round Room, who pointed them out to me in another connexion.

The passages have been arranged under the dates of performance, following the format of Miss M. S. Steele's *Plays and Masques at Court*. Since there are no textual questions at issue, I have expanded all contractions.

   1. 1610/1, 1 January (Tuesday). Banquetting House, Whitehall. *Oberon, the Fairy Prince*—Ben Jonson. See below under next entry.

   2. 1610/1, 3 February (Sunday). Banquetting House, Whitehall. *Love Freed from Ignorance and Folly*—Ben Jonson.

Two maskes are now in hande, the one for Newyearsnyght by ye Prynce, and 12 knyghts besyds him selfe, And the other for twefttnyght by ye Queens Majestie and her x Ladyes, besyds her selfe: The Mareshall Laverdine (who will be heere before the new yeare begyn, to take his Majestys oath to ye League, as my Lord Wotton hath alredy done in France), will beholde both theis Masks. every one in both ye Masks, doe furnish them selves on theyr owne charges, which will be very chargiable to them: My daughter Elizab: Gray is one, My d: of Arundell is excused by her beynge with chylde, and my d: of Pembroke, by her often beynge evell at ease, with a kynde of stytch or collique.[4]

The Prince's masque was performed as intended on 1 January, but the Marshal de Laverdin did not see it. He was present at the Queen's Masque which did not take place until 3 February.[5] Shrewsbury's letter confirms Chambers' conjecture that "the dresses of the main maskers... were probably paid for by the wearers".[6] It would appear from the list of masquers taking part in *Tethys Festival*[7] the previous June that the Countess of Pembroke had been "evell at ease" upon that occasion as well.

3. 1631/2, 12 January (Thursday). Lord Goring's. Unidentified Masque.

On Thursday night her Majesty had a masque of 6 Lords and as many ladyes presented her at my lord Gorings, my lord of Warwick being the chief.[8]

This performance was celebrated by Davenant, "In the Person of a Spy, At the Queens Entertainment by the Lord Goring".[9] Since he spoke of "this rude dull way to trouble you [the Queen] with gratitude", it seems likely that the masque was his own, though I have been unable to identify it. It might, of course, have been an extemporal masque.

4. 1631/2, 19 March (Monday). Trinity College, Cambridge. *The Rival Friends*—Peter Hausted.

On Munday the King and Queen heard and sawe Queens Colledge English Comedy upon Trinity Colledge stage in Cambridge; which being 7 howers long was very tedious to the Spectatours.[10]

Pory's letter confirms the information about the time, place and quality of this performance contained in Sir Simonds D'Ewes' autobiography.[11] (There are further allusions to the play under the entry on its companion piece by Randolph.)

5. 1631/2, 20 March (Tuesday). Trinity College, Cambridge. *The Jealous Lovers*—Thomas Randolph.

Trinity Colledge English Comedy acted before their Majesties on Tuesday in the afternoon was not onely more compendious, but more facetious, wherein they egregiously flouted them of Queens Colledge, and playd upon the Poets and players of this towne. At five of the Clock the same afternoon their Majesties departed to Roiston.[12]

Miss Steele and G. E. Bentley, following G. C. Moore Smith, incorrectly date the performance of Randolph's play as Thursday the 22nd. Moore Smith got his date from Cooper's *Annals of Cambridge*[13] which, in turn, was based on MS. Baker xxxiii. 235, "Particulars from Mr. Pern's Book Esqe Bedell viz. Funerals, Graces etc."[14] Pory's intelligence dovetails with D'Ewes' information that "the royal pair departed from Cambridge, Tuesday, March the 20th, in the afternoon".[15] Beadle Pern had greeted the King and Queen not on the 22nd, but on the 19th; and there was no return visit for the Randolph play.[16]

The plays were alluded to on the second and third of March by Henry Herbert[17] and John Flower,[18] and on the 24th Flower spoke of them as two English Comedies.[19] On 7 April Pory, in giving an account of the suicide of Dr Butts, the Vice-Chancellor, said that Holland had chidden Butts for allowing the "obscene, prophane, absurd, and tedious comedy" which the Queens' men had performed on the Trinity stage.[20]

6. 1632, 3 May (Thursday). The Cockpit-in-Court. Unknown play, by the King's Company.

On Thursday night my lo: Chamberlaine bestowed a feast and a playe upon the King and Queen at his lodging in the Cockpitt, which cost his lordship 1500[li]. This expense was noble both in respect of those that were feasted, and of him that made the feast.[21]

Thursday before 5 May was 3 May, and this performance, or at least the rehearsal for it, appears to have been paid for by the King himself, for there was a warrant to John Lowen, Joseph Taylor and Ellyard Swanston for plays given by the King's Company between 3 May 1632 and 3 March 1632/3 which started with "20[li] for rehersall of one at the Cockpitt by which meanes they lost their afternoone at the House".[22]

7. 1632, October, November. *The Magnetique Lady, or Humours Reconciled*—Ben Jonson.

Ben Jonson hath written a playe against the Terme called the Magnetick Lady.[23]

The Players of the Black fryers were on Thursday called before the high Commission at Lambeth, and were there bound over to answere such articles as should be objected against them. And it is said to be for uttring some prophane speaches in abuse of Scripture and wholly thinges, which they found penned, for them to act and playe, in Ben Jonsons newe comedy called the Magnetique lady.[24]

The play was licensed in October 1632, and the following month the Players were haled into the Court of High Commission. This reference seems to confirm Herbert's date of October 1633 for the second petition of the Players to the Court,[25] since it indicates that proceedings were not instituted until 15 November, 1632. Moreover, the Players seem here to be putting the onus on Jonson, which corresponds to their original defence.

8. 1632/3, 9 January (Wednesday). Somerset House. *The Shepheards Paradise*—Walter Montague.

The Queens Majesty with some of her ladies, and maides of honour is daylie practizing upon a Pastorall penned by Mr Walter Montague. And Taylour the prime actor at the Globe goes every day to teache them action.[26]

The pastorall penned by Mr Walter Montague (which is to be acted before the King at Denmarke house upon the 19th of 9ber being his Majesties birth-day, by the Queens Majesty her ladies, and maydes of honour) is extream long: for my lady Marques [of Hamilton] her part alone is as long as an ordinary playe.[27]

On Wedensday night his Majesty among other lordes meeting with mylord Privy seale at St Jameses, did highly congratulate and extoll unto him the rare and excellent partes of his sonne Mr Walter

Montague, appearing in that Pastorall which hee hath penned for her Majesty her Ladies, and maydes to acte upon his Majesties birthday. And it seemes his Majesty was in good earnest: for hee hath giuen him for that service 2000[li] out of the Queens portion-money, and her Majesty hath given him 500[li] out of her owne purse. Mr Taylour the Player hath also the making of a knight given him for teaching them how to act the Pastorall.[28]

This remarkable work, the only production of the season 1632–3, represented an extraordinary investment of time and money. Sometime before the middle of September Henrietta Maria and her ladies were daily at work on the pastoral, which, despite Pory's anticipation, was not finally presented until four months later. It brought unprecedented rewards both to its author and to Joseph Taylor, one of the leading actors in the King's Company.

Pory elucidates the implications of Taylor's court connexions, alluded to by Herbert and Marmion in their references to Taylor's appearance in *The Faithfull Shepherdess* at Somerset House on 6 January 1633/4.[29] Presumably the Queen's gift of the costumes was in addition to the King's gift of the making of a knight; how much Taylor received for that, and from whom, we do not know. Certainly it was the success of Montague's pastoral which led to the presentation of Fletcher's *Shepherdess* the following Twelfth Night. Marmion's statement that the *Shepherdess* was revived by Taylor's "cost and industry" may refer to a personal investment by the actor, perhaps the proceeds from the making of the knight.

A more important point is made by the letters: these are the only references which I have seen to professional dramatic coaching for a court production. Since this performance was in many ways unique, however, we cannot surmise that the practice was common.

9. 1632/3, 5 March (Shrove Tuesday). Somerset House. Unidentified Queen's Masque, possibly *The Shepheards Paradise*.

...the Queene entertains the King with a maske at Denmark house on tuesday night next.[30]

Miss Steele[31] takes the Venetian Ambassador's "public hall" to mean Whitehall, and speculates that this may have been the second performance of *The Shepheards Paradise*. The fact that it was presented "at Denmark house" strengthens the probability of that conjecture, for it was there that "a roome" was "purposely made" for the pastoral.[32]

10. 1634, October. A Spanish Comedy.

From this Court no newes, but (thanked bee God) all is well, and a Spannish companie of Comedians are to play in Spanish before their Majesties.[33]

On 23 December 1635 a warrant for 10[li] was made "unto Iohn Nauarro for himself and the rest of the Company of Spanish Players for A play presented before his Maty."[34] It would appear from the lapse of time between Weckherlin's report and the warrant that Navarro and his Company, though they gave only one performance at Court, stayed in England for over a year. Weckherlin wrote from Hampton Court, whence the Court returned to London on Thursday, 30 October 1634.[35] It seems probable, therefore, that the performance took place between 22 and 29 October.

11. 1634/5, 10 February (Shrove Tuesday). Banquetting House, Whitehall. *The Temple of Love*—William Davenant.

The Queene is preparing a Maske to present the King withall.[36]

The Queene intends to present to his Majesty a Maske, but having not yet made choise of her Ladies, it will not bee made before Shrovetyde.[37]

Upon Christmas day, the old Countesse of Leicester dyed, at Drayton, now all her childrens children to the third, and forth generation, put them selves into blacks, and because of this mourning the lady of Carlile, doth excuse her being of the Queenes maske at Candlemas.[38]

These excerpts, showing Weckherlin's intimate knowledge of the court schedule, explicate Garrard's report that the Countesses of Northumberland and Carlisle were not to be in the masque for "they have got their Friends to excuse them, and it is not ill taken."[39] The Countess of Leicester was Lettice Knollys, the maternal grandmother of the Countess of Carlisle and of her brother, the Earl of Northumberland.

12. 1637/8, 7 January (Sunday). Masquing House, Whitehall. *Britannia Triumphans*—William Davenant.

Wee haue a stately buylding toward in Whytehall (but more stately for forme and use then for matter or substance being all of wood) to be imployd only for maskes and dancing, whyle the bancketting is to be reserved only or cheefly for Audiences, with apprehension of his Majesty that torches, wyth theyr smoake may disluster the pictures and guyldings there, which are sayd to haue cost above ten thousand poundes.

This fabrick is placed (that I may rightly fix your lordships imagination and fancy of it) wythin some ten foot of the bancetting howse, extending in lenght toward the hall and gard chamber about a hundred and ten foot, in bredth: ten or twelue foot into the fyrst court; and about fyve and forty into that of the preaching place.[40]

The king will be in his owne person in a maske this Christmas. And soe will the Queene be likewise in a maske in her owne person this Christmas. for there will be two severall masks. And a faire large Roome of Timber is newly and suddenly built for that purpose betweene the bancquetting house and the gard chamber, taking upp halfe the bass, or first Court and halfe the Court in the preaching place.[41]

Upon Monday next being the 8th of this instant moneth, the kings maske will be at Whitehall.[42]

This duty of the season discharged, [he has sent New Year greetings] I owe another of my charge, not impertinant (I persweade my self thoughe tedious perhaps) for your lordships knowledg. it is of the puntillios, rysing this last Maske, both from the Frenche and Spanish Ambassadors about inviting and placing, thus. Five or six dayes before the Mask was to be presented by the king and a dozen of his lords and nobles: I repayred to my lord Chamberlin, and wyth him to his Majesty, for resolution how the Ambassadors were to be treated at it. when remembring his Majesty of his pleasure signified to me the day before for an audience demanded and assignd the Spanish and intimating how fit it would be (for avoydance of surprise in case he shoulde offer his presence at the Maske) that I should receyve instructions how to governe my self and my answeres if he should discover a disposition to be at it or an expectation to be formally invited to it; his Majesty gave me for answere that I knew well enoughe it had never bene his custome to invite Ambassadors to those intertaynments, for the troubles sake they brought with them, but that whosoever of them should come should be welcome as privat Persons, yet not without the regard due to theyr publick qualityes for theyr placing or otherwyse. I obiected that if the Frenche should meet the Spanish upon the same floare where there was a right hand and a left, they both contending for the right, myght rayse perhaps some disturbance to the assembly; It was answered that if the Frenche Ambassador should seat him self below among the ladyes (as it was lykely he would by example of other Ambassadors of his nation coming uninvited and privat) the Spanish could not refuse a place that should be offred above in a Box (as they call it) with the Countess of Arondell.

The next day that I might feele the pulse of the Spaniard and bring the difference to some Terme of accommodation, I went to him to his house at Chelsey and falling, after other purpose, upon that of the Mask towards, asked him if he ment not to be at it, Yes (quod he) very willingly if I may have the invitation that becomes my quality. The king (I replyd,) never invites any Ambassadors to Masks, but suche as come to them are sure to be welcome: I shall not be sure of that (answerd he agayne) unless his Majesty shall do me the honour to invite me, and then I doubt not but he will doe me the right to protect me, which I cannot promise my selfe so assuredly, if I shall be there as a Privat Person, and receyving (perhaps) an affront from some that will not stick to offer it shall too late fly to his Majesty for defence (as for a publick Minister) when I have made my self privat by coming thether uninvited.

With this his scrupulosity acquaynting the King and his Majesty commanding me to leave him to his owne way, I was twoo or three dayes after assaylled by his steward who presenting me a list (wyth his lords particular recommendation) of one or twoo and twenty persons (all except three under title of Dons) they were introduced by a Tourndoore into the fyrst entry of the Maske-Roome (not the bancketting house but another buylt, next it, to save that and the pictures in it from harme by smoaking) where I bestowing them awhyle for theyr after ascent to a place appointed for them on the left hand of the kings chayre somwhat behynd and over it; certayne of the better sort of them, (ignorant of the way) tooke to the right hand, and entring there a doore (too readyly opened by Mr Controller), the rest following, they (altogether) passed up to a stand kept for the Frenche, where once seated I could not with civility remove them, thoughe in discourse to myselfe and wyth expression to Mr Controller of some doubt of exception to follow from the Frenche, I wished it otherwyse; and for prevention of worse went immediatly to the Frenche Ambassador (then in Court and in company of his Gentlemen attendeng my call for theyr placing) when he asking me apart how him self should be placed. I told him that coming thether as a domestick privat and uninvited he myght be pleased to seat him self domestically among the ladyes; but (quod he) how will you dispose of my Gentlemen? in a stand (answered I) provided for them apart from the Spaniards to avoyd the disturbance that may possibly grow from theyr mingling. I but (replyed he) if myne have not the right hand and be not placed neerer the King and Queenes seat then the Spaniard nor they nor I are lyke to be there, and so I must be bold to tell the Queen. I desyred him to contayne him self awhyle tyll I should make a reuew for remedy (thoughe the error were not (I sayd) of my making) and therupon retourning to the Hall, acquaynted my lord Chamberlin wyth the French Ambassadors formality and exception (which his lordship and other thought over curious, the Ambassador of Spayne him self being not present and the other of France being to be there as privat) pointing to a place capable of seaven or eyght of the Frenche, on the right of the queene amongst some gentlewomen, which was bothe neerer and more in sight then that taken by the Spaniards it was approved-of, and possessed by them, to theyr satisfaction and wythout the others

PLATE III

A. TIMON BESIEGED BY HIS CREDITORS

B. ALCIBIADES PLEADS WITH
THE SENATORS

C. TIMON TURNS ON HIS FALSE FRIENDS AT THE MOCK-BANQUET
'TIMON OF ATHENS', THE OLD VIC, 1956. PRODUCED BY MICHAEL BENTHALL
AND DESIGNED BY LESLIE HURRY

PLATE IV

A. TIMON THROWS GOLD TO ALCIBIADES (LEFT) WHO IS ACCOMPANIED BY
TIMANDRA AND PHRYNIA

B. TIMON IN THE WOODS RAILS AT
APEMANTUS

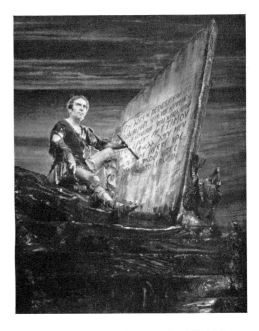

C. TIMON CHISELS HIS EPITAPH

exception, as eyther not observing or not regarding so small a difference. what wyll be stood upon at the next mask, to be presented by the Queen and her ladyes at Shrovetyde, I neyther wayghe nor apprehend, allors comme allors, I have told your lordship this for your intertaynment, having no knowledg of other matter worth it, nor is this so, but as it may perhaps afford subiect of question or discours (whether the Spanish Ambassadors puntillio for his invitation or the Frenches exception for his Followers placing were the more material, so leave it and the rest, to close all with an unfeigned assurance that I am....⁴³

The tale my last told your lordship of the Spanishe Ambassadors puntillio in his absence from the kings maske and of that of the Frenche in affecting and gayning the aduantage of place for his followers before the others, so tooke up my tyme as I could not tell other particulers I then intended.⁴⁴

Finet's description and placing of the new Masquing House do indeed "rightly fix" our "imagination and fancy of it". Through his vivid relation of the Ambassadors' punctillios, we can see the "Tourndoore" into the ante-room and the doors on the right (and left) leading into the main room, which contained the stands, the royal chairs, and, above, the boxes.

The last two letters disprove Garrard's statement to Wentworth that "The French and Spanish Ambassadors were both at the King's Mask".⁴⁵

13. 1637/8, 6 February (Shrove Tuesday). Masquing House, Whitehall. *Luminalia, or the Festival of Light*—William Davenant.
See the second and fourth citations under entry 12.

The Queenes maske wilbe performed againe at Easter and purposely reserved (as tis said) for the entertainment of the Dutches of Sheverez.⁴⁶

Your lordship thanks me for my so particuler relation of our Spaniards puntillios here, at the Kings Mask; those since at the Queens would deserve thanks indeed (had I tyme to tell them) for the mirths sake they would afford your lordship in theyr description. how gravely the Ambassador pretended to the iust number of his seruants to be intromitted, as at the Mask before; how lowdly my lord Chamberlin chaffed at his singularity, and how resolutly he notwithstanding limited them to the number in Noas Arck of eyght persons only; how patiently I satt attending in the porters lodge to prevent the thronging entrance at the Gate of the whole number of 21: stood uppon, and how silently two only crept in at the wicket, to make theyr claime, while nineteene sat without (coached) tyll I telling those twoo, of my lord Chamberlins absolute Order for admission of no more then eyght (as of no more of the Frenche, nobly and readyly assented to by that Ambassador) they all (as they sayd they had a direct command from theyr lord and Master) retournd together to theyr aboad at Chelsy, leaving the House eased of theyr Press, and the Ladyes pleased wyth the absence of theyr litle pleasing faces; but I should trouble your lordship and my self to wyth the particuler relation of these fopperyes; so I leave them.⁴⁷

Miss Steele does not record a performance at Easter, and it may be that Henrietta Maria's project did not materialize. Her fickle favourite, the Duchess of Chevreuse, cordially detested by the English nobility and assiduously attended by Walter Montague and Mr Crofts, rose and fell in her esteem during 1638; and Finet believed by December of that year that the Duchess would soon be leaving, put to rout by the Countess of Carlisle.

14. 1638, 28 July (Saturday). Somerset House. Unidentified play by the Queen's Company.

...the Venetian Ambassador and his lady; he lyes yet at Caron house Incognito and shee came three dayes since invited or at least allowed to come to a play sett forth by the Queen at Somerset house under the same maske, but wyth none on her face, which was greedily lookt on.[48]

The Venetian Ambassador's wife who came to court incognito (but without a mask) probably saw one of the seven plays of the season 1638–39 for which Henrietta Maria's Company was paid on 6 March 1639/40.[49]

During the twenty-seven-year period from January 1610/11 until July 1638, 14 plays and masques are mentioned.[50] Of these, five are unidentified (3, 6, 9, 10 and 14), three of them not listed by Miss Steele (3, 6 and 14). New dates are provided by 5 and 10,[51] and other new material by seven entries (3, 7, 8, 9, 10, 12 and 14). Five of the performances were graced by the Queen (2, 8, 9, 11 and 13), and one by the King (12). Prince Henry appeared in one masque (1). There were five plays acted before the King and Queen (4, 5, 6, 10 and 14).

Of the thirteen performances that actually took place (7 does not refer to a performance), three were presented at Somerset House (8, 9, and 14), and six at Whitehall, namely, three in the Banqueting House (1, 2 and 11), two in the Masquing House (12 and 13) and one in the Cockpit (6). Two were performed at Trinity College, Cambridge (4 and 5), one at Hampton Court (10) and one at Lord Goring's (3).

The value of this record is considerable; and we can be grateful that Lord Scudamore and his heirs not only purchased but also preserved the newsletters on which it is based.

NOTES

1. See Matthew Gibson, *A View of the Ancient and Present State of the Churches of Door, Home-Lacy and Hempsted* (1727).

2. See H. R. Trevor-Roper, 'Five Letters of Sir Thomas Bodley', *The Bodleian Library Record*, II, 134–9. In the first of the letters (the spelling has been modernized) there is a reference to the Oxford dramas which were presented to James from 27 through to 30 August 1605: "Their tragedy and comedies were very clerkly penned, but not so well acted, and somewhat over tedious, one only excepted."

The plays were *Alba*, a pastoral, *Ajax Flagellifer*, a tragedy, *Vertumnus, sive Annus Recurrens* and *The Queenes Arcadia*. James liked only the last.

There are a few words in these letters which I read differently from Trevor-Roper, e.g. in the first letter (C 115/M 20/7594), I read "if *wishing* would prevail" for "*writing*"; "not tenable *with* a garrison of *500* men" for "*without a garrison of seamen*"; "army is *infested*" for "*infected*"; "order of *placing* the books" for "*planning*"; in the third letter (C 115/M 20/7591), "*the* pattern of a true *repentant*" for "*that* pattern of a true *repentance*"; "as much as *any* confessor" for "as much as confessor"; "*at* Holme Lacy" for "*in*"; "which is hotly *rejected* by" for "*resisted*"; "never be *accorded*" for "*acceded to*"; "this *surcease* of arms" for "*surrender*"; "*thank* you more *effectually*" for "*shake* you more *affectionately*"; in the fourth letter (C 115/M 20/7592), "*good* leisure" for "*great*"; "to *chat* it out" for "*talk*"; and in the fifth letter (C 115/M 20/7593), "spark of *conceit*" for "*consent*". After "long absence" appears "from hence". There are other differences and additions which are not worthy of note.

3. *Archbishop Laud, 1573–1645* (1940). I wish to thank the Deputy Keeper of the Public Records for permission to publish these papers.

4. C 115/N 2/8519. Gilbert, Earl of Shrewsbury to Sir John Scudamore. 10 December 1610.

5. *The Elizabethan Stage* (Oxford, 1923), III, 385. Chambers assigns the latter correctly to 3 February at I, 173 and III, 386, but incorrectly to 2 February at IV, 125.

6. *Ibid.* III, 387. In his discussion of the cost of *Oberon*, Chambers cites Peter Cunningham's extracts from *The Accounts of the Revels at Court*...(Shakespeare Soc. 1842), viii. Herford and Simpson (x, 521) call Cunningham's version of the accounts very inaccurate; however, A.O. 1 Privy Purse/2021/2, which they cite as their source, and E 351/2794, which David Cook pointed out to me is an identical account on parchment (there are three minor differences in spelling), reveal that Cunningham's figures are entirely accurate though he added a comma and read 'o' for an 'e' in "rybbens". Herford and Simpson's transcript which, unlike Cunningham's, follows the format of the original contains the following errors: "mercers cci$^{\text{xx}}_{\text{ij}}$li viij^{s} v^{d}" for "cci^{xx} ix^{li} viij^{s} v^{d}"; "embroderers iiij^{xx} li xvj^{s} ix^{d}" for "ii^{xx} ix^{li} xvj^{d}"; "devysor for the *same* Maske" for "devyser for the *saide* Maske"; and the total in the margin is not "'m^{l} iiij^{xx} vii^{li}, vi^{s}, x^{d}'" i.e. £1087. 6s. 10d." but "m iiij^{xx} xii^{li} vi^{s} x^{d}" or £1092. 6s. 10d.

7. Chambers, III, 283.

8. C 115/M 35/8390. John Pory to Viscount Scudamore. 14 January 1631/2. John Pory was a professional news-writer who corresponded regularly with Joseph Mead, Sir Thomas Puckering, Lord Brooke, Sir Robert Cotton and others from 1624 until 1635. Scudamore employed him only for the year 1632. On 25 December, Pory acknowledged receipt of £10, and cancelled Scudamore's subscription. (C 115/M 35/8422.) There are 27 references to him in *The Letters of John Chamberlain*. Ed. by N. E. McClure (Philadelphia, 1939).

9. *Works*, 1673, part I, p. 318. A. H. Nethercot, *Sir William D'avenant*, p. 184, dates the poem about October 1637, but on no evidence which he makes explicit.

10. C 115/M 35/8397. Pory to Scudamore. 24 March 1631/2.

11. *The Autobiography and Correspondence of Sir Simonds D'Ewes*. Ed. by James Orchard Halliwell (1845), II, 67.

12. C 115/M 35/8397. Pory to Scudamore. 24 March 1631/2.

13. III, 249, 250.

14. *A Catalogue of the Manuscripts preserved in the Library of the University of Cambridge*, V, 375. This repeats the date of 22 March.

15. *Autobiography*, II, 67.

16. Pory noted in an earlier letter that the play by Hausted was to have been presented on 7 March, the anniversary of the day on which James I had entered Cambridge in 1614/15; but the Earl of Holland, the Chancellor of the University, had been thrown off his horse on to his head, so the visit had had to be postponed. C 115/M 35/8396.

17. This Henry Herbert on 15 August 1629 wrote to Scudamore of a letter which he had received from Sir Henry Herbert. The present correspondent seems to have been a wine merchant. C 115/N 3/8545, 8547, 8548.

18. C 115/M 31/8148. John Flower, another professional news-writer, corresponded weekly with Scudamore from the Fall of 1629 until early 1634. On 11 May 1633 he acknowledged receipt of £11, and on 12 April 1634 wrote that he was unable to do Scudamore much further service because of "the death of my friend". C 115/M 31/8151, 8173.

19. C 115/M 32/8191. 20. C 115/M 35/8383.

21. C 115/M 35/8402. Pory to Scudamore. 5 May 1632.

22. *Malone Society Collections*, II, 360, a transcription of LC 5/132/325. Though, as J. Q. Adams, *Shakespearean Playhouses* (p. 408, n. 2), points out, the Cockpit living quarters were not identical with the Cockpit-in-Court (The Theatre Royal), it seems likely, since the theatre had been open since 5 November 1630 (Bentley, I, 28, n. 1) and was the scene of much activity, that the play alluded to above was presented in the Cockpit-in-Court.

23. C 115/M 35/8411. Pory to Scudamore. 15 September 1632.

24. C 115/M 35/8418. Same to same. 17 November 1632.

25. Bentley, IV, 618–20.

26. C 115/M 35/8411. Pory to Scudamore. 15 September 1632.

27. C 115/M 35/8424. Same to same. No date, but probably 27 October 1632.

28. C 115/M 35/8416. Same to same. 3 November 1632. 29. Bentley, II, 595.

30. C 115/M 32/8206. Flower to Scudamore. 2 March 1632/3.

31. *Plays and Masques at Court*, p. 244. 32. *MSC*, II, 359, a transcription of LC 5/132.

33. C 115/M 37/8467. Weckherlin at Hampton Court to Scudamore. 22 October 1634. Georg Rudolph Weckherlin (1584–1653) was an under-secretary of State from 1624–41. In 1644 he was made Secretary for foreign tongues, was displaced by Milton in 1649, and in 1652 was Milton's assistant for nine months. A complete edition of his letters is being prepared by L. W. Forster.

34. *MSC.* II, 377, a transcription of LC 5/134/90. 35. *CSP* (Venetian), 1632–36, p. 296.

36. C 115/M 37/8474. Weckherlin at Whitehall to Scudamore. 6 December 1634.

37. C 115/M 37/8475. Same to same. 19 December 1634.

38. C 115/M 36/8447. E. Rossingham to Scudamore. 3 January 1634/5. George Garrard wrote to Wentworth on 7 February 1637/8: "Lately an Horseman in the Street riding through the *Strand*, called a Porter to him, delivering a Letter to him to carry to Sir *Toby Matthew's* Lodgings, who would hardly receive it, not knowing from whom it came; but he did, laying it aside that Night on his Table, next Morning sent for two or three Friends, with whom he consulted what he should do with it: One to burn it; he opined to send it to one of the Secretaries; after much Debate, it was agreed to open it, but he told them that they must come upon Oath, to witness what was contained in it, if any Thing against the King or State. The Letter was underwritten, your humble Servant, *Rossingham*, who is Successor to *John Pory*, and is the most known Writer of News we have, a very honest Man, whom your Lordship knows." *The Earl of Strafforde's Letters and Dispatches, with an Essay towards His Life, by Sir George Radcliffe*, ed. by William Knowler (London, 1740), II, 149. I am at work on a biography of the object of this suspicion, Sir Tobie Matthew.

39. *Strafforde Letters*, I, 360.

40. C 115/N 8/8810. Sir John Finet to Scudamore in Paris. 1 November 1637. Sir John Finet (1571–1641) succeeded Sir Lewis Lewkenor as Master of Ceremonies on 12 March 1625/6. He consistently signed himself "Finet" not "Finett" as he is now known.

41. C 115/N 4/8619. Ja: Burghe to Scudamore. 5 December 1637. I have not been able to identify James Burghe with any certainty. He sent Scudamore news from 1636 to 1638.

42. C 115/N 4/8621. Same to same. 3 January 1637/8.

43. C 115/N 8/8814. Finet to Scudamore. 18 January 1637/8.

44. C 115/N 8/8815. Same to same. 24 January 1637/8.

45. *Strafforde Letters*, II, 148.

46. C 115/N 4/8622. Burghe to Scudamore. 14 February 1637/8.

47. C 115/N 8/8816. Finet to Scudamore. 21 February 1637/8.

48. C 115/N 8/8821. Finet to Scudamore. 31 July 1638.

49. *Malone Society Collections*, II, 392. An amusing evidence of the addiction of Royalty to masques is provided by Pory, 31 March 1632. "I sawe in a letter that came along with Sir Jacob [Ashley], that the King of Sweden and his company being one night in a merry mood, would needs make an Extemporall maske, the king himselfe putting on the habit of a Spaniard, his Queen of a Burgers wife, the King of Bohemia of a Jesuite, the Duke of Saxon Weymar of a Dutche host, Duke Augustus of a woodman, the Earle of Hanaw of a Buffon, and some ten or twelve mor in antique habits." C 115/M 35/8398.

50. There are other less interesting, on the whole merely corroborative, references to the following plays and masques (listed chronologically) which I hope to publish elsewhere: Daniel's *Tethys Festival*, Jonson's *Neptune's Triumph for the Return of Albion*, Middleton's *A Game at Chesse*, A Pastoral of the Queen's (Shrove Tuesday, 1625/6), The Duke's Masque, The Duke's Play, The Queen's Masque, The Queen's Play (5, 6, 16 and 19 November 1626), A Masque of the Queen's (14 or 15 January 1626/7), Jonson's *Love's Triumph through Callipolis* and *Chloridia*, Townshend's *Albion's Triumph* and *Tempe Restored* and Shirley's *The Triumph of Peace*. There is also one further, repetitive reference to Montague's *The Shepheards Paradise*.

51. Miss Steele (p. 253) lists Navarro's play under "The Season 1635–1636".

INTERNATIONAL NOTES

A selection has been made from the reports received from our correspondents, those which present material of a particularly interesting kind being printed in their entirety, or largely so. It should be emphasized that the choice of countries to be thus represented has depended on the nature of the information presented in the reports, not upon either the importance of the countries concerned or upon the character of the reports themselves.

Australia

An event of outstanding importance took place in April 1956 with the production of *Twelfth Night* in Sydney by Hugh Hunt on behalf of the Australian Elizabethan Theatre Trust. This production, in a repertory with two other plays, enjoyed a nine months' tour of Australia, visiting all the capital cities and many others.

Though Dinah Shearing as Viola justly won high praise, it was the production rather than the performances which made theatrical history. Within living memory there had been no native Australian production of a play by Shakespeare which could hope to stand comparison with the imports from Stratford and the Old Vic. This is not to deny many excellent performances by the Alan Wilkie and John Alden Companies —both splendid troupers who have devoted themselves to Shakespeare without adequate resources. Hunt, with Elaine Haxton as designer, gave Australia its first home-made production, setting and costumes which for elegance, taste and delight would have won laurels in Stratford or London.

Miss Haxton cleverly contrived a single outdoor set which combined harmoniously the two moods of this play. It was at once solid enough for the low humours of Sir Toby and yet light and courtly enough to give romantic colour to the love scenes. How the one dovetailed and slid into the other as if by magic gave a chuckle of pleasure but never detracted attention from the words where they were the important discipline. Where partial distraction could be permitted (as in some of the Toby Belch scenes) Hunt introduced comic apparatus in the shape of a barrel and a ladder. In Act II, Scene iii a new atmosphere was created without our being taken out of the main surroundings and without any loss of speed. The barrel might have symbolized Belch's depravity and the ladder the base degrees of Malvolio's ambition, yet none of this fanciful imagining was necessary, because all the business and invention were contained within the action and dialogue of the play at its entertainment level.

ERNEST W. BURBRIDGE

Austria

During the annual Festival in June 1956 the Vienna State Opera offered the first performance of Frank Martin's opera, *The Tempest*, where Shakespeare's text appears almost in its entirety. The only addition is an elaborate ballet in the third act, suggested by the maskers who bring in the banquet offered by Prospero. The luxurious Vienna performance found a very warm welcome.

A new interest is being taken here in those plays of Shakespeare where the idea of mercy forms the main subject. *Measure for Measure* and *The Merchant of Venice* appeared in the repertory of the Vienna Burgtheater and the Innsbruck Landestheater, and found an appreciative audience. In the latter, Shylock is no longer represented as broken by the verdict in the trial scene; rather is he overwhelmed. He is shown as not being able to grasp the fact that he will not have to lose his life, as suggested by the letter of the law, and that even his fortune will remain in the hands of his only natural heir and her husband. Producers here have followed a suggestion by Richard Flatter.

The Burgtheater, late in the year, revived *Othello* with Ewald Balser as Othello, Albin Skoda as Iago, Käthe Gold as Desdemona. It is a performance in which everything spectacular and theatrical is avoided. Balser's Othello is a noble Oriental, Skoda's Iago an unscrupulous, rather modern cool schemer who wants to get ahead and does not care what means he uses; Desdemona becomes a victim of circumstances she cannot understand. The Burgtheater will tour various German cities with its *Othello* early in 1957.　　KARL BRUNNER

Canada

Three very significant events occurred in Canada during 1956, all of which will have an important effect on Shakespearian study and production.

In the first place, the Stratford (Ontario) Shakespeare Festival decided to build a permanent theatre after four very successful seasons in a large theatre-tent. The initial estimate for the building, which will preserve the original open stage designed by Tanya Moiseiwitsch and Tyrone Guthrie in 1953, was for $800,000. This has since been raised to one and a half million dollars. The fund is now nearly complete and the permanent theatre, now building, will be in use for the 1957 season.

The last season in the tent saw two productions, one of *The Merry Wives of Windsor* which had a great deal to commend it since it was treated as high comedy and played very convincingly. The other was *Henry V* with a Canadian actor Christopher Plummer in the main role, and with French-Canadian actors taking the roles of the French courtiers. This latter innovation proved a great success, showing the mercurial quality of French-Canadian acting to perfection. There were certain difficulties for the listener as he heard blank verse being spoken with the accent shifted as a French-Canadian shifts it. But this minor irritation was forgotten in the effect of the last scenes in the play, where French-Canada might well have been speaking in its present-day voice as Burgundy urged the English to submerge their differences and to live together in productive peace—a situation which as yet barely prevails in this bi-lingual country with two distinct cultures.

The second great step forward has been the founding of the Canadian Players, a group of travelling repertory players drawn from the Festival company who have toured Canada and the United States extensively. Their productions are without scenery and costumed in somewhat modernistic dress. The plays can thus be given almost anywhere and have a speed and élan wholly commendable. In the course of their two seasons this group has played *Macbeth*, *Hamlet* and *Othello* in such varying places as Espanola, Ontario; Cold Lake, Saskatchewan (which lived up to its name by greeting the company with temperatures thirty degrees below zero);

Washington, D.C. and Lexington, Kentucky. This group of players, under the direction of Douglas Campbell, a former member of the Old Vic and the husband of Ann Casson, has provided top-quality productions in a country where, apart from what amateur groups have presented, there has been no Shakespeare played outside of the main centres, and often not professionally even there.

The third event has been the setting up of a Canada Council. This Council will have the same sort of function in Canada as the Arts Council of Great Britain. Started with a capital fund of $100,000,000 by the Dominion Government, it will spend the interest on this sum solely in helping to promote the arts and in giving fellowships and other help to the humanities departments of Canadian universities.

In other words, 1956 saw the arts recognized as something important in Canada—important enough for funds to be set aside by governments to see that they have a chance to survive in what is still a booming, pioneer land. And the impetus for this has, without any question whatsoever, come from the success of the Stratford Shakespeare Festival which proved its worth by being invited to the Edinburgh Festival in 1956 with its production of *Henry V*.　　ARNOLD EDINBOROUGH

Czechoslovakia

There are sixty-three professional acting companies in Czechoslovakia, and during 1956 forty Shakespearian productions were staged in their theatres. The most popular play proved this time to be *Much Ado About Nothing* (in seven theatres); then came *A Midsummer Night's Dream* (six); *Othello* (five); *Romeo and Juliet* and *The Merry Wives of Windsor* (four); *The Merchant of Venice* and *Twelfth Night* (three); *The Two Gentlemen of Verona*, *As You Like It* and *Hamlet* (two); *Measure for Measure*, *Macbeth* and *Antony and Cleopatra* (one). Two Czech composers have written music to ballets on Shakespearian themes—D. C. Vackár for *A Midsummer Night's Dream* and Jan Hanuš for *Othello*. Several new editions of Shakespeare appeared (one with illustrations by John Gilbert) and, at last, the *Complete Works*, translated by J. V. Sládek and others (see *Shakespeare Survey*, 9), is being prepared for press by O. Vočadlo.

　　　　　　　　　　　　　　BRETISLAV HODEK

Finland

Shakespeare's position as the most popular non-Finnish playwright remains unchallenged: statistics drawn up by the Central Federation of Finnish Theatre Associations at the end of 1956 show that for the past ten years Shakespeare has been by far the leading foreign author on the Finnish stage. Several of his plays figure yearly in the repertories of the thirty-three state-subsidized theatres and of the thousands of amateur companies.

The most popular Shakespeare productions in 1956 were those of *The Taming of the Shrew, The Tempest, The Merchant of Venice, A Midsummer Night's Dream,* and *As You Like It. The Tempest,* produced at the Finnish National Theatre at the end of 1955 to mark the ninetieth birthday of Jean Sibelius, the composer, whose stage music was played unabridged by a full-size symphony orchestra, continued to attract full audiences in the spring season of 1956. Urho Somersalmi's Prospero was an outstanding achievement. The Finnish text was revised for the occasion by the producer, Arvi Kivimaa. Other remarkable productions were those of *The Taming of the Shrew* at the Turku Municipal Theatre and the Helsinki Popular Theatre, in both of which the frame story was omitted. The Turku production by Jouko Paavola aimed at lightness and liveliness of tone, while in Helsinki Gloru Leppänen tried to reproduce a rich Renaissance atmosphere. Combining word and movement in remarkable harmony, the production proved a success also on an open-air stage in the summer.

RAFAEL KOSKIMIES

France

This year no Shakespearian production in Paris reached the standard of Jean Vilar's *Macbeth,* which I discussed in last year's notes. But no company deserves greater praise than 'La Guilde', which performed *King John* in Salle Pelleport, in the popular district of Ménilmontant (July 1956). Members of La Guilde are young amateurs in the best sense of the word and, to quote a critic, are capable of a sincerity which is no longer found among professionals. Producer, decorator and actors carry disinterestedness to the point of remaining anonymous.

Performances of *Coriolanus* at the Comédie Française in 1934 occasioned violent scenes, a section of the public hailing the play as a satire of democracy. This time Jean Meyer's production fell flat. The actors were not outstanding, and the setting, a complex structure of plain wood, white against a black background, with staircases at unusual angles, became an easy butt for the critics. This creaking carpentry, which provided such perilous sitting accommodation for the senators, seems to have been raised as a belated tribute to the Russian constructivists of thirty years ago, yet it was conceived by the producer as a return to the conditions of the Elizabethan stage. I should rather say it was an unsuccessful attempt to escape from the stage routine of the Comédie Française. While the 'synthetic setting' represented an effort to liberate Shakespeare from stage conventions which were not his own, its already outmoded modernism clashed with the pseudo-Corneille version by Piachaud in unrhymed *alexandrins.*

This unfortunate experiment helps us to understand why French producers usually seem freer and happier in their treatment of Shakespeare in open-air performances. There is no need to reconcile the Elizabethan conception with that of our classics, or to tone down the poetry: cosmic imagery seems no longer out of place, and there is no stage tradition to take into account. Vilar's *Richard II* and *Macbeth,* as presented in Paris at the Théâtre National Populaire, owed a great deal of their beauty to the original productions in Avignon and most critics expressed a sense of loss when the shows were transferred from the façade of the Palais des Papes to the stage of the Palais de Chaillot. They had the same feeling when Raymond Hermantier, as a guest of Vilar's, revived at Chaillot *Julius Caesar,* which he had directed the previous year in the arena of Nîmes. The adaptable set was simple and well suited to the crowd scenes. But the show was marred by bad taste and ludicrous effects. The colossal statue of Caesar was hideous, the thunder and lightning was also on a gigantic scale and Casca could be seen grovelling with fear, Caesar fought for his life like D'Artagnan and succumbed after a prolonged fencing act. Hermantier loves a part to tear a cat in, and as Mark Antony he ranted and foamed to his heart's content; he did not deliver the famous speech as a cunning politician, but worked himself up to a fury and ended by swaying threateningly into the air the litter upon which was stretched a dummy representing Caesar's corpse.

Only two more indoor productions came to my notice. There were a few performances of *Measure for Measure* at the 'Bouffes Parisiens' (June 1956) in an adaptation by J. Houbart and J. L. Richard, the producer. And I hear that *Hamlet* has just been acted in Rennes and other towns of Brittany by the 'Centre Dramatique de l'Ouest' in a version by Hubert Gignoux, the director of the company. I have already mentioned the good work of the 'Centres Dramatiques' in the provinces. The 'Stages Nationaux d'Art Dramatique' also contribute to raising the standards of theatrical life outside Paris by combining the instruction of amateurs with the preparation of festival productions—usually during the summer vacations—the work of a dramatic and an artistic group being combined. In Louviers *The Knight of the Burning Pestle* was presented in a modernized version, in which the hero became a chivalrous cowboy: it may well have been greater fun than Shakespeare in modern dress. René Jeauneau, the instructor of the 'Stage' in Carcassonne, set himself a more ambitious task: *Measure for Measure* was given there in the open-air theatre (a reconstruction of the antique) with the famous towers and battlements as a background. Organ music, transmitted from the fourteenth-century basilica, provided an impressive opening to the play as adapted by Jean Lescure. In Nérac, with its memories of the court of Navarre, *Love's Labour's Lost* was considered most appropriate. It was performed, under the direction of Jean Lagénie, on a simple platform surrounded with trees.

Gabriel Monnet, the instructor of the 'Stage' in Annecy, asked why he had not used the castle's architecture as an element of décor in his performance of *Hamlet* (1955), answered that natural and architectural surroundings created a certain quality of atmosphere, but that details should not be made artificially to coincide with dramatic action. As most of the summer festivals came into existence in order to take advantage of the attraction of monuments or natural scenery, it is unlikely that many producers will resist this temptation and will make Monnet's subtle but artistically valid distinction. For instance, when Jacques Charon produced André Obey's adaptation of *Richard III* in the courtyard of the castle of Angers, he made use as part of the décor of a certain tower which was supposed to represent the Tower of London. Douking chose the massive Tour Royale dominating the bay of Toulon as a setting for his *Othello* (19–25 July 1956): battlements, streamers flying in the evening air and a vast expanse of sea created an appropriate atmosphere for certain scenes—perhaps at the expense of the conflict in the soul of the protagonist, impersonated by Gamil Ratib, a gifted young actor whose handsome and powerful features, though more Egyptian than Moorish, provided the required exotic note.

Talking of exoticism leads us to mention the festival of Baalbek which, according to a journalist of the Middle East, "was the greatest political victory of Libanus since Libanus came into existence". There, some fifty miles from Beirut, Jean Marchat, at the head of a French company, produced and acted the title part of *Julius Caesar* in a version by Georges Beaume on the steps of the temple of Jupiter, surrounded by the ruins of Heliopolis. After Baalbek the island of Bendor, off the coast of Bandol, will, by festival standards, seem a rather shabby place for a Roman play. Jacques Dacqmine and his company carried indifference to natural

settings to the extent of playing *Coriolanus* against a background of rocks and trees: maybe it was a way of reminding some people that the play is the thing. *Twelfth Night* was one of the plays of the 'Nuits de Bourgogne' in Dijon and other towns (June to August 1956) and Jean Denincz produced *Romeo and Juliet* in the courtyard of the Ancien Evéché at Blois.

This survey of Shakespearian performances owes a great deal to the assistance of Mlle Moudouès who kindly placed at my disposal the resources of the Centre de Documentation of the Société d'Histoire du Théâtre.

JEAN JACQUOT

Germany

Two unrelated trends in this year's Shakespeare activity in Germany demand notice. The first is the gradual replacement of the long-established Schlegel-Tieck-Baudissin translation by other more modern versions—especially those of Hans Rothe and Richard Flatter. Not only does this affect the productions generally, but also results in increased popularity for certain plays: for example, the large number of presentations of *The Comedy of Errors* may well be explained by the success of Rothe's adaptation. The general interest in these new versions of Shakespeare is indicated by the fact that the ninety-second volume of the *Shakespeare-Jahrbuch* is devoted to the history of Shakespeare translation in Germany and the problems involved in this task. The second trend is a striking predilection for the "dark comedies", especially *Measure for Measure*. Quite frequently these are treated as dramas presenting social problems and philosophies in harmony with the views of modern political cliques. The attempt to interpret Shakespeare in this way is not, however, confined to the treatment of the dark comedies: thus, for example, Gisela Kurtzweig tries to argue that Katharine's behaviour in *The Taming of the Shrew* is due to her aversion to the social hypocrisy of her father and Bianca, while Petruchio is similarly motivated—the result being that "both of these characters respect one another because of their uprightness".

During the year only a relatively small number of the 159 productions were of the histories and the Roman plays. The early comedies still maintain their place, in a diversity of modes. *A Midsummer Night's Dream* at Berlin was given as romantic a tone as possible by Fritz Wisten (with Mendelssohn's music); the same play presented by Günther Meincke at Osnabrück had the stress laid on its poetry and laughter; while at Annaberg, under the impress of Gerhard Pröhl, it was given a somewhat tragic flavour. As compared with the ninety-four productions of comedies there were only fifty-one of the tragedies, with *Romeo and Juliet* (twelve productions) and *Othello* (nine productions) maintaining their traditional popularity. It is worthy of note that *King Lear*, which has rarely been performed in recent years, seems to be of increasing interest to the public.

KARL BRINKMANN

Greece

In this country four of Shakespeare's plays have been presented during the year 1956: *Twelfth Night*, translated by Basil Rotas, produced at the Arts Theatre, Athens, directed by Charles Koun; *A Midsummer Night's Dream*, translated by Basil Rotas, produced at the National Gardens Theatre, Athens, directed by Dinos Yannopoulos; *The Taming of the Shrew*, translated by Cleandros Karthaios, at the National Gardens Theatre, Athens, directed by Nicos Hatziscos; and *Othello*, translated by Cleandros Karthaios, produced at the Kotopouli Theatre, Athens, directed by Demetrios Myrat.

GEORGE THEOTOKAS

Italy

Vittorio Gassman, whose interpretation of *Hamlet* was discussed in *Shakespeare Survey*, 7, gave an outstanding production of *Othello* at the Teatro Quirino in Rome (first night, 31 October 1956), with himself, Salvo Randone and Anna Maria Ferrero in the cast. The peculiarity of this production is that Gassman and Randone alternate in the roles of Othello and Iago. Gassman is good in both roles, but particularly in that of Iago, to which he gives a little of Hamlet's ambiguity. Randone as Othello offers the curious personality of a meditative, restrained (one would almost say, retired) general, who is suddenly seized by a fit of madness. Anna Maria Ferrero is a very convincing Desdemona, not over-stressing her sweet devotion to the point of foolishness. The setting by Giulio Coltellacci, with certain attempts at symbolism (nets and grates hinting at Othello's soul in the fetters of jealousy), was not particularly effective; the costumes, mostly after Giorgione's paintings, gave a pleasant shock of recognition to the cultured part of the audience. Unfortunately the text, a prose version by Salvatore Quasimodo, in its endeavour to supply the actors with an easy-flowing medium flattened out the imaginative power of the original.

In July 1956 *The Winter's Tale* (translated by C. V. Ludovici) was produced in the Vittoriale in Gardone, with Lilla Brignone, Gianni Santuccio and Maria Letizia Celli in the chief parts.

MARIO PRAZ

Japan

In January 1956, Bungakuza, one of the largest theatrical companies in Tokyo, presented *Hamlet* in a Japanese translation by Tsuneari Fukuda, who also acted as the producer. This proved most successful. It is noteworthy that NHK (the Japan Broadcasting Corporation) has presented five Shakespeare plays in translation: *Hamlet*, *King Lear*, *Othello*, *Macbeth* and *A Midsummer Night's Dream*. Each play was given two hours of broadcasting time, and the fact that rarely is so much allowed for any drama demonstrates the increasing interest in Shakespeare among students and the general public.

JIRO OZU

Norway

Three plays have been staged in 1956, all of them comedies: *The Taming of the Shrew* in Bergen (2 March), *As You Like It* at the Open Air Stage in Oslo (23 June), and *Twelfth Night* at the National Theatre in Oslo (28 September). *The Shrew* enjoyed the benefit of a superb translation, sparkling with wit and humour, by Gunnar Larsen, a colourful decor by P. Schwab, and a vigorous Petruchio created by Ola Isene. The Frogner Park in Oslo provided a sufficiently rustic frame for *As You Like It*, where the two outstanding performances were the charming Rosalind of Inger Marie Anderson and the buoyant Orlando of an outstanding Danish guest, Erik Mork. By far the best of the three productions, however, was *Twelfth Night*, with Wenche Foss as a very enchanting Viola and Per Aabel as Malvolio—the latter placed just in the borderland between comedy and tragedy where Chaplin excels.

LORENTZ ECKHOFF

Poland

Although 1956 has been rather a Shaw than a Shakespeare year, the Warsaw theatre has seen a much-disputed performance of *Romeo and Juliet* aiming at a radical modernization of the play, and *The Comedy of Errors* in a new version by Andrzej Makarewicz.

The Państwowy Instytut Wydawniczy has added four new volumes to its collection—*Romeo and Juliet*, *King Lear* (both translated by Zofia Siwicka), *Othello* (by Krystyna Berwińska) and *Richard II* (by Władysław Tarnawski). All of these have high artistic and philological value.

A remarkable critical and historical contribution is Witold Chwalewik's study, *Poland in Shakespeare's Hamlet*, published by the Ossolineum in Wrocław: this seeks to explore the significance of the character of Polonius and the elective monarchy, reminiscent of Polish procedure.

STANISŁAW HELSZTYŃSKI

South Africa

Shakespeare continues to attract good audiences in South Africa, even though the majority of the productions are still in the hands of amateurs. The professional companies, when they risk a 'Shakespeare', as a cultural variation from their modern commercial successes, are prudent enough to select from the plays prescribed for the Matriculation Examinations. *Hamlet, Macbeth, The Tempest, Julius Caesar, The Merchant of Venice, A Midsummer Night's Dream, Twelfth Night, The Taming of the Shrew, Much Ado About Nothing* and *The Merry Wives of Windsor* have been the stock-in-trade for the last half-century. At least two dozen of Shakespeare's plays have never been seen on the stage in South Africa.

There never was such a realistic shipwreck on the stage as Leslie French produced for the first scene of *The Tempest* at the Johannesburg Repertory Theatre. In the masque the car of Juno descended from the heavens, not without some creaking of the engines, and a full ballet was added, which somewhat marred the balance of the production. In Cape Town French also produced *The Taming of the Shrew* with robustiously comic effect. The popularity of this play never seems to wane, and another production of it was uproariously received at the Children's Theatre in Johannesburg, probably by the same audience as disturbed the peace of the M.C.C. cricketers at the Wanderers.   A. C. PARTRIDGE

Sweden

The leading companies seem to have forgotten Shakespeare during the past year, but our national travelling company, the Riksteatern, and various provincial playhouses have been active. The Riksteatern presented a *Twelfth Night* last autumn with Margareta Fahlén as a pretty Olivia and Gunnar Björnstrand as a fine Malvolio. Later on it toured with *Othello*, and this proved a great success. The leading roles were taken by the experienced actors Holger Löwenadler (Othello) and Hans Stråät (Iago).

An open-air performance of *A Midsummer Night's Dream*, produced by Kolbjörn Knudsen, benefited from having one of Gothenburg's many beautiful parks as a setting. Berit Frodi as Puck was very effective, acting with a kind of whipcord grace.

Recently *The Merchant of Venice* appeared at the Uppsala Municipal Theatre. The producer, Josef Halfen, treated it as a pure comedy. Even Georg Årlin's Shylock, with just a touch of tragedy, could find a place within this frame. A weak point was perhaps that the lyrical tone, at least in the Jessica-Lorenzo scenes,

seemed to fade away. And still more recently the Folkets Hus Teater of Gothenburg has given us a beautifully designed *Much Ado About Nothing*.
          NILS MOLIN

Switzerland

1956 was again a lean year. There were no Shakespeare productions in the French-speaking part of the country and none in Zürich. *The Winter's Tale* had a short run at the Bern Municipal Theatre, and *The Taming of the Shrew* a longer one at St-Gall. At Bâle, a students' performance of *The Comedy of Errors* in the summer and a *Hamlet* staged by the Stadttheater both aroused a good deal of excitement. The comedy was acted one evening in the University gardens and the same actor played the two Antipholuses, a gramophone with a loud-speaker representing the Syracuse twin in the last scene. The *Hamlet* production, with Adolf Spalinger in the title role, was highly experimental. Instead of the usual scenery, there was a system of curtains with concentric red circles on the floor under elaborate lighting. Unfortunately the company did not quite come up to the requirements set by the near-abstraction of the setting.   GEORGES BONNARD

U.S.A.

That Broadway did not have a very profitable American production of Shakespeare may be a matter of concern to the professional producer, but those who follow Shakespeare's fortunes on the stage do not measure the popularity of Shakespeare by box-office receipts and final profits. Broadway is not New York just as the West End is not London. The metropolitan area had an interestingly varied Shakespearian fare. At the East River Park Amphitheatre 25,000 persons, "about 90% of whom had never before seen a live play", saw free performances of *Julius Caesar* and *The Taming of the Shrew* in a two-month programme which cost only $2,000—the forty-five Equity members receiving no salary for their services. The still successful Shakespeare-wrights offered *Macbeth* and *Romeo and Juliet*, while other groups presented *Macbeth, Twelfth Night, Much Ado, As You Like It* and *The Two Gentlemen of Verona*.

The American Shakespeare Festival Theatre and Academy at Stratford, Connecticut, came of age in its second season and entertained over 100,000—an increase of 30,000 over last year. *King John, Measure for Measure*, and *The Taming of the Shrew* received greater critical acclaim than did last year's productions. A steeply raked stage, a larger apron, unusual scenery which consisted merely of varying arrangements of 'venetian blinds', lively direction by John Houseman assisted by Jack Landau and Norman Lloyd, and a versatile cast produced results which will lead to accomplishing for the United States what the Old Vic and Stratford-upon-Avon companies have done for England—the maintenance of a year-round repertory of Shakespeare.

Festivals in widely separated areas of the United States still continue to offer plays to enthusiastic and devoted patrons. Topeka, Kansas, had its first Festival with a production of *The Tempest*; Hofstra College had its fifth with *Richard III* on John C. Adams' famous replica-of-the-Globe stage; Memphis, Tennessee, had its fifth with *As You Like It*; and Philadelphia continued its outdoor series with *Timon of Athens*, *A Midsummer Night's Dream*, and *Antony and Cleopatra*.

At its fifth Annual Festival the Antioch Area Theatre (Antioch College, Yellow Springs, Ohio) became the first American company to present all the First Folio plays, *Pericles*, and *The Two Noble Kinsmen*. (The three parts of *Henry VI* had been condensed into one play.) The eleven-week season offered *King Lear*, *Much Ado*, *Hamlet*, *All's Well*, *Love's Labour's Lost*, *Measure for Measure*, and *The Comedy of Errors* to a campus audience of 35,000. Arthur Lithgow's production of *King Lear*, starring the versatile Ellis Rabb, was hailed by the *Saturday Review* as "the best American production of the play in our time".

The 14,000 who attended the seventh Annual Festival at the 'Old Globe' in San Diego, California, were treated to an unusual *Midsummer Night's Dream* in which the fairy kingdom characters were clad as Japanese Kabukis and the lovers as modern-dress military school students.

At Ashland, Oregon, the sixteenth Annual Festival—the oldest in the United States—offered *Richard III*, *Love's Labour's Lost*, *Titus Andronicus*, and *Cymbeline* on an outdoor stage modelled on the Elizabethan Fortune play-house.

Elsewhere in the U.S.A. there were an unusual number of offerings. There was an *Othello* with an all-Negro cast, *A Midsummer Night's Dream* with an all-female cast, a musical version of *The Tempest*, a *Julius Caesar* in a Unitarian Church with aisles and choir pressed into service, another *Dream* with a *corps de ballet* and Mendelssohn's music, and still another presented completely in ballet form on an outdoor stage with a large blue moon hanging in a tree, a thirty-foot cobweb, a moat of dyed blue-green water separating the stage from the audience, and at the back of the stage a red fountain to which little children dressed as animals came to drink. Even the Restoration adapters might have raised their eyebrows at some of these effects. A *Hamlet* at Baylor University deserves special mention. There were three masked Hamlets, each one showing by repetition and pantomime a facet of the character—"the warrior, the sharp-witted prince, and the neurotic philosopher". Burgess Meredith meanwhile played the central Hamlet, a composite of them all. There was also a 'tormented conscience' character acting with Claudius. A steeply raked central stage and side stages almost completely surrounded the spectators—who were thoughtfully provided with swivel chairs. LOUIS MARDER

HAMLET COSTUMES : A CORRECTION

By RAYMOND MANDER AND JOE MITCHENSON

[The following notes refer to the article on 'Hamlet Costumes' by D. A. Russell in *Shakespeare Survey*, 9.]

In his 'Hamlet Costumes from Garrick to Gielgud', D. A. Russell makes reference to our *Hamlet Through the Ages* (1952; second impression, revised and enlarged, 1955). Though not actually quoting us wrongly, he does by certain mistakes give the impression that we must be in error in our information. We are glad of this opportunity to correct a number of factual errors in the article, which, lest they might lead others astray, need correction. We propose to deal with the text and illustrations together in order, and to note only factual errors, not those of interpretation.

1. Plate I, 2 is not an engraving of Samuel Foote, who only played Hamlet during his first engagement at the Haymarket in 1744. It is a picture of John F. Foote, who played Hamlet at Drury Lane on 12 November 1802. This completely destroys the author's idea that any costume other than contemporary dress was used before the advent of Kemble in 1783.

2. Plate I, 3. Henderson is depicted in the grave-yard scene, in which Hamlet would naturally not be wearing royal insignia, being hastily returned from England.

3. John Philip Kemble made his London début as Hamlet at Drury Lane in 1783. The engraving I, 4 is dated 1785 and presumably represents this production. He did not assume management of Drury Lane until

1788. So the 'Van Dyck' costume was not, as stated, first worn then. The author has followed and quoted Doran's mis-statement (though, to be fair to Doran, we should note that Kemble did wear the Order of the Elephant and sash etc. in 1783, though *not* contemporary Court clothes).

Boaden, writing in 1825, states that in 1783 Kemble did not wear the then familiar 'Van Dyck' costume but contemporary Court dress; but he does not say when the Van Dyck costume came into use, or even that Kemble introduced it! The only evidence is the print dated March 1785. Kemble played Hamlet nine times in quick succession in 1783, and a further three times before the end of the season in 1784. In the 1784–5 season he only played it three times before the publication of the engraving.

We can find no evidence to show that the 'new' costume was an innovation for the second season, though no one seems to have remarked on it on either occasion.

4. Plate I, 5. Henry Erskine Johnson. The engraving illustrated, though published in 1817, is from a drawing made when the actor first appeared in London in 1798. There is another print of him at Edinburgh in 1795 which shows an even more interesting transitional costume. (*Hamlet Through the Ages*, 2nd ed., p. 62.)

5. Plate I, 7. This is not a *genuine* print of Charles Kemble, but a version by an unscrupulous engraver of the famous Lawrence portrait of John Philip Kemble painted in 1800, with the face of Charles substituted. Charles first acted Hamlet in 1803 but the engraving is a later fake.

6. Edmund Kean. Plate I, 9 dates from 1814. He went to Paris in 1828, but did *not* act Hamlet. It was Kemble who had played the part there in 1827 and Macready in 1828 (before Kean's visit).

7. Charles Kean. There is a picture of him (on the Battlements) in the 1838 production, showing the first version of the Tunic costume, which he introduced (*Hamlet Through the Ages*, 2nd ed., p. 27). This has no Elizabethan trimmings. But another lithograph of the same production (the scene with Rosencrantz and Guildenstern) shows the full Elizabethan lace collar, etc., as does a painting done in Liverpool in 1838 (which we illustrated, p. 104), and a head dated 1839 (Haymarket Theatre). This might indicate a change of costume during the action of the play. The Plate I, 12 dates from 1850.

8. Plate I, 10 dates from 1849, not 'early '40's', as stated.

9. Plate II, 13. Phelps' costuming dates from 1847 and the engraving from about 1853.

10. Charles Dillon played Hamlet at the Lyceum, 1857, from which time the engraving II, 16 dates. Not 'at the Surrey in the '60's'.

11. Plate II, 18 represents Herman Vezin as Laertes, not 'Hamlet, 1859'. He acted Laertes to Fechter's Hamlet at the Princess' Theatre in 1861. The similarity of the design of the costume to that of Fechter shows a production which had some artistic unity. Note the *Phrygian cap*—obviously worn on Laertes' return from France after the death of Polonius (a 'Cap of Liberty'— he was leading a revolt!).

12. Plate II, 21. The author expresses surprise to "find a Hamlet such as Allerton's dressed in the accepted style —'Elizabethan costume of the late nineteenth century'". This places Allerton among the famous actors to which reference has been made. After some hours of research we have found that a Charles Allerton appeared in London for three performances as Hamlet, at the Princess' Theatre in June 1868, and took the Lyceum for a few weeks the following year. He was described as "from the Theatre Royal, Dublin, Birmingham and Brighton". *The Era* remarks that his performance was not above the level they had been accustomed to see given by talented amateurs, adding that it was regarded "as the eccentricity of a well-intentioned gentleman, rather than as the serious effort of a young actor". On his second attempt, reference was made to "the long-suffering public". It would seem to have been a scratch production with a poor supporting company, so his costume can hardly be said to be significant. It looks like something left over from at least forty years before. The point of showing the costuming of Hamlet should surely be to reflect important revivals of integrity, or the attitude of actors of standing.

13. Plate II, 21 and text. Irving's first London Hamlet was in 1874. He inaugurated his own management of the Lyceum with a revival in 1878, but continued at intervals to act the part till 1885. Unless this is stated, the challenge of Edwin Booth (1880), which precedes Wilson Barrett (1884), is not appropriate.

14. Plate III, 26, 27, 28 and text. Bernhardt did not play Hamlet until 1899, hence the reference to Tree in 1892 is inappropriate.

15. Plate III, 33 and 34. The Ernest Milton photograph dates from 1925, and that of George Hayes from his Stratford Seasons, 1928–30. The tunic costume was still being worn by Duncan Yarrow with the H. V. Neilson company (the heir to the Benson Company) as late as 1939.

16. The undated photographs of Matheson Lang (London) and Walter Hampton (New York) date from 1909 and 1918 respectively.

17. Plate III, 35. The modern-dress Hamlet was *presented* by Sir Barry Jackson: it was produced by H. K. Ayliff.

SHAKESPEARE PRODUCTIONS IN THE UNITED KINGDOM: 1956

A List compiled from its Records by the Shakespeare Memorial Library, Birmingham

JANUARY

23   *The Merchant of Venice:* Sheffield Repertory Company at The Playhouse, Sheffield. *Producer:* GEOFFREY OST.

30   *The Comedy of Errors:* The Playhouse, Oxford. *Producer:* PETER WOOD.

FEBRUARY

13   *As You Like It:* Nottingham Playhouse Company (on tour). Sponsored by the Arts Council. *Producer:* JOHN HARRISON.

14   *King Lear:* Bristol Old Vic Company, at the Theatre Royal, Bristol. *Producer:* JOHN MOODY.

     Julius Caesar: The Library Theatre, Manchester. *Producer:* DAVID SCASE.

     Julius Caesar: Citizen's Theatre, Glasgow. *Producer:* RICHARD MATHEWS.

21   *Othello:* The Old Vic Company, at the Old Vic Theatre, London. *Producer:* MICHAEL BENTHALL.

27   *Macbeth:* Guildford Theatre Company. *Producer:* BRYAN BAILEY.

MARCH

5   *Othello:* Perth Repertory Theatre Company (on tour), Orkney and Shetland Islands. *Producer:* DAVID STEUART.

12   *Troilus and Cressida:* The Marlowe Society, at the Arts Theatre, Cambridge. (Producer and actors are anonymous.)

13   *A Midsummer Night's Dream:* Northampton Repertory Theatre. *Producer:* ALEX REEVE.

14   *Romeo and Juliet:* Sloane School, London. *Producer:* GUY BOAS.

16   *Richard II:* Norwich Players, Maddermarket Theatre, Norwich. *Producer:* FRANK HARWOOD.

19   *Othello:* Ipswich Theatre. *Producer:* VAL MAY.

28   *The Comedy of Errors:* The Arts Theatre Club, London. Adapted as a comic operetta by Lionel Harris and Robert McNab. Music by Julian Slade. *Producer:* LIONEL HARRIS.

APRIL

3   *Troilus and Cressida:* The Old Vic Company, at the Old Vic Theatre, London. (Afterwards on tour in the United States of America and Canada.) *Producer:* TYRONE GUTHRIE.

10   *Hamlet:* Shakespeare Memorial Theatre, Stratford-upon-Avon. *Producer:* MICHAEL LANGHAM.

17   *The Merchant of Venice:* Shakespeare Memorial Theatre, Stratford-upon-Avon. *Producer:* MARGARET WEBSTER.

     Julius Caesar: Birmingham Repertory Theatre. *Producer:* BERNARD HEPTON.

     Twelfth Night: Dundee Repertory Theatre. *Producer:* GEORGE HOLST.

MAY

8   *Hamlet:* Liverpool Repertory Company. *Producer:* WILLARD STOKER.

14   *The Merchant of Venice:* Salisbury Arts Theatre. *Producer:* JOHN MAXWELL.

22   *Macbeth:* The Old Vic Company, at the Old Vic Theatre, London. (Afterwards on tour in the United States of America and Canada.) *Producer:* MICHAEL BENTHALL.

28   *As You Like It:* Folio Theatre Company, Regent's Park Open Air Theatre, London. *Producer:* ROBERT ATKINS.

29   *Othello:* Shakespeare Memorial Theatre, Stratford-upon-Avon. *Producer:* GLEN BYAM SHAW.

JUNE

1   *King Lear:* Harrow School. *Producer:* RONALD WATKINS.

5   *The Merchant of Venice:* Oxford University Dramatic Society. *Producer:* DAPHNE LEVENS.

12   *Romeo and Juliet:* The Old Vic Company, at the Old Vic Theatre, London. (Afterwards on tour in the United States of America and Canada.) *Producer:* ROBERT HELPMANN.

18   *Macbeth:* Rugby School. *Producers:* T. A. BUCKNEY and T. P. LAW.

22   *Othello:* The Norwich Players, at the Maddermarket Theatre, Norwich. *Producer:* FRANK HARWOOD.

JULY

3   *Richard II:* The Old Vic Company, at the Old Vic Theatre, London. (Afterwards on tour in the United States of America and Canada.) *Producer:* MICHAEL BENTHALL.

     Love's Labour's Lost: Shakespeare Memorial Theatre, Stratford-upon-Avon. *Producer:* PETER HALL.

23   *Twelfth Night:* Folio Theatre Company, Regent's Park Open Air Theatre, London. *Producers:* ROBERT ATKINS and ANDREW LEIGH.

AUGUST

4   *Timon of Athens:* The Marlowe Society, at the Arts Theatre, Cambridge. *Producer:* TONY WHITE.

14   *Measure for Measure:* Shakespeare Memorial Theatre, Stratford-upon-Avon. *Producer:* ANTHONY QUAYLE.

28   *Henry V:* Shakespearian Festival Company, Stratford, Ontario, at the Edinburgh Festival. *Producer:* MICHAEL LANGHAM.

SEPTEMBER

5   *Timon of Athens:* The Old Vic Company, at the Old Vic Theatre, London. *Producer:* MICHAEL BENTHALL.

10   *Henry V:* The Youth Theatre, at Toynbee Hall Theatre, London. *Producer:* MICHAEL CROFT.

11   *Cymbeline:* The Old Vic Company, at the Old Vic Theatre, London. *Producer:* MICHAEL BENTHALL.

24   *A Midsummer Night's Dream:* Perth Repertory Theatre Company at Perth and Kirkcaldy. *Producer:* EDMUND BAILEY.

SHAKESPEARE PRODUCTIONS IN THE UNITED KINGDOM

OCTOBER

Exact date not known. *The Tempest:* David Lewis New Theatre Company, Liverpool. *Producer:* THOMAS G. READ.

8   *The Tempest:* Guildford Theatre Company.

15   *Measure for Measure:* Drama Department of Bristol University at the Theatre of Bristol University Union, Bristol. *Producer:* NEVILL COGHILL.

16   *Richard II:* Citizen's Theatre, Glasgow. *Producer:* RICHARD MATHEWS.

22   *Othello:* Leatherhead Repertory Company Ltd. *Producer:* JORDAN LAWRENCE.

23   *Coriolanus:* Birmingham Repertory Theatre. *Producer:* BERNARD HEPTON.

     Much Ado About Nothing: The Old Vic Company, at the Old Vic Theatre, London. *Producer:* DENIS CAREY.

NOVEMBER

7   *Macbeth:* The County Theatre Company at Stanford Hall Theatre, Nottingham. *Producer:* JOHN GRIFFIN.

13   *The Tempest:* The Library Theatre, Manchester. *Producer:* DAVID SCASE.

16   *The Winter's Tale:* The Maddermarket Theatre, Norwich. *Producer:* FRANK HARWOOD.

     Macbeth: Repton School. *Producer:* R. T. FISHER.

19   *The Tempest:* Bradford Civic Playhouse. *Producer:* ANTHONY HAIGH.

27   *Othello:* Bristol Old Vic Company, at the Theatre Royal, Bristol. *Producer:* JOHN MOODY.

28   *Twelfth Night:* Nottingham University Dramatic Society, in the Great Hall, Nottingham University. *Producers:* J. R. BAKER and D. J. HANSON.

29   *The Merry Wives of Windsor:* The Amateur Dramatic Company of the University of Cambridge, at the A.D.C. Theatre. *Producer:* CLIVE PERRY.

DECEMBER

3   *Othello:* Theatre Royal, Lincoln. *Producer:* JOHN HALE.

     Henry V: Manchester University Drama Group, for the Manchester University Arts Festival, in the Free Trade Hall, Manchester. *Producer:* J. L. CULE.

8   *The Merchant of Venice:* The People's Theatre, Newcastle-upon-Tyne. *Producer:* ARTHUR KAY.

11   *The Merchant of Venice:* The Old Vic Company, at the Old Vic Theatre, London. *Producer:* MICHAEL BENTHALL.

27   *Twelfth Night:* Jack Rose Repertory Players, at the Royal Pavilion, Blackpool. *Producer:* ARTHUR LESLIE.

UNTO CAESAR:
A REVIEW OF RECENT PRODUCTIONS

BY

ROY WALKER

Major Shakespearian productions run from knight to knight. The Old Vic 1956–7 season opened with a production by the theatre's director, Michael Benthall, which brought back Sir Ralph Richardson to Shakespeare's stage in *Timon of Athens*. The final production of the Stratford-upon-Avon 1957 season restored Sir John Gielgud's Prospero (much changed since he was seen at the Old Vic in 1940) in a production of *The Tempest* by Peter Brook which had Drury Lane stamped all over it and was to transfer to that capacious cavern for what was once the pantomime season.

Sir Ralph's Timon and Sir John's Prospero were cousins once removed. Richardson's misanthrope in the wilderness was no vituperative, half-naked poor Tom. In his sheepskin coat he was protected against rough weather if not from man's ingratitude. His revulsion from human greed for gold was a molten melancholy that seethed inside him, not a volcano spitting scalding satire on all comers. Gielgud's Prospero came half-way back to meet him. Until the end this was no rich-robed and short-tempered magician but an ascetic hermit in brief tunic, burning with resentment of past wrongs which threatened to overthrow his reason altogether. These two performances, in fact, invited some reconsideration of the transition from one play to the other in Shakespeare's mind, the dive from the beached verge of the salt flood and the not altogether sea-changed surfacing on the shores of the enchanted isle.

Until this Peter Brook production of *The Tempest* reached Drury Lane, the event of the 1957 London season, as far as Shakespeare was concerned (or, if you prefer, partly concerned), was the revival of the same producer's *Titus Andronicus*, with Sir Laurence Olivier as the human sea of grief and rage, about which Richard David wrote in *Shakespeare Survey* 10. This was the final production at the Stoll Theatre, where it arrived only fairly fresh from a triumphal progress through Europe. If the Roman acting honours of the year remained securely with Sir Laurence, sinking Caesar had some of his trophies salvaged, in the year of the 2000th anniversary of his assassination, in Glen Byam Shaw's first production of that greater Roman tragedy, at Stratford-upon-Avon.

Timon of Athens was part of the five-year plan which the Old Vic will have completed by the time these lines are published. It is to be regretted that no attempt was made to present the Folio plays in any sort of significant order. What Herbert Farjeon wrote in 1923, when the Old Vic was completing its first full cycle, was either not remembered or not heeded:

Now suppose that Miss Baylis and Mr Atkins were to treat the complete series as a series of chronicle plays, regarding the thing chronicled as the development of a great artist and a human soul. Suppose they were to address themselves to the task of producing all the plays chronologically, in the order in

128

PLATE V

150. *Iulius Cæsar Veneris beneficio in Cometam mutatur.*

A. CAESAR'S SOUL IS MADE A STAR. AN EARLY SEVENTEENTH-CENTURY ILLUSTRATION
OF THE CLIMAX OF OVID'S 'METAMORPHOSES' (ANTWERP, 1606)

B. 'JULIUS CAESAR', SHAKESPEARE MEMORIAL THEATRE, 1957
PRODUCED BY GLEN BYAM SHAW, DESIGNED BY MOTLEY

PLATE VI

A. 'AS YOU LIKE IT', SHAKESPEARE MEMORIAL THEATRE, 1957.
PRODUCED BY GLEN BYAM SHAW, DESIGNED BY MOTLEY

B. 'CYMBELINE', SHAKESPEARE MEMORIAL THEATRE, 1957. PRODUCED BY
PETER HALL, DESIGNED BY LILA DE NOBILI

PLATE VII

A. 'KING JOHN', SHAKESPEARE MEMORIAL THEATRE, 1957. PRODUCED
BY DOUGLAS SEALE, DESIGNED BY AUDREY CRUDDAS

B. 'THE TEMPEST', SHAKESPEARE MEMORIAL THEATRE, 1957.
PRODUCED AND DESIGNED BY PETER BROOK

PLATE VIII

'THE TEMPEST', SHAKESPEARE MEMORIAL THEATRE, 1957. PROSPERO AND MIRANDA

which they are debatably believed to have been written. Not only would the public be afforded an exciting opportunity of following the development of Shakespeare's mind as it developed during his lifetime, but students of the theatre would be afforded an extraordinarily valuable opportunity of following the development of his stage-craft.[1]

No doubt box-office considerations and the strategy of attracting star actors between more profitable engagements make this sort of planning difficult, but certainly more might have been done. A fully patterned cycle, whether in conjectural order of composition or by the arrangement of the Comedies, Histories and Tragedies in significant groups, is outside the scope of a theatre that has to pay its way, even if it receives an Arts Council subsidy. It is something that the B.B.C. could do, and should perhaps be preparing to do in 1964; but at present sound broadcasting is in retreat all along the cultural front.

By cutting some 500 of its 2300 lines, Michael Benthall ran through *Timon of Athens* in two hours, including a single interval of fifteen minutes. The deletions included what may be regarded as the definitive announcement of the theme of the play and a whole scene of some importance. Some minor characters were amalgamated and the ending of the play was boldly remodelled.

The first heavy stroke of the producer's pencil made Timon's entry cut short the opening dialogue of the Painter and Poet. There was no talk of artistic images of the fall of the truly great man when the mood of Fortune changes. It might be argued that modern audiences do not want the moral of a dramatic fable at the outset. But can any actor of Timon spare the tribute, spoken before he comes on (and not, therefore, in flattery), to "his good and gracious Nature"? And can any satisfactory production of the play dispense with the preliminary raising of the particular instance which we are to see into a general rule: "'Tis common". The effect, if not also the intention, of omitting this choric opening dialogue is to slant the drama away from its theme of man's ingratitude towards the tragedy of a particular fault in the protagonist which invites a general censure. The producer's trimming of Timon's exchanges with Apemantus and excision of the dialogue of abuse between the two Lords and that churlish philosopher, which should close the first scene, does no such damage, except to deprive the scene of its deliberate final emphasis on Timon (who has left the stage and, again, is not being flattered): "The noblest mind he carries, That ever govern'd man".

In the banquet scene which follows, Apemantus' carbolic commentary was reduced, and Act II lost little by cutting out the dialogue in which Apemantus and the Fool are involved with the creditors. In fact the scene gained by leaving the crucial interview between Timon and his Steward uninterrupted. There is no dramatic difficulty in taking the Steward's proper presentation of his accounts for granted, and the sole function of the indifferent dialogue with the Fool seems to be to mark time while that statement of accounts is supposed to take place.

The action so far had been acceptably staged in the hall of Timon's house, on one side of which was placed a tall and somewhat awe-inspiring statue of a goddess, presumably a stand-in for Fortune. Now a drop curtain depicting the outer walls of the city was lowered and lighted, but no scene was played before it. After a few moments it rose to reveal a street scene of which the main feature was the central portal and steps of Timon's house. The range of three steps was the same as for the interior scene, and was not enough to allow any symbolic effect of moving down the steps as reverses of Fortune followed thick and fast. This open-air scene worked very well to give a free flow to the first five scenes of Act III. Instead of three servants, this production entrusted all the begging to Timon's steward, who was of course addressed as Flavius where the text names the others. A climax to the three dialogues in the street was provided by bringing on Sempronius in a palanquin where he was lounging with a paramour. No pause or scene-change was necessary for the fourth scene, in which the creditors pounded upon Timon's door, with Flavius taking the lines of Servilius and Timon appearing in a plain grey robe which made an effective contrast with the rich crimson he wore in the earlier scenes. The dialogue between the Senators (accompanied by a bald, stripped, dark-skinned executioner who seemed to have wandered in from *Hassan*) and Alcibiades was also played in the street. The drop curtain was used as before, with no action in front of it, while the scene was shifted back to Timon's hall for the mock banquet.

Timon, in red robes again, served not water but only clouds of steam; he overturned tables, pulled down curtains and set the house afire. As he finally advanced to the forestage the drop curtain was lowered once more, semi-transparent where it was lighted from behind, to produce a most effective stage-picture. Through the walls of Athens, outside which Timon now stood, could be seen to one side the ruins of the banquet in the lurid light of flames flickering off-stage. On the other side the enigmatic white goddess gazed inscrutably on the scene of destruction. Timon went straight on from his speech near the end of Act III to the denunciation that opens Act IV. Throwing aside his cloak only, he made his departure from this City of Destruction by descending into the pit at the front of the stage, and the curtain fell for the single long interval.

The producer's decision to give a clear visual contrast between the city scenes of the first half and the wilderness scenes of the second half dictated the omission of IV, ii, the scene in which the steward shares his own remaining coins among Timon's other former servants. Instead the curtain rose upon the wilderness, or as the stage direction has it "in the woods". As soon as this scene was revealed it became evident that the production had not only cut the lines but missed the poetic point about the hero who is spurned down the slope of Fortune's Hill and ignored by those who had previously been his beneficiaries. Timon in Athens was on the same level as his fellows throughout, but for the insignificant range of three or four steps. Timon in exile had the vantage of a central rocky mound, to the top of which he frequently resorted. If the intention had been to show that Timon's last state was, despite appearances, better than his first, the placing might have been justified. But if this was in the producer's mind it was hardly the impression Sir Ralph Richardson left on his audience. The general effect of the scene, which included a long brown fringe of what looked rather like seaweed hung up to dry, and of the actor's armless sheepskin coat and bare cross-gartered legs, was more reminiscent of Robinson Crusoe than of the naked outcast Timon.

Sir Ralph's delivery of Timon's long speeches and his judgements on those who came to visit him were spoken with a quiet irony more effective than the negligent extravagance of the first half. After the name-calling contest with Apemantus, which culminated in a vigorous exchange of stones, the churlish philosopher did not stay to bandy further insults. Instead, there was a brief black-out in which the festoon was raised and the rocky buttress was now seen against a cyclorama sky. This might or might not have been at the verge of the salt sea, there was neither sight nor sound of the ocean.

Timon had set up on his rocky stronghold a huge slab, like a tombstone, on which he was carving his epitaph as he spoke the lines up to "make thine Epitaph, That death in me, at others' lives may laugh". A cut of some twenty lines allowed the three Bandits to interrupt the speech at this point. Richardson's uncanny stillness as he sat looking down unseen upon them, listening to their avaricious interchanges, gave him a memorable moment of moral superiority, which the thieves sensed when they looked up and met his quietly accusing gaze.

In the next interview, the last long speech of the steward was omitted, and there was a cut of some thirty lines early in the scene with the Poet and the Painter. The Steward and the Senators departed sadly on "Trouble him no further..." and Timon resumed his chiselling for his final speech, " Come not to me again...let my gravestone be your Oracle...Timon hath done his reign", in a last ray of the setting sun.

There was a black-out while the actor left the stage, and to preserve unity of place the short scene of the Senators' report back to Athens (v, ii) was omitted. Only the first two lines of v, iii were spoken by the Soldier, who was interrupted by the entry of Alcibiades and his forces, not before Athens but at the base of Timon's rocky retreat, where they were confronted by the frightened Senators and people who enter from the opposite side of the stage. Alcibiades rejected the Athenian pleas for mercy and ordered the assault; but at this moment the Soldier, who had climbed up to examine the inscription, called urgently to him and Alcibiades halted the attack to read the epitaph himself. It was this reminder of human mortality that melted the banished general to pity, a bold rehandling of the end of the play which at least tied the main and sub-plots together in a theatrically effective way.

In the text of the play as we have it, Alcibiades relents for no dramatically adequate reason, and Michael Benthall's solution therefore deserves serious consideration. But whether the change which makes Timon's death the cause of that change of heart is an acceptable image of the death of misanthropy bringing forth new mercy, or whether it is only a last irony that the man who willed the destruction of Athens should be the inadvertent means of saving the city, remains a dangerous dramatic ambiguity.

Whatever its intention, the impression made by this production on audiences who had small knowledge of the play was that Timon was entirely to blame. The early scenes suggested to them not the noble magnanimity of a largess universal like the sun, only a reckless extravagance. Yet it was presumably the poet's intention to show how selfish society drives out true generosity (and makes of it a judgement on itself); much as, in the preceding play, the mob drives out military heroism and discipline in Coriolanus, whose story is echoed (with a happier ending) in the Alcibiades sub-plot of *Timon of Athens*. Modern middle-class audiences have been indoctrinated with ideals of prudence and economy and are, moreover, suffering the effects of inflation and a credit squeeze ! But something more might be done for Timon's credit by making the friendship of his beneficiaries seem plausible while they can still feed on Timon's means, so that we share some of his disillusionment at their unmasking.

Michael Benthall certainly avoided the gross mistake of Tyrone Guthrie's production at the Old Vic four years earlier, when the cultural *élite* of Athens was a pack of comic scarecrows. Nor was Richardson, as André Morell had been, like some devout peasant who had won a chariot-pool and set up as a one-man Athenian Arts Council, a fool and his money soon parted. But if the role of Timon calls for a display of active magnanimity, like Antony's, in the first part, and an active agony, like Philoctetes', in the second, Richardson remained too near the middle of the road throughout. His negligent prodigality at first and his half-amused irony later failed to scale the heights or reach the depths of the poetry, and his occasionally careless delivery, as well as that of a company far from strong even by recent Old Vic standards, came in for deserved censure from some critics.

No major play of Shakespeare's has suffered more from democratic distortion than *Julius Caesar*. It seems improbable that the sympathies of the Elizabethan poet and his audience would be hostile to the ageing, sick and childless personal ruler, brutally and treacherously assassinated by professed friends who then plunge their country into the dread cycle of civil wars that ends only with the disruption and downfall of the Republic. Although Hazlitt supposed that Shakespeare painted an entirely antipathetic portrait of Caesar, it was still possible, before two world wars darkened the scene, to recognize, as MacCallum did in 1910, that "Shakespeare makes it abundantly clear that the rule of the single master-mind is the only admissible solution for the problem of the time".[2] The Hazlitt tradition reached its patriotic peak in Dover Wilson's 1949 edition of the play. Meanwhile it had spread to the stage. After Orson Welles' 1937 modern-dress production (in which, of course, this powerful actor elected to play Brutus), other modern-dress *Caesars* in this country, and most costume productions too, presented the drama as the democratic doing-in of a diabolical dictator. They could therefore make nothing of the celestial portents and still less of the fifth act in which the spirit of the dead dictator inconveniently triumphs.

Now that the dogs of war are on the leash again there are signs of scholarly reaction on both sides of the Atlantic. In 1953 Virgil Whitaker argued that Shakespeare meant Caesar to seem "a great and good ruler"[3] and in the new Arden edition two years later T. S. Dorsch agreed that "Shakespeare wishes us to admire his Caesar".[4] A similar rehabilitation on the stage was overdue. It was peculiarly appropriate that this should be achieved in the year of the 2000th anniversary of the assassination, and in the Shakespeare Memorial Theatre at Stratford-upon-Avon, where Glen Byam Shaw produced the play. The main interest of this production lay in its bold centralization of Caesar, who became the real as well as the nominal protagonist, and in the means employed to keep this presence dramatically alive on the stage after the actual murder, with a consequent gain in coherency and in the significance of the last act.

Glen Byam Shaw's interpretation began at the beginning of the play. The curtain rose on a stage dominated by a larger-than-life statue of Caesar, raised on a tall plinth in the centre of the stage. After the disrobing of this image by the envious tribunes, this statue pivoted backwards out of sight, the two walls of grey stone parted and against the blue sky at the back the living Caesar was acclaimed. The statue might easily have dwarfed the human figure, but the magnificence of the gold-embroidered crimson toga and the majesty of Cyril Luckham's bearing made him the incarnation of an immutable and pivotal principle of order. This ordered Rome was visible in the massive fluted monoliths of light grey stone, ranged outwards from Caesar as their personal centre in two symmetrical lines, continued in the tall stone portals flanking the fore-stage. Here was the wide perspective of Caesar's Rome with Caesar himself the keystone.

When the procession had passed, that centre was unfilled while Cassius, effectively played as a 'little Caesar', a Corsican upstart, by Geoffrey Keen, manœuvred for the advantage of height with a Brutus (Alec Clunes) who was every inch Caesar's angel in presence and noble innocence.

At the end of this scene of lurking disorder, the sky darkened with supernatural speed and an ominous patch of crimson appeared above the place where Caesar had stood. Cassius' defiance of the lightning was posed at stage-centre and met with a crackling blaze of white light from heaven, a warning which went unheeded by the arch-plotter.

The foremost monoliths converged again to close the main stage and leave the fore-stage for Brutus' orchard, but the central niche where Caesar's image had been was now eloquently empty while Brutus struggled to put away loyalty and friendship. When this orchard wall parted to reveal the interior of Caesar's house, the central entrance was hung with a divided crimson curtain, behind which was visible a head of Caesar, now isolated on a pedestal of his own height. The front walls converged again and Artemidorus paused before the empty niche to read over his warning to Caesar. They reopened on the Senate, with a raised central throne, its back a solid sheet of gleaming gold, on which Caesar took his place with his head high against the blue sky beyond. As he fell to the assassins' swords there was a fierce crackle of lightning from the clear sky, which was then rapidly overcast.

When the scene changed to the Forum, the two lines of monoliths had fallen back in disorder, leaving a wider gap in the centre. Caesar's central throne had now given place to the popular pulpit from which successive demagogues harangued the changeable many who lined the front of the stage in dark silhouette, as though under a sinister shadow that had fallen on all Rome. Caesar's catafalque, the body shrouded with the crimson, gold-ornamented robe, was laid on the centre of the fore-stage, below the pulpit. As Antony (Richard Johnson) passionately roused the mob to blood, the sky reddened, and at the climactic cry "Here was Caesar! when comes such another?" he was standing a little off-centre in front of the now empty pulpit, his right arm thrust straight up to heaven; and suddenly in the true centre of the sky the northern star shone out alone. After the tumultuous exit the stage was empty and silent for a moment with the star shining distantly down. The poet Cinna half turned his head towards it as he entered saying "I dreamt to-night that I did feast with Caesar". Back surged the mob, now bearing lighted torches, bobbing and blazing symbols of disorder, the wandering fires of an earth from which the unmoved mover had been withdrawn. The interval arrived with an unforgettable stage picture of the murdered poet, flopped brokenly over the front of the pulpit like a discarded glove-puppet, and the star, blazing brighter in a sky that turned from blue to black, shining down in silent comment on the grim scene of chaos come again.

The second half opened with the triumvirate standing apart with their backs to a huge suspended map of the Mediterranean. Antony was in front of Italy, Octavius before the Balkans, Lepidus over against Asia Minor; the stretches of sea between the actors subtly suggested the space that always separated them, and the pattern of civil wars to come. Rome was now gone without a trace, and it was in a blood-red tent near Sardis that Brutus contended with Cassius and saw Caesar's ghost, which materialized in the open mouth of the tent, against the sky. When this tent was struck the bare stage was broken only by a low ridge of fissured rock which rose to a slight eminence a little off-centre. It was from here that Octavius and Antony, with their troops and standards, saw Brutus and Cassius coming down to battle in the plains where dusty death awaits them. Cassius fell, then Brutus, their own swords turned against them by friendly hands, in the same central area and general posture as Caesar was, but further downstage, on a lower level. When Brutus came upon Cassius' body and exclaimed "O Julius Caesar, thou art mighty yet !", the northern star suddenly appeared again. There it remained, so that the final curtain recalled and resolved the first-half curtain. The dead body of the tragically deluded liberator lay in the centre of the stage, not in Rome but in the wilderness he had helped to make of Rome, and high above him shone out the star of whose true-fixed and resting quality there is no fellow in the firmament.[5]

The 1957 Stratford-upon-Avon season had opened with Glen Byam Shaw's other production, a freshened version of his production of *As You Like It* five years before, with Peggy Ashcroft as Rosalind. There is nothing incredible in a forest that comes into leaf and in which strains of music are heard when such a Rosalind arrives in it. Miss Ashcroft's Ganymede was neither boy-player nor pantomime principal, but a whole human in which everyone could find a love to his liking. The production abounded in quiet touches of poetry. It was natural enough for Jaques to get up from the stool on which he was sitting while he spoke of the seven ages of man, so that old Adam could rest there. But when we saw how soon his figure sitting there had been replaced by the image of the pantaloon we knew that a lifetime is too soon spent to be wasted in melancholy moralizing. It was natural, too—only no one else had thought of it—that when Rosalind turned to stride off at the end of her first encounter with Orlando in the forest she should be hauled back by the doublet while Orlando offered his arm to Celia, the lady who must take precedence over the charming youth.

Peggy Ashcroft also appeared at Stratford as Imogen, that later heroine who flies to the country in masculine attire, in a more complex comedy of nature cure. Peter Hall had decided that the only possible course with *Cymbeline* was to make it "as archetypal and fairy storyish as possible" and this, with the help of his designer, Lila de Nobili, he did to considerable effect. The audience entering the theatre was confronted with a charmingly painted curtain between two colossal trees whose massive branches almost met overhead. The curtains parted not on "two Gentlemen" but a score of fantastic fairy-tale figures. The black-robed Queen, Joan Miller's best performance of the season, with dead white face and splayed white fingers, looked in her black dress like some arcane transformation of Titania into Lady Macbeth. Geoffrey Keen's handsome Iachimo was in black, too, while Posthumus (Richard Johnson) was in white, with Imogen an enchanting vision in white, silver and blue. The composite setting had a dreamlike quality, and allowed the action to flow without interruption, but the atmosphere of fantasy weakened a little towards the end, and the higher level of the scene was not used to much effect.

Douglas Seale of the Birmingham Repertory Theatre continued his conquest of the Histories with a *Richard III* at the Old Vic, more notable for the producer's handling of the lamenting women than for Robert Helpmann's too consistently melodramatic Crookback, and a *King John* at Stratford in a permanent set somewhat reminiscent of that used on the same stage for the Lancastrian tetralogy in 1951. A battlemented centrepiece made a suitably medieval fortress, on whose gates were blazoned the rival heraldries of France and England, and the entry from below stage level and up through this central opening was particularly effective in the dungeon scene. Robert Harris was a by no means unlikeable King John, Joan Miller gave an intelligent and effective but not at all poetic rendering of Constance, and Alec Clunes was a hearty, healthy Bastard from first to last.

Peter Brook's production of *The Tempest*, the last of the Stratford 1957 season, was perhaps the most controversial. He is not, like Byam Shaw, the sort of producer who has the art that conceals art. Brook writes his own personality all over a play and is therefore likely to succeed or fail to the extent to which the play responds to his temperament. Having made a great impression with his *Titus Andronicus* production, for which he also designed the scenery and costumes and composed the music, he set about *The Tempest* in the same fashion. Never have the Ariel songs sounded more dreary, the masque been more eerie, or the scenery more obtrusively scenic. But, as usual, Brook knew what he wanted and why he wanted it, and the interpretation of Prospero superbly delivered by Sir John Gielgud, a man whose wrongs haunted him through the winding caverns and overgrown jungles of the mind, largely justified the strangely subterranean settings and tangled hothouse vegetation. Only a Miranda in a sarong struck a jarring note for which no justification could be discovered in the producer's score. An ashen Ariel and an anthropoidal Caliban were explicable as projections of Prospero's disordered imagination. Stephano and Trinculo (Patrick Wymark and Clive Revill) were simply the best comics to undertake these parts in recent years. Revill in particular enhanced his reputation with a series of performances of which his Cloten in *Cymbeline* was the most outstanding.

NOTES

1. Herbert Farjeon, *The Shakespearean Scene* (1949), pp. 113–14.
2. M. W. MacCallum, *Shakespeare's Roman Plays* (1910), p. 214.
3. Virgil K. Whitaker, *Shakespeare's Use of Learning* (1953), p. 234.
4. T. S. Dorsch (ed.), *Julius Caesar* (1955), p. xxxviii.
5. It is necessary for the reviewer to disclose an interest. The present writer suggested to Mr Byam Shaw the parallel between 'that bright Occidental star', as the Jacobean translators of the Bible called the Queen, and the Caesar whose soul was taken up and made a star in the climax of Ovid's *Metamorphoses*, an episode to which Shakespeare refers in the opening scene of *1 Henry VI*. He also suggested that the northern star speech in *Julius Caesar* draws poetically on that Ovidian climax, and that the promise that the ghost will appear again at Philippi may have been kept by displaying an emblematic star in "the heavens". (For a more elaborate staging of the transfiguration of a soul into a star on the stage, see the stage-direction for the death of Hercules in Thomas Heywood's *The Brazen Age*.) Ways in which a comparable effect might be provided for modern audiences with present-day lighting equipment were also discussed. But a suggested interpretation is one thing; imaginative transformation is another. Mr Byam Shaw transmuted the argument into his own art. If I am open to suspicion of being prejudiced in favour of the result, I may at least point out that the general opinion of responsible critics was that the production was conspicuously successful in its rendering of the true values of the play.

THE YEAR'S CONTRIBUTIONS TO
SHAKESPEARIAN STUDY

1. CRITICAL STUDIES

reviewed by KENNETH MUIR

Bonamy Dobrée, alarmed at some recent criticism of Shakespeare, reminds us, in a civilized essay,[1] that the plays were, after all, written to be enjoyed; and Ernest Barker, equally alarmed by the application of the techniques of classical scholarship to the text of Shakespeare, asks for the use of imagination and common sense in the interpretation of the plays.[2] Although these warnings are salutary, there are a few books published each year which add to our understanding without detracting from our enjoyment. In the period under review the most stimulating criticism is to be found in M. M. Mahood's study of Shakespeare's quibbles.[3] Expanding her essay entitled 'The Fatal Cleopatra', and applying its ideas to five plays and the sonnets, Miss Mahood provides the first comprehensive study of the subject. Not only does she throw light on scores of passages, but she also increases our understanding of the subtlety and complexity of Shakespeare's style and meaning. In her last chapter she outlines Shakespeare's changing attitude to the problem of meaning, and shows that in the tragic period there is a conflict between "the world of words and the world of facts".

Geoffrey Bush, writing on Shakespeare and the natural condition, "circles around his subject", we are told, "in a spiral, touching, in each revolution, once more on themes he has mentioned earlier".[4] This makes the book easy to read and difficult to summarize, but it contains some genuine insights into the tragedies and an interesting chapter on "comedy and the perfect image". F. E. Halliday has written yet another of his useful books on Shakespeare,[5] this time a life illustrated with many well-chosen illustrations. Max Lüthi provides a critical analysis of every play in the canon,[6] his main thesis being that Shakespeare achieved a unique fusion of medieval, renaissance, and baroque elements, and it is illustrated by discussion, often original and perceptive, of each play. A new edition has appeared of T. S. Eliot's Elizabethan essays.[7]

Some light is thrown on Shakespeare's comic method by John V. Curry's painstaking study of the use of deception by Elizabethan dramatists.[8] There are a number of articles on individual comedies. Sidney Thomas, disagreeing with T. W. Baldwin, thinks that *The Comedy of Errors* was first performed on 28 December 1594;[9] and John S. Weld believes that the reference to

---

[1] 'On (Not) Enjoying Shakespeare', *Essays and Studies* (1956), pp. 39–55.
[2] 'Literary Criticism', *Times Literary Supplement*, 4 May 1956, p. 269.
[3] *Shakespeare's Word-Play* (Methuen, 1957).
[4] *Shakespeare and the Natural Condition* (Harvard University Press; Cumberlege, 1956).
[5] *Shakespeare. A Pictorial Biography* (Thames and Hudson, 1956).
[6] *Shakespeares Dramen* (Berlin: Walter de Gruyter and Co., 1957).
[7] *Essays on Elizabethan Drama* (New York: Harcourt, Brace and Co., 1956).
[8] *Deception in Elizabethan Comedy* (Chicago: Loyola University Press, 1955).
[9] 'The Date of *The Comedy of Errors*', *Shakespeare Quarterly*, VII (Autumn 1956), 377–84.

"Old Adam new apparelled" means "What, have you got the sergeant, who in his leather coat symbolized your unregenerate nature, new clothed as liberator?"[1] Georges A. Bonnard discusses the meaning of the *Dream* and concludes that Shakespeare weighs "the rival claims of imagination and sober vision" and decides "in favour of the latter while giving the former its due".[2] Howard Nemerov finds a great deal of subtle significance in the marriage of Theseus and Hippolyta.[3] Hilda M. Hulme ingeniously defends three original readings in *The Merchant of Venice*,[4] glossing *wit* (II, i, 18) as 'witword' (testament), *rage* (II, i, 35) as 'wild folly', and *mean* (III, v, 82) as 'married life'. Norman A. Brittin accuses Draper of making Shakespeare look like a naturalistic novelist, and of treating the characters in *Twelfth Night* as real people.[5] David L. Stevenson, in an interesting re-assessment of *Measure for Measure*,[6] rejects both the findings of historical critics and Christian apologists and suggests that the play has affinities with Jonson's satiric comedies. His interpretation is partially spoilt by his anxiety to discount a religious interpretation, which makes him find an Aristotelian, rather than a scriptural, reference in the title, by his calling Claudio's comparison of lust to ratsbane a wry jest, and by his finding Juliet's moving words of repentance "morally colourless". Stevenson also defends two Folio readings— "mortality of imprisonment" and "some run from brakes of Ice" which he takes to refer to Angelo "who takes his origin in thickets of ice".[7] Norman N. Holland proposes *die* for *do* (I, iii, 43).[8] Karl F. Thompson, following Malone, shows that Cressida's betrayal acts as a purge of Troilus' love-sickness.[9]

Little has been written about the histories. Arthur Suzman has an interesting study of the imagery and symbolism connected with rising and falling in *Richard II*;[10] Robert A. Greenberg examines one passage in some detail;[11] and I. B. Cauthen, Jr. suggests that Thomas Digges' *Stratioticos* was a possible source of "moat defensive", though the idea is to be found elsewhere.[12] Johannes Kleinstück has a subtle analysis of the means by which Shakespeare presents the character of Bolingbroke, "a man who was not conscious of his own aims", but who knew instinctively "what line to take".[13] Matthew McDiarmid shows that as two passages in *King John* were influenced by a passage in Kyd's *Cornelia* it must have been written later.[14] Ernest Schanzer argues convincingly that the death-scene of the same play was influenced by some lines

[1] '"Old Adam New Apparelled"', *ibid.* pp. 453–6.

[2] 'Shakespeare's Purpose in *Midsummer-Night's Dream*', *Shakespeare Jahrbuch*, XCII (1956), 268–79.

[3] 'The Marriage of Theseus and Hippolyta', *The Kenyon Review* (Autumn 1956), pp. 633–41.

[4] 'Wit, Rage, Mean: Three Notes on *The Merchant of Venice*', *Neophilologus* (January 1957), pp. 46–50.

[5] 'The *Twelfth Night* of Shakespeare and of Professor Draper', *Shakespeare Quarterly*, VII (Spring 1956), 211–16.

[6] 'Design and Structure in *Measure for Measure*: A New Appraisal', *E.L.H.* XXIII (December 1956), 256–78.

[7] 'On Restoring Two Folio Readings in *Measure for Measure*', *Shakespeare Quarterly*, VII (Autumn 1956), 445–8.

[8] '"Do" or "Die" in *Measure for Measure*, I, iii, 43', *Notes and Queries* (February 1957), p. 52.

[9] 'Cressid's Diet', *ibid.* (September 1956), pp. 378–9.

[10] 'Imagery and Symbolism in *Richard II*', *Shakespeare Quarterly*, VII (Autumn 1956), 355–70.

[11] 'Shakespeare's *Richard II*, IV, i, 244–50', *The Explicator*, XV (February 1957).

[12] 'Shakespeare's "Moat Defensive"', *Notes and Queries* (October 1956), pp. 419–20.

[13] 'The Character of Henry Bolingbroke', *Neophilologus* (January 1957), pp. 51–6.

[14] 'A Reconsidered Parallel between Shakespeare's "King John" and Kyd's "Cornelia"', *Notes and Queries* (December 1956), pp. 507–8.

in Seneca's *Hercules Oetaeus*.[1] Harold Jenkins, in a poised and witty inaugural lecture, argues that *Henry IV*

is both one play and two. Part 1 begins an action which it finds it has no scope for but which Part 2 rounds off. But with one half of the action already concluded in Part 1, there is a danger of a gap in Part 2. To stop the gap Part 2 expands the unfinished story of Falstaff and reduplicates what is already finished in the story of the Prince. The two parts are complementary, they are also independent and even incompatible.[2]

John S. Tuckey defends the Folio reading of the passage describing the dying Falstaff by glossing *pen* as 'mountain', *and* as 'on', and *table* as 'tableland'.[3] Peter Ure, naturally sceptical of this, defends the Theobald emendation.[4] Hilda M. Hulme suspects some, surely inappropriate, bawdy puns;[5] and F. W. Bateson still prefers 'talkd' to 'babld'.[6] Robert A. Law takes issue with Warren D. Smith and shows that the choruses in *Henry V* were authentic and that they refer to Essex rather than to Mountjoy.[7]

There have been several valuable books on tragedy. T. R. Henn covers a wide field, ranging from Aristotle to Anouilh and offering sensible solutions to many of the problems on which he touches, though he does not always succeed in synthesizing conflicting views.[8] His brief discussion of Shakespeare is condensed into seven general propositions, which may be summarized still further: Shakespearian tragedy is caused by a violation of order as a result of sin; in this sin there is an element of 'unripeness'; and the emergence of evil through personality into action has complicated reactions on "the most remote and improbable lives". This is a stimulating, and sometimes a brilliant, book; but Henn occasionally appears to demand that the reader should fill in the outlines he provides. H. D. F. Kitto's book contains, in addition to his study of six Greek plays—which is more satisfying than his previous book—a comparison of Greek and Elizabethan tragedy and a long essay on *Hamlet* in which he stresses the religious aspect of the play, concerned as it is with the corroding power of sin.[9] It is, perhaps, the most impressive of recent interpretations of the play. Brents Stirling writes on the interplay of theme and character in Shakespearian tragedy, and his book includes studies of *Julius Caesar, Hamlet, Othello* and of three other plays.[10] He analyses imagery in relation to plot and character, and much of what he has to say is both subtle and new; but in stressing what has not been pointed out before he often mistakes a peripheral for the central meaning of the play.

Irving Ribner takes issue with recent critics on the subject of *Julius Caesar* and claims that Caesar is "the noble hero overthrown by his pride and ambition" and that Brutus "brings only greater tragedy to Rome" through "his own insufficiency and because of the depravity of the

[1] '"Hercules Oetaeus" and "King John"', *ibid.* p. 509.
[2] *The Structural Problem in Shakespeare's Henry the Fourth* (Methuen, 1956).
[3] '"Table of Greene Fields" Explained', *Essays in Criticism*, VI (October 1956), 486–91.
[4] *Ibid.* VII (April 1957), 223–4.   [5] *Ibid.* pp. 222–3.
[6] *Ibid.* pp. 225–6.
[7] 'The Choruses in *Henry the Fifth*', *The University of Texas Studies in English*, XXV (1956), 11–21.
[8] *The Harvest of Tragedy* (Methuen, 1956).   [9] *Form and Meaning in Drama* (Methuen, 1956).
[10] *Unity in Shakespearian Tragedy* (Columbia University Press; Cumberlege, 1956).

Roman people".[1] Shakespeare did not see in the murder of Caesar "a vindication of monarchy as a divinely favoured institution". The *Shakespeare Survey* articles on *Hamlet* included Clifford Leech's judicious retrospect which concludes with the recognition that "simplification must be recognized for what it is" since the play was "written by more than one, perhaps written by Shakespeare more than once".[2] R. A. Foakes has a valuable study of the imagery and style of the play, in which he stresses the contrast between public and private speech.[3] Carl Anders Dymling has a detailed discussion of Hamlet's age, in which he argues that the discrepancies are due to the telescoping of time.[4] Hamlet in the course of the play

ages both emotionally, intellectually, and purely physically in a way that is inconceivable in the period of the time embraced by the action.

James J. McKenzie, on the other hand, brushing the evidence of Hamlet's youth on one side, argues that he was thirty.[5] Warren V. Shepard gives various examples from the play of actions being turned against their originators.[6] Leo Kirschbaum has a subtle analysis of the relationship between Hamlet and Ophelia, arguing that Shakespeare was deliberately ambiguous in his presentation of it.[7] The best essay in Richard Flatter's new book[8] presents arguments in favour of the view that Gertrude was an accomplice in the murder of her husband, and he argues that Hamlet's fear of finding his mother a murderess is the cause of his melancholy. Her "incestuous sheets" were cause enough. In another essay he tries to prove that Shakespeare was the best actor of his company—even though he did not get the best parts. A third essay traces Shakespeare's development from the assertion of justice and order as ultimate values to a belief in forgiveness. James L. Donovan discusses whether "Not shriving time allow'd" should be regarded as part of the forged letter and argues that Hamlet is tainted with evil.[9] Alwin Thaler has a useful note on "In my mind's eye, Horatio".[10] William Montgomerie discusses the element of the folk play and of ritual to be found in *Hamlet*,[11] and he has a number of interesting notes on the hobby-horse, on "a king of shreds and patches", and on other passages, some of them rather fanciful. Josephine Bennett avers that Polonius's precepts would be familiar to every schoolboy from his reading of the *Ad Demonicum* of Isocrates.[12] K. A. Rockwell proposes to read "Are of all most select" in a famous crux (I, iii, 74);[13] and Winifred M. T. Nowottny suggests that the dying

[1] 'Political Issues in *Julius Caesar*', *Journal of English and Germanic Philology*, LVI (January 1957), 10–22.
[2] 'Studies in *Hamlet*, 1901–1955', *Shakespeare Survey*, 9 (1956), 1–15.
[3] '*Hamlet* and the Court of Elsinore', *ibid.* pp. 35–43.
[4] *Hamlet's Age* (Stockholm: Zetterlund and Thelanders Boktryckeri A-B, 1956).
[5] 'Hamlet's Age Again', *Notes and Queries* (April 1956), pp. 151–2.
[6] 'Hoisting the Engineer with his own Petar', *Shakespeare Quarterly*, VII (Spring 1956), 281–5.
[7] 'Hamlet and Ophelia', *Philological Quarterly*, XXV (October 1956).
[8] *Triumph der Gnade* (Vienna: Verlag Kurt Desch, 1956).
[9] 'A Note on Hamlet's "Not Shriving Time Allow'd"', *Notes and Queries* (November 1956), pp. 467–9.
[10] '"In my Mind's Eye, Horatio"', *Shakespeare Quarterly*, VII (Autumn 1956), 351–4.
[11] 'Folk Play and Ritual in "Hamlet"', *Folk-Lore*, LXVII (December 1956), 214–27.
[12] 'These Few Precepts', *Shakespeare Quarterly*, VII (Spring 1956), 275–6.
[13] '*Hamlet*, I, iii, 74: "Of a Most Select"', *Notes and Queries* (February 1957), p. 84.

Hamlet should say "O God, Horatio...shall't leave behind me!"[1] Harold Jenkins argues pleasantly that only one of the gravediggers deserves the title.[2] Friedrich Knorr thinks that *Hamlet* criticism has been too much concerned with the Prince, Shakespeare's main concern being with the wrong done to the Danish people by a criminal usurper and the eventual re-establishment of order on the accession of Fortinbras.[3] Few will share Knorr's confidence that this interpretation leaves no part of the play unexplained. Helen Gardner's British Academy Lecture[4] is a restatement, lucid, eloquent, and wise, of the older view that Othello was essentially noble, arguing that modern critics who stress the inadequacy of the hero's nobility disregard "the play's most distinctive quality". In a slighter essay[5] on Brabantio, Aerol Arnold stresses the importance of Shakespeare's invention of the incident "in which Brabantio forces Desdemona to choose Othello publicly". Albert F. Sproule suggests that only three days are needed for the action at Cyprus if we assume that Bianca came with Cassio from Venice.[6] This, however, does not solve all the time difficulties in the play. Theodore C. Hoepfner glosses Othello's *naked* (v, ii, 261) as 'unarmoured', rather than 'unarmed', though the words can be synonymous.[7] R. W. Zandvoort gives us a sensible survey of recent criticism of *King Lear*, though it is arguable he is not quite fair to imagistic and allegorical critics.[8] Abraham Schechter has an extraordinary essay on the play, dedicated to the spirit of William Blake, which is not, in so far as I understand it, literary criticism, but some kind of prophetic utterance.[9] S. K. Heninger, Jr. explicates the opening lines of III, ii.[10] Leo Kirschbaum argues forcibly that Banquo and Edgar should not be regarded as coherent characters, but as dramatic functions;[11] but S. Nagarajan makes a gallant attempt to defend the character of Banquo from such criticism.[12] With these essays may be grouped Robert Langbaum's well-reasoned analysis of the tension between character and action in several of Shakespeare's plays.[13] Ernest Schanzer has four interesting notes on passages in *Macbeth*, including convincing explanations of "the warder of the brain" and of "understood relations" by birds.[14]

Alan Warner writes on the ambivalence of *Antony and Cleopatra*,[15] and insists that in spite of

[1] 'The Application of Textual Theory to Hamlet's Dying Words', *Modern Language Review*, LII (April 1957), 161–7. A. D. Fitton Brown, 'Two Points of Interpretation', *Notes and Queries* (February 1957), p. 51, discusses passages in *Hamlet* and *Othello*.

[2] 'How Many Grave-Diggers has *Hamlet*?', *Modern Language Review*, LI (October 1956), 562–5.

[3] 'Über Shakespeares "Hamlet"', *Donum autumnale II, Jahresgabe der Coburger Dienstagsgesellschaft* (1956), pp. 1–66.

[4] 'The Noble Moor', *Proceedings of the British Academy*, XLI (1956), 189–205.

[5] 'The Function of Brabantio in *Othello*', *Shakespeare Quarterly*, VIII (Winter 1957), 51–6.

[6] 'A Time Scheme for *Othello*', ibid. VII (Spring 1956), 217–26.

[7] 'An *Othello* Gloss', *Notes and Queries* (November 1956), p. 470.

[8] '*King Lear*: The Scholars and the Critics', *Mededelingen der Koninklijke Nederlandse Akademie van Witenschappen, Afd. Letterkunde*, XIX (1956), 229–44.

[9] *King Lear: Warning or Prophecy?* (New York: Press of Theo. Gaus' Sons, 1956).

[10] 'Shakespeare's *King Lear*, III, ii, 1–9', *The Explicator*, XV (October 1956).

[11] 'Banquo and Edgar: Character or Function?', *Essays in Criticism*, VII (January 1957), 1–21.

[12] 'A Note on Banquo', *Shakespeare Quarterly*, VII (Autumn 1956), 371–6.

[13] 'Character versus Action in Shakespeare', ibid. VIII (Winter 1957), 57–69.

[14] 'Four Notes on "Macbeth"', *Modern Language Review*, LII (April 1957), 223–7.

[15] 'A Note on *Antony and Cleopatra*', *English*, XI (Spring 1957), 139–44.

the "rottenness at the core" of Antony's passion "we cannot read the play as a moral lesson against lust". Elizabeth S. Donno, on the other hand, agrees with J. Dover Wilson that the play is Shakespeare's 'Hymn to Man'.[1] Thomas P. Harrison calls attention to the influence of Marlowe's *Dido* on the play, especially in the scenes in which Antony tries to break from Cleopatra.[2] Alfredo Obertello provides an accurate Italian translation, and writes of it as a baroque tragedy.[3] Maurice Charney has a noteworthy article on the function of imagery in *Coriolanus*.[4] Ralph Behrens argues that in the Queen's speeches in *Cymbeline* III, i, Shakespeare is speaking directly to the audience but that Cloten's are not altogether out of character.[5]

A few articles on general topics may be mentioned briefly. R. W. Zandvoort had a note,[6] overlooked by my predecessor, on Portia's portrait, in which he stressed the point that Shakespeare shared the Renaissance view that painting should be as lifelike as possible. The *Jahrbuch* has a series of articles on translations of Shakespeare into German,[7] French,[8] Norwegian,[9] Swedish,[10] and Italian;[11] Otakar Vočadlo discusses translations and performances in Czechoslovakia;[12] and Edvard Beyer analyses with great insight general difficulties of translation in relation to Scandinavian versions.[13] Carl Fehrman surveys work on Shakespeare's imagery;[14] and Curt A. Zimansky has provided an excellent, and most useful, edition of Rymer's criticism.[15] Finally, Paul E. Bennet, applying Yule's statistical tests of literary vocabulary, arrives at the comforting con-

---

[1] 'Cleopatra Again', *Shakespeare Quarterly*, VII (Spring 1956), 227–33.

[2] 'Shakespeare and Marlowe's *Dido, Queen of Carthage*', *The University of Texas Studies in English*, XXXV (1956), 57–63.

[3] *La Tragedia di Antonio e Cleopatra* (Arnoldo Mondadori, 1957).

[4] 'The Dramatic Use of Imagery in Shakespeare's *Coriolanus*', *ELH* (September 1956), pp. 183–93. John M. Steadman has a note on 'The Fairies' Midwife: *Romeo and Juliet*, I, iv', *Notes and Queries* (October 1956), p. 424.

[5] 'On Possible Inconsistencies in Two Character Portrayals in *Cymbeline*', *Notes and Queries* (September 1956), pp. 379–80. E. E. Duncan-Jones, *ibid.* (February 1957), p. 64, glosses 'Forlorn' in the same play.

[6] *Rivista di Letterature Moderne*, II (September 1951), 351–6.

[7] Siegfried Korninger, 'Shakespeare und seine deutschen Übersetzer', *Shakespeare Jahrbuch*, XCII (1956), 19–44. Käthe Strickler, 'Deutsche Shakespeare-Übersetzungen im letzten Jahrhundert', *ibid.* pp. 45–89. Edna Purdie, 'Observations on some Eighteenth-Century German Versions of the Witches' Scenes in *Macbeth*', *ibid.* pp. 96–109. Henry Lüdeke, 'Gundolf, Flatter und Shakespeares *Macbeth*', *ibid.* pp. 110–27. Irmentraud Candidus und Erika Roller, 'Der Sommernachtstraum in deutscher Übersetzung von Wieland bis Flatter', *ibid.* pp. 128–45. Friedrich Hoffman, 'Stefan Georges Übertragung der Shakespeare-Sonette', *ibid.* pp. 146–56. Walter Josten, 'Schwierigkeiten der Shakespeare-Übersetzung', *ibid.* pp. 168–74. Hans Rudolf Hilty, 'Zur Behandlung der Eigennamen in Shakespeare-Übersetzungen', *ibid.* pp. 255–67. Rudolf Schaller, 'Gedanken zur Übertragung Shakespeares in unsere Sprache', *ibid.* pp. 305–13.

[8] Elisabeth Brock-Sulzer, 'André Gide als Übersetzer Shakespeares', *ibid.* pp. 207–19.

[9] Lorentz Eckhoff, 'Shakespeare in Norwegian Translations', *ibid.* pp. 244–54.

[10] Nils Molin, 'Shakespeare translated into Swedish', *ibid.* pp. 232–43.

[11] Mario Praz, 'Shakespeare Translations in Italy', *ibid.* pp. 220–31.

[12] 'Shakespeare and Bohemia', *Shakespeare Survey*, 9 (1956), 101–110.

[13] *Problemer omkring oversettelser av Shakespeares dramatikk* (Bergen: A. S. John Griegs Boktrykkeri, 1956).

[14] 'The Study of Shakespeare's Imagery', *Modern Spraak*, LII (1957), 7–20.

[15] Thomas Rymer, *The Critical Works*, edited by Curt A. Zimansky (New Haven: Yale University Press; London: Cumberlege, 1956).

clusion that *Julius Caesar* and *As You Like It* were written by the same man.[1] He intends to apply the tests to doubtful plays.

It should be added that R. B. Heilman's important book[2] on *Othello* arrived too late to be reviewed this year.

2. SHAKESPEARE'S LIFE, TIMES AND STAGE

reviewed by R. A. FOAKES

In his handsomely produced pictorial biography of Shakespeare,[3] F. E. Halliday dresses up the facts with some genially sentimental speculation, discovering the profound effect on the playwright of the death of Hamnet, and the inspiration his grand-daughter provided for the last plays; it is all most enjoyable and should have a wide appeal to Stratford audiences fresh from the theatre. At least this book shows how many facts are known about Shakespeare's life, and perhaps not many more will be discovered; this year has produced only a further note on his possible acquaintances.[4] But in view of the endless spate of speculation which is so often presented as if it were fact, Robert Adger Law has performed a useful service in comparing three recent works relating to Shakespeare's early life and career, and showing not only that each is unfounded, but that they mutually contradict one another.[5] It is not easy for critics to avoid some prejudice or distortion in their account of the poet, as is brought out by Horst Oppel,[6] who surveys a variety of beliefs ranging from the assertion that he was the most characteristic figure of his age, to the claim that he was the least typical: these extreme attitudes illustrate the difficulty of seeing Shakespeare as fully belonging to his own age, and also as a unique artist distanced by his universality from his contemporaries, and Oppel suggests that a right perspective would reconcile both views. A right perspective eludes W. Schrickx,[7] who presents a Shakespeare too passionately interested in the squabbles of Harvey, Nashe and Greene to be credible. He would relate *Love's Labour's Lost* and an early draft of *As You Like It*, dating these in 1592–3, to their pamphlet war, finding parallels and allusions everywhere; the trouble is that assumptions multiplied do not approach certainty, as the author seems to think, and their importance for the interpretation of the plays is at best marginal. But while few will accept his argument, many will refer to the material he has gathered, which throws some light on the confused literary relationships of the early 1590's.

---

[1] 'The Statistical Measurement of a stylistic Trait in *Julius Caesar* and *As You Like It*', *Shakespeare Quarterly*, VIII, (Winter 1957), 51–6. Other articles which may be mentioned include: Andrew S. Cairncross, '"The Tempest", III, i, 15, and "Romeo and Juliet", I, i, 121–8', *ibid.* VII (Autumn 1956), 448–50; Edward Stone, '*Moby Dick* and Shakespeare: A Remonstrance', *ibid.* pp. 445–8.

[2] *Magic in the Web* (1957).

[3] *Shakespeare. A Pictorial Biography* (Thames and Hudson, 1956).

[4] H. A. Shield, 'Links with Shakespeare, XIV', *Notes and Queries* (October 1956), pp. 421–3.

[5] 'Guessing about the Youthful Shakespeare', *University of Texas Studies in English*, XXXIV (1955), 43–50.

[6] '"One of the least typical of all Elizabethans": Probleme und Perspektiven der Shakespeare-Forschung', *Anglia*, LXXIV (1956), 16–65.

[7] *Shakespeare's Early Contemporaries. The Background of the Harvey-Nashe Polemic and Love's Labour's Lost* (Antwerp: Nederlandsche Boekhandel, 1956).

The question of a balanced perspective is always involved in the study of Shakespeare's sources, and especially in that pursuit of vague parallels or uncertain echoes which keeps a host of commentators busy. Kenneth Muir's study of *Shakespeare's Sources*[1] provides a much needed point of orientation, and will be very widely used. He modestly disclaims any critical intent, but frequently the importance of sources in relation to critical judgements is displayed. The book brings together a mass of recent discovery, devoting most space to the tragedies, and, perhaps understandably, rather too much to sources the author has already noticed or analysed, for instance the use of Harsnett's *Declaration* in *King Lear*. He is also too ready at times to accept a commonplace verbal resemblance as a mark of indebtedness, but demonstrates effectively that Shakespeare was capable of using as many as ten sources for one play, and of conflating several in a few lines, and should make us more aware of the poet as a shaping artist. In spite of its immense value, this is ultimately a rather disappointing work, for it is neither a full critical study of Shakespeare's use of sources, nor an adequate book of reference, but something between the two; it is a great pity that so useful a survey should be inadequately indexed.

Muir refers in his book to the evidence collected by Ernest Schanzer of Shakespeare's use of Appian's *Civil Wars* in portraying Antony in *Julius Caesar* and Pompey in *Antony and Cleopatra*: the extent of the borrowings can now be studied in Schanzer's edition of relevant extracts.[2] Both Muir and Schanzer contribute some further notes. The former finds further evidence of debts to Erasmus in *Measure for Measure*,[3] to Lewkenor's translation of Contarini in *Othello*,[4] to Studley's translation of Seneca in *Macbeth*,[5] and to Brooke's *Romeus and Juliet* in *Romeo and Juliet*;[6] the latter tracks Senecan influences in *King John*,[7] finds further parallels between the Countess of Pembroke's *Antonius* and *Antony and Cleopatra*,[8] and enlarges on Shakespeare's use of Holinshed in *Macbeth*.[9] Other critics observe possible echoes or allusions in *King John*,[10] *Richard II*,[11] *Hamlet*,[12] *Julius Caesar*,[13] *The Winter's Tale*,[14] and in Sonnet CXXIX.[15] Most of these deal with slight verbal parallels or similarities of image or reference which do not compel belief. The connexions seem less tenuous in a few other articles: Haldeen Braddy[16] finds a likeness

---

[1] *Shakespeare's Sources. I. Comedies and Tragedies* (Methuen, 1957).

[2] *Shakespeare's Appian. A Selection from the Tudor Translation of Appian's Civil Wars* (Liverpool University Reprints, 1956).

[3] 'Shakespeare and Erasmus', *Notes and Queries* (October 1956), pp. 424–5.

[4] 'Shakespeare and Lewkenor', *Review of English Studies*, new series, VII (April 1956), 182–3.

[5] 'Seneca and Shakespeare', *Notes and Queries* (June 1956), pp. 243–4.

[6] 'Arthur Brooke and the Imagery of Romeo and Juliet', ibid. pp. 241–3.

[7] '"Hercules Oetaeus" and "King John"', *Notes and Queries* (December 1956), pp. 509–10.

[8] 'Antony and Cleopatra and the Countess of Pembroke's Antonius', *Notes and Queries* (April 1956), pp. 153–4.

[9] 'Four Notes on Macbeth', *Modern Language Review*, LII (April 1957), 223–7.

[10] Matthew P. McDiarmid, 'A Reconsidered Parallel between Shakespeare's King John and Kyd's Cornelia', *Notes and Queries* (December 1956), pp. 507–8.

[11] I. B. Cauthen Junior, 'Shakespeare's "Moat Defensive" (Richard II, II, i, 43–9)', *Notes and Queries* (October 1956), pp. 419–20.

[12] W. Montgomerie, 'Lucianus, Nephew to the King', *Notes and Queries* (April 1956), pp. 149–51.

[13] J. C. Maxwell, 'Julius Caesar and Elyot's Governour', ibid. p. 147.

[14] Ernst Kunstler, 'Julio Romano im Wintermärchen', *Shakespeare Jahrbuch*, XCII (1956), 291–8.

[15] Charles A. O. Fox, 'Thomas Lodge and Shakespeare', *Notes and Queries* (May 1956), p. 190.

[16] 'Shakespeare's Puck and Froissart's Orthon', *Shakespeare Quarterly*, VII (Spring 1956), 276–80.

between Shakespeare's Puck and the character Orthon who figures in a tale in Froissart's chronicles; F. D. Hoeniger[1] shows a relationship between *Cymbeline* and Bandello, and notices an analogue for this play in a *commedia dell'arte* based on the same tale in the *Decameron* that Shakespeare used; S. Musgrove[2] points out that Edgar, Edmund and Oswald, the only Anglo-Saxon names in *Lear*, are to be found in Camden's *Remains*.

Studies of the background of ideas available in literature or in tradition in Shakespeare's time often seem better related than the pursuit of sources to that balanced perspective Horst Oppel had in mind. Several valuable works of this kind have appeared in the past year. The reprint of Willard Farnham's *The Medieval Heritage of Elizabethan Tragedy*[3] twenty years after it was first published deserves to be welcomed: it is an important book mainly for its commanding display of the development of tragedy in the context of the growth of the idea of human responsibility. It shows how medieval conceptions of tragedy as the necessary and inexplicable fall of the great, imaged in the wheel of fortune, or the necessary and fully explicable fall of man as a consequence of sin, reflected in exhortations to scorn the world, were absorbed and transformed; a growing emphasis is traced in morality and interlude on God's justice rather than his mercy, and the book brings out the character of what are seen as the twin mainsprings of Elizabethan tragedy, ambition and revenge, and indicates how the drama came to "focus upon human character" as the shaper of tragic destiny. Two other studies of pre-Shakespearian drama range less widely. Agostino Lombardo[4] writes in enthusiastic appreciation of some miracle plays, moralities and interludes, and has a long chapter on *Gorboduc*, bringing out what Shakespeare may have learned from them; his praise of *Gorboduc* is excessive, but the superiority of Sackville over Norton as a poet-dramatist, the originality of the play, and its relation to *The Mirror for Magistrates*, are well brought out. F. M. Salter, who has collected much information on the Chester cycle of plays,[5] argues that they date from the 1380's and not from the 1320's as Chambers believed, and that they were never secularized, but lingered after the Reformation only because of their popularity, the new church being hostile to them as Popish. Like Lombardo, his judgement is swayed by his enthusiasm, and he finds the greatest art where most critics can see only an elementary artifice.

W. G. Meader[6] attempts to relate love in Shakespeare's plays to the tradition of courtly love, basing his discussion on a description of the stages of courtship as formalized by Andreas Capellanus. He has some perceptive pages on *Troilus and Cressida*, but otherwise the discussion is conducted on a very elementary level, demonstrates what is well known, employs false critical criteria, such as sincerity, and reveals a failure properly to read Shakespeare, whose dramatic code is equated with that of Hollywood. In a book that has much less direct reference to Shakespeare, Gordon Worth O'Brien[7] says much more that is of value. He traces the development of the

[1] 'Two Notes on *Cymbeline*', *Shakespeare Quarterly*, VIII (Winter 1957), 132–3.

[2] 'The Nomenclature of *King Lear*', *Review of English Studies*, new series, VII (July 1956), 294–8.

[3] Oxford: Blackwell, 1956.

[4] *Il Dramma Pre-Shakespeariano. Studi sul Teatro Inglese dal Medioevo al Rinascimento* (Venice: Neri Pozza Editore, 1957).

[5] *Medieval Drama in Chester* (University of Toronto Press, 1955).

[6] *Courtship in Shakespeare: In Relation to the Tradition of Courtly Love* (New York: Columbia University, King's Crown Press, 1954).

[7] *Renaissance Poetics and the Problem of Power* (Chicago: Institute of Elizabethan Studies, Publication Number Two, 1956).

concept of the dignity of man as "absolute power disposed to creative ends by discipline and clear intelligence", which, in his view, lies behind the grandest utterances of Shakespeare and Milton. This development is described in two ways, in terms of the specific image of a mirror or speculum, passing into the phrase "clear spirit", and in terms of a transference of the image of correspondence between man and the world "from the obligation of man to dominate the passions of his little world to his obligation to preserve the harmony of the cosmos itself". Man becomes a god in potentiality (Faustus, Adam), and his tragic sin is to prevent his time, to desire to possess now the assimilation of man into god promised to him—an assimilation which finds a dramatic image in Prospero. This is a book which contains many interesting perceptions, but it sadly needs an index. Siegfried Korninger's study[1] is in some ways complementary to it, for this provides a survey of seventeenth-century poetry, showing how, in its sharpening of perception of details of the natural scene, tending towards minute and exact description, and in its sense of the expansion of the universe and the world in the evidence of astronomers and voyagers, this poetry reflects a new Baconian outlook on the world in terms of natural science.

More directly concerned with Shakespeare's own age is Allardyce Nicoll's anthology[2] of extracts from Elizabethan writers, carefully arranged for sequence or contrast, and interspersed with illustrations from paintings, title-pages, plans, and documents, all well chosen to form an integral part of the book. Each extract or illustration is numbered, and full references are given in notes at the end, which do not get in the reader's way, but will tempt him to explore. It is probably the fullest, and certainly the best presented anthology of its kind, and deserves to be popular with those who have interests of any kind in the age. Paul Jorgensen develops a minor theme at too great length in *Shakespeare's Military World*.[3] A great deal of scholarship has gone into his discussions of military rank, of ideal concepts of war and peace, of the status of the soldier in society, especially the difficult and ambiguous place of the Elizabethan captain, and of the way in which Shakespeare employs the ideas and attitudes concerning war that were available to him. The light this throws on the plays is mostly of a kind that will be more useful in editorial commentary than in critical discussion. The most interesting parts of the book critically are those on *Timon of Athens* and *Coriolanus*. *Timon* is seen in terms of a Renaissance concept of war and peace as belonging to a necessary cycle of events; society in the play is "rank with Plenty, Pride and Envy", and this brings disaster to Timon, and can only be cured by war in the figure of Alcibiades, "less a person than an impersonal force". *Coriolanus* is related to contemporary views of the soldier's ineptitude in peace.

Two important articles are concerned with the dating of plays. In one, E. A. J. Honigmann[4] reconsiders the evidence for the dating of *Hamlet*, which he would place between mid-1599 and February 1601, after *Julius Caesar* was composed, and before the execution of the Earl of Essex, a terminal date based upon a re-interpretation of Gabriel Harvey's note referring to the play in his copy of Speght's 1598 edition of Chaucer. Sidney Thomas[5] goes against the recent tendency

---

[1] *Die Naturauffassung in der Englischen Dichtung des 17. Jahrhunderts* (Vienna: Wiener Beiträge zur Englischen Philologie, Band LXIV, 1956).

[2] *The Elizabethans* (Cambridge University Press, 1957).

[3] University of California Press and Cambridge University Press, 1956.

[4] 'The Date of *Hamlet*', *Shakespeare Survey*, 9 (1956), 24–34.

[5] 'The Date of *The Comedy of Errors*', *Shakespeare Quarterly*, VII (Autumn 1956), 377–84.

to push forward the dates of Shakespeare's plays by arguing strongly for December 1594 as the date of the first production of *The Comedy of Errors*: his main points are that the well-known allusion to trouble in France was as appropriate in this year as earlier, that the use of legal terms and of classical sources would appeal to a Gray's Inn audience, and that the 1595 edition of Warner's translation of the *Menaechmi* was not the first, which may well have been available in 1594. Further exploration of the background of Shakespeare's plays has been made in a number of articles. John E. Hankins[1] writes on the ultimate derivation in medieval visions of the after-world and in Virgil of Shakespeare's images of purgatory and the torments of hell. In a survey of the poet's allusions to Turks, J. W. Draper[2] reveals only that he shared traditional attitudes. John S. Weld[3] and S. K. Heninger Junior[4] seek to explain two difficult passages in *The Comedy of Errors* in terms of traditional ideas and imagery. A useful service is performed by John P. Cutts[5] in printing the contemporary musical settings he has found of songs in Middleton's *The Witch*, in *2 Henry IV* and *The Winter's Tale*.

Relatively little has been written about the Elizabethan stage in the past year. John Cranford Adams is fighting a losing battle, if not supporting a lost cause, in maintaining his conception of the structure of the Globe and the staging of plays there; but he makes a sharp and well-presented retort[6] to Richard Hosley,[7] asserting that the entire 242 lines of the balcony scene in *Romeo and Juliet* (Act III, Scene v) were played on what he thinks of as a multiple upper-stage of window and gallery. Irwin Smith,[8] who seems to be of Adams' school of thought, claims that there were gates which folded back within the inner-stage; like Adams, he relies on dubious evidence; he takes much too literally author's stage-directions and references in dialogue, which do not indicate a need for real gates. Hosley has returned to the fray with a general argument,[9] based on a few allusions, on de Witt's drawing of the Swan, and on the frontispieces to *Roxana* and *The Wits* (1662), that the gallery over the stage was used primarily and always as a Lord's Room, and "only secondarily, occasionally, and then for relatively short periods as a raised production-area", at which times it had both functions simultaneously. The evidence is not sufficient, is of doubtful validity, assumes an identity of practice in numerous theatres, and is open to alternative interpretation, but for all this, it amounts to something. Another opponent of Adams, G. F. Reynolds, seeks to reconstruct the original staging of *Hamlet*,[10] which he thinks was acted almost

---

[1] 'The Pains of the Afterworld: Fire, Wind and Ice in Milton and Shakespeare', *PMLA*, LXXI (June 1956), 482–95.

[2] 'Shakespeare and the Turk', *Journal of English and Germanic Philology*, LV (October 1956), 523–32.

[3] 'Old Adam New Apparelled', *Shakespeare Quarterly*, VII (Autumn 1956), 453–6.

[4] 'The Heart's Meteors, a Microcosm: Macrocosm Analogy', *Shakespeare Quarterly*, VII (Spring 1956), 273–5.

[5] 'The Original Music to Middleton's *The Witch*', *Shakespeare Quarterly*, VII (Spring 1956), 203–9; 'The Original Music of a Song in *2 Henry IV*', *Shakespeare Quarterly*, VII (Autumn 1956), 385–92; 'An Unpublished Contemporary Setting of a Shakespeare Song', *Shakespeare Survey*, 9 (1956), 86–9.

[6] 'Shakespeare's Use of the Upper Stage in *Romeo and Juliet*, III, v', *Shakespeare Quarterly*, VII (Spring 1956), 145–52.

[7] See *Shakespeare Survey*, 9 (1956), 146.

[8] '"Gates" on Shakespeare's Stage', *Shakespeare Quarterly*, VII (Spring 1956), 159–76.

[9] 'The Gallery over the Stage in the Public Playhouse of Shakespeare's Time', *Shakespeare Quarterly*, VIII (Winter 1957), 15–31.

[10] '*Hamlet* at the Globe', *Shakespeare Survey*, 9 (1956), 49–53.

entirely on the outer stage. Ernest Schanzer points out in an important note[1] the ways in which a mistranslation of Thomas Platter's account of his visit to a London theatre in 1599 has given rise to misconceptions such as that the audience was standing in the galleries, and that a tent was a permanent feature on the Elizabethan stage.

Later productions of Shakespeare's plays, and their influence, are receiving much attention. The publication of the second part of Charles Beecher Hogan's catalogue[2] of eighteenth-century performances in London completes a necessary guide: the "virtually complete day-by-day run of playbills" for the period 1751–1800 dealt with in this volume has provided the author with a vast mass of material which is reduced to order in the form of a pleasant and lucid reference-work. It follows the same plan as the first part; a calendar of performances at the various theatres is followed by a detailed tabulation, with cast-lists, of productions of each play, and an index of references to actors and to characters in the plays. An appendix on the relative popularity of the plays shows that as a group the Greek and Roman plays were least popular in the century, and that *Love's Labour's Lost* had the unique distinction of not being acted at all. Arthur H. Scouten[3] complains that Hogan's presentation of his statistics by year and not by theatrical season may give a false impression of events, and he re-assesses the various waves of popularity of Shakespeare's plays up to 1750, suggesting that the flood of cheap reprints by Tonson and Walker in the late 1730's and 1740's was more important than the influence of Garrick in stimulating stage revivals. Emett L. Avery has a parallel note[4] on the influence of a Ladies' Club in encouraging productions in 1736 and the next few years. The importance of Garrick's 1769 Jubilee in exciting French and German interest in Shakespeare is well described by Martha Winburn England,[5] and the record of French interest in, distortion of, and adaptation of *Hamlet* is traced from this time to the end of the nineteenth century by Paul Benchettrit.[6] Further articles on this play include D. A. Russell's account[7] of the costuming of Hamlet since Garrick's time, E. Martin Browne's review[8] of interpretations of the part by English actors since 1913, and Joseph Patrick Roppolo's survey[9] of productions in New Orleans from 1820 to 1865.

The main theme of the 1956 *Shakespeare Jahrbuch* is the translation of Shakespeare's plays. The articles include a statement by a theatre director[10] of the reasons why the Schlegel-Tieck-Baudissin versions are still used on the stage. He argues that to adapt only distorts without recreating Shakespeare. Hedwig Schwarz, on the other hand, pleads[11] that adaptation to the modern stage

---

[1] 'Thomas Platter's Observations on the Elizabethan Stage', *Notes and Queries* (November 1956), pp. 465–7.

[2] *Shakespeare in the Theatre 1701–1800. Volume II. A Record of Performances in London 1751–1800* (Clarendon Press: Oxford University Press, 1957).

[3] 'The Increase in Popularity of Shakespeare's Plays in the Eighteenth Century: A *Caveat* for Interpreters of Stage History', *Shakespeare Quarterly*, VII (Spring 1956), 189–202.

[4] 'The Shakespeare Ladies' Club', *ibid.* pp. 153–8.

[5] 'Garrick's Stratford Jubilee: Reactions in France and Germany', *Shakespeare Survey*, 9 (1956), 90–100.

[6] '*Hamlet* at the Comédie Française: 1769–1896', *Shakespeare Survey*, 9 (1956), 59–68.

[7] 'Hamlet Costumes from Garrick to Gielgud', *ibid.* pp. 54–8.

[8] 'English Hamlets of the Twentieth Century', *ibid.* pp. 16–23.

[9] '*Hamlet* in New Orleans', *Tulane Studies in English*, VI (1956), 71–86.

[10] K. G. Kachler, 'Weshalb immer noch die Shakespeare-Übertragungen der Romantiker vorzuziehen sind' *Shakespeare Jahrbuch*, XCII (1956), 90–5.

[11] 'Arbeit für Shakespeare durch Shakespeare-Bearbeitungen', *ibid.* pp. 175–83.

and audience is necessary. K. H. Ruppel[1] writes on the effect the use of Shakespeare's plays for librettos had on the form of Verdi's operas, and W. M. Merchant[2] argues that a valid style of décor needs to be worked out for modern productions of Shakespeare, which now rely casually on various elements in "the visual history of the stage" in the past three centuries. Also of relevance to modern staging is Saxon Walker's discussion[3] of mimicry and heraldry in *1 Henry IV*, which, in his view, express the "opposing claims" exerted upon Prince Hal by Falstaff, the King and Hotspur, and the conflict between the King and the rebels. To complete their tribute to William Poel, J. Isaacs has edited for the Society for Theatre Research his prompt-book of *Der Bestrafte Brudermord*.[4] This is historically interesting as one of the two "first productions ever" for which Poel was responsible, and it shows something of his methods; but one wonders if a prompt-book of a Shakespeare play, though less fully annotated than this, might have been more valuable.

Commentary on current production grows, especially now that *Shakespeare Jahrbuch* and *Shakespeare Quarterly* report extensively on activities in Germany[5] and in the United States.[6] The second season at Stratford, Connecticut, seems to have been much better than the first, and this festival will no doubt be raising in the critic as high hopes as the established ones at Stratford, Ontario, and Stratford-upon-Avon, hopes never quite fulfilled.[7] Kenneth Muir[8] in particular is severe upon what he sees as faults of over-production, inadequate acting, and inconsistency of style at the English festival. The most perceptive criticism remains that of Richard David,[9] who draws some conclusions regarding the nature of Shakespeare's tragedy from the London and Stratford productions of *Macbeth* in 1954 and 1955.

A few miscellaneous notes deserve mention. Two new seventeenth-century allusions to Shakespeare have been observed.[10] The exact date of the court performance which Leslie Hotson identifies with *Twelfth Night* is still being discussed, and the evidence points to Christmas 1600/1 rather than 1601/2.[11] Edward Alleyn Loomis seeks to identify as a real ship the 'Tiger'

---

[1] 'Verdi und Shakespeare', *Shakespeare Jahrbuch*, XCII (1956), pp. 7–18.

[2] 'Visual Elements in Shakespeare Studies', *ibid.* pp. 280–90.

[3] 'Mime and Heraldry in Henry IV, Part 1', *English*, XI (Autumn 1956), 91–6.

[4] *William Poel's Prompt-Book of Fratricide Punished* (Society for Theatre Research, 1956). This is available to members only.

[5] In addition to a general review of German productions in 1955–6 by Wolfgang Stroedel, there are reports on post-war productions in Stuttgart by K. H. Ruppel and in Lower Saxony by Reimar Hollmann, as well as a note on recent activity on the Swiss stage by Gunther Schoop, in *Shakespeare Jahrbuch*, XCII (1956), 299–326.

[6] The most interesting reports are those by A. C. Sprague on what seems to have been a poor season on the New York stage, and by Robert D. Horn on the flourishing festival in Oregon, *Shakespeare Quarterly*, VII (Autumn 1956), 393–8 and 415–18. The general survey of 'Elizabethan Drama: 1956' by J. A. Bryant Junior, *Sewanee Review*, LXV (Winter 1957), pp. 152–60, should also be noted.

[7] These are reviewed respectively by Richard Hosley, Arnold Edinborough and John Russell Brown in *Shakespeare Quarterly*, VII (Autumn 1956), 399–410.

[8] 'Stratford 1956', *Essays in Criticism*, VII (January 1957), 113–18.

[9] 'The Tragic Curve', *Shakespeare Survey*, 9 (1956), 122–31.

[10] G. B. Harrison, 'A New Shakespeare Allusion', *Shakespeare Quarterly*, VIII (Winter 1957), 127; J. C. Maxwell, 'An Uncollected Shakespeare Allusion', *Notes and Queries* (June 1956), p. 231.

[11] G. R. Batho, '*Twelfth Night* and the Duke of Northumberland's MS.', *Notes and Queries* (April 1956), p. 178.

referred to in *Macbeth*.[1] J. C. Maxwell has an interesting article[2] on Shakespeare's ghost-scenes, suggesting that their effectiveness is a result of a clash between sophisticated theories and popular beliefs, which the dramatist brilliantly combines and exploits. Finally, the world-wide interest in Shakespeare is illustrated by an article devoted to his allusions to medicine in the *Medical Journal of Malaya*.[3]

3. TEXTUAL STUDIES

reviewed by JAMES G. McMANAWAY

Two volumes have now been added to the New Cambridge Shakespeare: *Pericles*, edited by J. C. Maxwell,[4] and *Othello*, jointly edited by Alice Walker and John Dover Wilson. Editing *Pericles* is a thankless job. The only text is a wretched report, and no one but himself is likely to be satisfied with any editor's solution of the problem of single or dual authorship. Maxwell is conservative in rejecting the suggestion that there was an *Ur-Pericles* and in believing in dual authorship. He is sound in dismissing George Wilkins, author of a prose romance about Pericles that is essentially a narrative report of the King's Men's play, as a collaborator; and he is courageous in checking doubtful readings in the play against the text of the novel. He disagrees with Mr Philip Edwards, a believer in Shakespeare's sole authorship, who has argued that the extant text is the product of two reporters, the first of whom did incalculably greater damage to Shakespeare's Acts I and II than his fellow did to Acts III–V; and although he corrects Edwards in some details he does not, in my opinion, upset his hypothesis. Maxwell cannot decide whether Shakespeare had a collaborator or took a poor play and after touching up the first part wrote the last three acts afresh. If there was a collaborator, Maxwell inclines towards Thomas Heywood, though he admits that he cannot explain how a dramatist for the Queen's Men offered a manuscript to the King's or acquiesced in Shakespeare's rewriting it. In many places, the editor found his text hopelessly corrupt; elsewhere he has introduced "a large number of emendations, especially metrical regularizations...even when the hopes of getting back to the authentic text are very slight" (p. 97). This attitude reminds one of the banquet served a condemned prisoner on the eve of his execution. No attempt is made to solve the very serious bibliographical problems of the first quarto.

In the edition of *Othello*,[5] the General Editor has written the Introduction and contributed a scattering of signed notes, and Miss Walker has been "responsible for the preparation of the text together with everything in the volume that comes after the text". There was collaboration on the Notes and Glossary. What Miss Walker has done must be considered in connexion with her essay in *Shakespeare Survey*, 5, and with Chapter VII of her *Textual Problems in the First Folio*. *Othello* is one of the troublesome but fascinating plays surviving in two (or more) substantive

---

[1] 'Master of the Tiger', *Shakespeare Quarterly*, VII (Autumn 1956), 457.
[2] 'The Ghost from the Grave: A Note on Shakespeare's Apparitions', *Durham University Journal*, new series, XVII (March 1956), 55–9.
[3] B. R. Sreenivasan, 'Shakespeare on Medicine', *Medical Journal of Malaya*, X (June 1956), 279–88.
[4] J. C. Maxwell, ed., *Pericles Prince of Tyre* (The New Shakespeare), Cambridge University Press, 1956.
[5] Alice Walker and John Dover Wilson, eds., *Othello* (The New Shakespeare), Cambridge University Press, 1957.

texts. Miss Walker's business has been to discover, if possible, the source and nature of the copy Walkley used in printing Q1 (1622), with what this quarto was collated in preparation of F and how carefully, and the amount of corruption introduced into the text—or permitted to remain there—by the various scribes and compositors participating. Her exhaustive analyses lead her to the following conclusions.

Q. seems...to represent a licentious transcript of a late acting version of *Othello* further mangled in its printing....The main virtue of F. seems to derive from the collation of an example of Q. with a respectable manuscript....That this manuscript stood at no more than one remove from Shakespeare's foul papers seems likely....I...incline to the conclusion that the MS. used for collation was a fair copy, anterior to the prompt book....That F. preserves the better text has never been seriously in doubt.... That F. is not an entirely trustworthy text is, however, only too clear from its numerous manifest errors.

These widely scattered excerpts give, I think, a fair picture of Miss Walker's editorial position. That the text she produces is eclectic is inevitable. Over and above the more-or-less readily detectable errors introduced in Q by Walkley's scribe and compositor, those introduced by Jaggard's shop and by the expurgator, and the collator's miscorrections of Q, there are, the editors estimate, about 70 to 80 errors in Q that were undetected by the collator (10% of the some 700 errors in Q). Miss Walker's repeated challenge to editors to emend boldly has had a marked influence on recent volumes in the New Cambridge and the New Arden series, and she has been no laggard in attacking corruption in *Othello*. She adopts, for example, forty-six emendations of readings common to QF, only eight of which are now usual, though many were proposed or adopted by the eighteenth-century editors (see pp. 134–5).

It is possible, I think, that Miss Walker underestimates the significance of the permissive stage directions at I, iii, 120, 'Exit two or three', and I, iii, 170, 'and the rest', as evidence that Q was set from a transcript of foul papers. Such directions do occur in *The First Part of the Contention*, as she says, but in this play and others like it they are descriptive notes of a reporter trying to eke out his text, not, as she supposes in *Othello*, "the work of a book-keeper who saved himself time and trouble by using his memory rather than his eyes" (*Textual Problems*, p. 151). She certainly errs in rejecting C. K. Hinman's identification of Jaggard's apprentice compositor E (p. 123, n. 3; p. 132, n. 1), for it is not based on preferential spellings but on identifiable pieces of type and other objective evidence. Some of the corruption formerly charged against compositor B must in future be allocated to E.

The three current additions to the New Arden Shakespeare are histories: *2 Henry VI*, *Richard II* and *Henry VIII*. The Introduction to *2 Henry VI* by A. S. Cairncross is admirable.[1] The problems of authorship and transmission of text of this play have defied solution, and although Cairncross calls his work merely "a contribution to a more comprehensive solution of the problem", he gives the most comprehensive and, to at least one reader, the most nearly satisfactory account that has been offered. Briefly, he thinks that Shakespeare is the sole author of the play, written about 1590. His manuscript was marked for revision in many places by the censor, and a shortened

---

[1] Andrew S. Cairncross, ed., *The Second Part of King Henry VI* (New Arden), London: Methuen, 1956.

version was performed with success. After the bankruptcy of Pembroke's company in 1593, a reported text was put together by the actors who had played Warwick, Suffolk—Clifford, Armourer—Spirit—Mayor—Vaux—Scales, and York (added by Cairncross, who thinks some of the same agents are responsible for reporting *The True Tragedy*), and this was published in 1594 as *The First Part of the Contention*. At later dates, notably about 1600, other dangerous passages were altered. About 1621, Heminge and Condell delivered this heavily patched prompt book to Jaggard, but his compositors made scissors-and-paste use of pages from Q3 (supplemented by passages from Q2) of *The Contention* wherever possible, in accordance with their known preference for printed copy. The resultant text has many imperfections, but some of the faulty readings may be spotted and amended.[1] "The final result is of course unsatisfactory, but in the nature of the case it must be so. The main satisfaction, perhaps, is to know the worst, see how it happened, and do the best possible to repair some of the damage" (p. xlix). Major differences between Q and F are thus explained as the result of theatrical abridgement or of repeated intervention by a censor; corruptions, as the result of faulty reporting and inaccurate typesetting.

This is a plausible account, and Cairncross may be right, but I should feel easier in mind if he had named other plays that were subjected to censorship by the Revels Office after once being licensed. It seems more likely that politically dangerous passages may have been changed voluntarily by Shakespeare's company as a matter of prudence. I am far from certain that the prompt book was sent to Jaggard's shop to be used as copy; that, they would preserve because of the license it bore from the Revels Office. I suggest that a partial or complete transcript was made for use in conjunction with a marked quarto.

Cairncross says what has long been needed about Shakespeare's supposed plagiarism from Robert Greene and about Henry Chettle's apology. At worst, Shakespeare's debt was for words, such as Q's "Abradas, the great Masedonian Pyrate" (from Greene's *Menaphon*), that was changed in F to "Bargalus the strong Illyrian pirate" (from Cicero's *De Officiis*). And when Chettle wrote of Shakespeare's 'honesty' he was not thinking of plagiarism. "'Honestus', to these Elizabethans so familiar with their Horace, meant 'decent, gentlemanly'; and 'uprightness of dealing' has not quite the same business flavour as it has today" (p. xliii).

The problem confronting R. A. Foakes in editing *Henry VIII*[2] was very different, for the text of this play is notably free from the imperfections of *2 Henry VI*. There is only one substantive text, the First Folio, and that, Foakes believes, was a clean transcript of the author's foul papers, probably by a single scribe. The play is not, however, an easy one to edit. Since 1850 there has been a strong movement to give part of the play to John Fletcher or to Philip Massinger. Foakes meets the charges of the disintegrationists head-on and after cool examination of the evidence of vocabulary, contractions, speech-tags, style, and use of sources, not to mention the ways in which a scribe and the Folio compositors might alter the accidentals of a text, comes to the conclusion that one mind—and only one mind—produced the play. "If Fletcher has to be

---

[1] Cairncross's text is in some respects iconoclastic, for he has had the courage to emend in the light of his textual theory. See, for example, his readings and notes at I, i, 252; I, ii, 75–6; and III, ii, 407. Some of the editor's readings that restore the metre or improve the sense may appear at first sight to be 'improvements' like those made in the eighteenth century; but however similar the results, Cairncross has wholly different grounds of emendation.

[2] R. A. Foakes, ed., *King Henry VIII* (New Arden), London: Methuen, 1957.

introduced, then I think his share must have been considerably less than the usual division ascribes to him, and that he worked only as an occasional reviser or toucher-up, who perhaps contributed one or two scenes. . . . Throughout the remainder of this introduction Shakespeare is assumed to be the author" (pp. xxv, xxvi).

In editing *Richard II*, Peter Ure[1] was unfortunate in not being able to take into account M. W. Black's recent Variorum Edition, in view of the fact that Black collated a fourth copy of Q1 (that at Petworth House, never previously examined by scholars), for it contains D (i) in the uncorrected state. Two of the four variants recorded by Black show that the press corrector referred to copy at II, i, 194–6 and again at II, ii, 35–6 to restore omissions of more than a line. There are four other variants in this forme unnoted by Black (cf. *Shakespeare Survey*, 10, p. 151), one of which ("his owne disgrace" at II, i, 176) gives a reading the faulty alteration of which has kept editors guessing ever since. Ure bases his text, correctly, on Q1, which he thinks—with H. F. Brooks and A. S. Cairncross—suffers from memorial contamination at the hands of the scribe that copied Shakespeare's foul papers. This scribe, according to Brooks, also prepared the copy for Q1 of *Richard III* and was probably the bookholder of the company. The contamination manifests itself in metrically irregular lines and in passages containing exclamations and is most evident in II, ii and V, ii, where York is prominent. Many corrections are accepted from F, because, in the editor's opinion, a copy of Q3 (supplemented by three leaves of Q5) was collated with the manuscript prompt-book in preparation of the First Folio. From this prompt-book came also the good text of the Deposition Scene. Ure rejects Dr Richard E. Hasker's hypothesis that a worn prompt-book had been superseded by a marked copy of Q3 (later supplemented by leaves from Q5) and that this prompt-book itself served as copy for F; instead, he insists wisely that the manuscript prompt-book with the Deposition Scene, was "tenaciously preserved" in the playhouse.

With such strong convictions about the presence of contamination in the text and of the signs by which it may be recognized, Ure does not hesitate to amend suspected passages, even when Q readings are confirmed by F, for he thinks that the collation of Q3 (5) with the prompt-book was not meticulous. He may well be right at I, i, 204, a fairly simple case; the problem at V, iii, 40–5 is more complex, and though Ure advances strong arguments and produces a smooth passage he risks the charge of exalting the sanctity of regular iambic pentameters.

During the year, the Shakespeare Association of America has begun an experiment the outcome of which will be watched with interest. Mindful of the fact that neither individuals nor libraries can hope to keep fully abreast of Shakespeare scholarship, and that even the ample volumes of the New Variorum Shakespeare (begun in 1873 by Horace Howard Furness, continued by his son and namesake, and since 1936 issued under the auspices of the Modern Language Association of America) become outdated within a short time of publication, the Shakespeare Association commissioned the compilation of a *Supplement*[2] to the New Variorum *1 Henry IV* and published it as the summer number of *Shakespeare Quarterly*, with extra copies in cloth covers similar to

---

[1] Peter Ure, ed., *King Richard II* (New Arden), London: Methuen, 1956.
[2] G. Blakemore Evans, ed., *Supplement to Henry IV, Part 1. A New Variorum Edition of Shakespeare* (New York: Shakespeare Association of America, Inc., 1956).

volumes of the New Variorum. G. Blakemore Evans, the editor of this *Supplement*, has brought together in variorum form "with some degree of completeness all (mere nonsense aside) that has been written relating to the play from 1935 to July 1955". John Crow's review of the book concludes in part as follows:

It is all notes and no text—the pedant's dream....The book is what it sets out to be; it is intended not to divert, nor even to persuade, but to chronicle....If we wish to know—and teachers of Shakespeare simply have to know—what all the boys have been saying in the last twenty years, this books tells us and tells us admirably....I read it through and was enthralled with it and I shall regard it as a necessary part of my library. It led me to much that I had missed; it reminded me of much that had begun to grow hazy in my memory....[1]

If this volume proves sufficiently useful and popular, the Shakespeare Association of America may be encouraged to bring out Supplements to *2 Henry IV* and other of the New Variorum volumes.

Until recently there has been a shortage in the American market of paperback editions of single plays of Shakespeare. Volumes of the Penguin edition prepared by G. B. Harrison and of the Appleton–Century–Crofts series under the general editorship of R. C. Bald were first in the field. Of the three newcomers, the Pelican Shakespeare[2] issued under the direction of Alfred Harbage has brought out eight plays: *Richard II* edited by M. W. Black, *1 Henry IV* by M. A. Shaaber, *2 Henry IV* by A. G. Chester, *Henry V* by Louis B. Wright and Virginia Freund, *Macbeth* by Alfred Harbage, *Winter's Tale* by Baldwin Maxwell, *Measure for Measure* by R. C. Bald, and *Coriolanus* by Harry Levin. Each play is preceded by an essay by Harbage on 'Shakespeare and his Stage' and an Introduction of from four to eleven pages by the special editor, who has made his own choice of copy text and introduced emendations as needed. Spelling and punctuation are modernized. Notes are kept to a minimum and printed at the foot of the page. Only one play has yet to come from press in The Folger Library General Reader's Shakespeare: *King Lear*, edited by Louis B. Wright and Virginia Freund.[3] The Introduction of some thirty pages treats of the author, the Elizabethan stage, and the play in question, gives references for further reading, and contains the bulk of the fifteen to twenty reproductions intended to illustrate the play or the life and times of the author. The most noticeable innovation is the printing of notes and commentary on the pages facing the text. The third series to appear is the Yale Shakespeare, which has brought out six of its regular volumes in paper covers. *Hamlet*,[4] for example, is a re-issue of the 1954 printing of C. F. T. Brooke's 1947 revised edition. It gives a very full text with indication of passages omitted in Folio and Quarto 2, has footnotes and textual notes, and two appendices on the play, as well as fourteen pages of glossary. The spelling is modernized.

The records of the Company of Stationers of London have been consulted sporadically for a long time in the study of the history of English literature. Since the publication of Arber's *Transcripts of the Stationers' Register*, they have been used systematically, especially by students of

---

[1] *Shakespeare Quarterly*, VIII (Winter 1957), 91–4.
[2] The Pelican Shakespeare. Baltimore: Penguin Books, 1956, 1957.
[3] *The Tragedy of King Lear* (The Folger Library General Reader's Shakespeare), New York: Pocket Library, 1957.
[4] *Hamlet* (Yale Shakespeare). Yale University Press, 1954.

English drama. A new body of material was made available in Greg and Boswell's *Records of the Court of the Stationers' Company, 1576–1602*, and W. A. Jackson's edition of Court-Book C (now in preparation) will add still more to our knowledge. Meanwhile, there are many things unknown or imperfectly understood. Some of the more important of these are disclosed and explained in Sir Walter Greg's James P. Lyell Lectures in Bibliography of 1954–5.[1] These treat of Decrees and Ordinances, the Stationers' Records, Licensing for the Press, Entrance and Copyright, Imprints and Patents, the Hand of the Master of the Revels, and Blocking Entries. Some of these matters have been in dispute ever since the 'blocking entries' of James Roberts first came to notice. This is a book that must be read by anyone who wants to know why 'good' quartos of *Merry Wives* and *Henry V* were not published to displace the 'bad' ones, as happened in the case of *Hamlet*, for example; or how Bonian and Walley managed to bring out an edition of *Troilus*; or whether Edward Blount, as a sort of successor to Roberts, presented the prompt-books of *Pericles* and *Antony* at Stationers' Hall; or whether Walkley's *Othello* really had the sanction of the King's Men (Greg now has some doubts).

An essay of primary importance[2] introduces compositor E of the First Folio, whose hitherto shadowy existence was hinted at by E. E. Willoughby in 1932 and by Philip Williams in 1956. His was a prentice hand, Hinman tells us, and most of the pages he set exist in both an uncorrected and a corrected state: proof of the fact that Jaggard was aware of E's limitations and tried to catch his worst mistakes. He is known only in his work ("The evil that men do lives after them"): a page of *Titus*, the second setting of the last half-page of *Romeo*, part of *Troilus*, Act I of *Othello*, ten pages of *Lear*, and one and one-half pages of *Hamlet*. Of this, only *Titus*, III, ii was set from manuscript copy; all the rest was from printed copy, though the ten selected pages of *Lear* and presumably the page-and-a-half of *Hamlet* were marked copies of quartos and thus somewhat more difficult. This is the man. The final identification of compositor E, who in that title achieves more lasting fame than if his name and birthplace were known, is not simply a brilliant piece of bibliographical research that could hardly have been accomplished without the use of Hinman's collating machine and his vast accumulation of data about the printing of the First Folio. It gives meaning for the first time to the otherwise fantastically erratic sequence of formes through Jaggard's press as the First Folio moved to tardy completion.

In a poorly lithographed book that deserves formal print and clean reproductions, John Shroeder makes a valuable contribution to the study of the First Folio.[3] The book suffers from trying to combine instruction for the general reader with the solution of highly technical problems, but this should not detract from the praise of the author's perception that, by plotting through a thousand pages the course of the box rules that enclose the two columns of text in the First Folio, it might be possible to determine the order in which the formes were printed. It is Shroeder's misfortune that he excluded the centre rules from consideration and that he had not a collating machine to single out details that escape the unaided eye. In consequence of these things and of the fact that the story told by the rules must be supplemented by the evidence of

---

[1] *Some Aspects and Problems of London Publishing between 1550 and 1650*. Oxford University Press, 1956.

[2] Charlton K. Hinman, 'The Prentice Hand in the Tragedies of the Shakespeare First Folio: Compositor E', *Studies in Bibliography*, IX, 3–20.

[3] *The Great Folio of 1623: Shakespeare's Plays in the Printing House* (New Haven: The Shoe String Press, 1956).

broken types and the explanation of the part played by compositor E (whose existence was then unproved), Shroeder falls occasionally into error and has to concede that certain irregularities defy explanation. In his long review of the book,[1] Charlton Hinman points out the limitations of Shroeder's methods and corrects some of his mistakes but adds that "Mr Shroeder has demonstrated conclusively that *Julius Caesar* was printed before *Romeo and Juliet*; that part of *Richard III* and the whole of *Henry VIII* were printed only long after the other Histories and when all of *Macbeth* and part of *Hamlet* had completed their runs at the press; . . . that, indeed, irregularity was the rule rather than the exception throughout the printing of a large part of the great folio of 1623. This is important information, and its discoverer deserves high praise. . . ."

There has been general agreement that Q2 of *Romeo and Juliet* was printed in large part from a manuscript in Shakespeare's hand but that in one long passage, roughly from I, ii, 52 to I, iii, 35, the copy was a corresponding passage in Bad Quarto I. The terminal points of this passage are controversial, as is the extent to which Q1 may have contaminated Q2 elsewhere. A few hard facts about the printing of Q2 have been quarried by Paul L. Cantrell and George Walton Williams.[2] They give bibliographical evidence that all of Q2 except six pages was set by a compositor called A; the rest by compositor B. Then by analysis of the spellings of speech tags in Qq1, 2 they indicate the very strong probability that specified pages of Q2 were set from manuscript and are presumably free from Q1 contamination (barring, of course, casual consultation of Q1 by A or B). The results of this part of the investigation would be more usable if they had been presented in tabular form. Apart from the value of the study in the examination of the text, it is important as illustrating a new method of attacking a vexing problem. In a companion study[3] Professor Richard Hosley restates convincingly the reasons for rejecting the proposition that Q2 of *Romeo* was set from an annotated copy of Q1 and for believing that Shakespeare's foul sheets served as copy except for the passage, I, ii, 52 to I, iii, 35. Previous commentators had suggested I, ii, 46, 54, or 58 as the starting point. He gives several good examples of sporadic consultation of Q1 and coins and defines a useful term, "manuscript link" (pp. 133–4).

Titus Andronicus "is either Shakespeare's first play, an alternative to which I incline, or else the work of more than one author". This is the conclusion of R. F. Hill's examination of the rhetoric of the play,[4] and of a comparison of the use of rhetorical figures in it and in ten other of Shakespeare's plays usually dated 1590 to 1596. It is not surprising that *2* and *3 Henry VI* differ from *Titus* less than do *Richard II* or *Romeo*, for example, or that *1 Henry VI* (referred to only incidentally) shares certain characteristics with *Titus*. Certain usages occur much more or much less frequently in *Titus* than in the other plays. Hill refuses to commit himself on the question of authorship until studies similar to his have been made of the rhetorical habits of the other dramatists of the period (but what of anonymous plays, and of the plays that have not survived— may not the author of one of them be involved, if there be a second hand in *Titus*?); meanwhile, he is convinced that a date prior to 1590 should be assigned to *Titus*, with the possibility of a Shakespearian revision of his own play before the performance in January 1594.

[1] *Shakespeare Quarterly*, VIII, 219–22.
[2] 'The Printing of the Second Quarto of *Romeo and Juliet* (1599)', *Studies in Bibliography*, IX, 107–28.
[3] 'Quarto Copy for Q2 *Romeo and Juliet*', *Studies in Bibliography*, IX, 129–41.
[4] 'The Composition of *Titus Andronicus*', *Shakespeare Survey*, 10, pp. 60–70.

BOOKS RECEIVED

[Inclusion of a book in this list does not preclude its review in a subsequent volume]

BEYER, EDVARD. *Problemer omkring oversettelser av Shakespeares dramatikk* (Universitet I Bergen, Arbok 1956; Historisk-antikvarisk rekke, Nr. 3). (Bergen: A. S. John Griegs Boktrykkeri, 1956.)

BROWN, J. R. *Shakespeare and his Comedies* (London: Methuen, 1957).

CLEMEN, WOLFGANG. *Kommentar zu Shakespeares Richard III* (Göttingen: Vandenhoeck and Ruprecht, 1957).

COE, CHARLES NORTON. *Shakespeare's Villains* (New York: Bookman Associates, 1957).

DICKEY, FRANKLIN M. *Not Wisely But Too Well; Shakespeare's Love Tragedies* (San Marino, California: The Huntington Library, 1957).

DYMLING, CARL ANDERS. *Hamlet's Age* (Stockholm: Zetterlund and Thelanders Boktryckeri, 1956).

ELIOT, T. S. *Essays on Elizabethan Drama* (New York: Harcourt, Brace and Company, 1956).

FARNHAM, WILLARD. *The Medieval Heritage of Elizabethan Tragedy* (Oxford: Basil Blackwell, 1956).

FRIEDMAN, WILLIAM F. and ELIZEBETH S. *The Shakespearean Ciphers Examined* (Cambridge University Press, 1957).

JACQUOT, JEAN (Editor). *Les Fêtes de la Renaissance* (Paris: Éditions du Centre National de la Recherche Scientifique, 1957).

KORNINGER, SIEGFRIED. *Die Naturauffasung in der Englischen Dichtung Des 17 Jahrhunderts* (Vienna-Stuttgart: Wilhelm Braumüller, 1956).

KORNINGER, SIEGFRIED. *Studies in English Language and Literature: presented to Professor Karl Brunner* (Vienna: Wilhelm Braumuller, 1957).

LOMBARDO, AGOSTINO. *Il Dramma Pre-Shakespeariano* (Venice: Neri Pozza, 1957).

LÜTHI, MAX. *Shakespeares Dramen* (Berlin: Walter de Gruyter and Co., 1957).

MUIR, KENNETH. *Shakespeare's Sources*, Volume One, Comedies and Tragedies (London: Methuen, 1957).

NICOLL, ALLARDYCE. *The Elizabethans* (Cambridge University Press, 1957).

O'BRIEN, GORDON WORTH. *Renaissance Poetics and the Problem of Power* (Chicago: Institute of Elizabethan Studies, 1956).

POEL, WILLIAM. *Prompt-Book of "Fratricide Punished"*. Edited by J. Isaacs (London: Society for Theatre Research, 1956).

RYMER, THOMAS. *The Critical Works*. Edited by Curt A. Zimansky (Oxford University Press, 1956).

SCHUTE, WILLIAM M. *Joyce and Shakespeare: a study in the meaning of "Ulysses"* (Oxford University Press, 1957).

SHAKESPEARE, WILLIAM
  (New Arden Shakespeare):
    King Henry VI, Part 2, edited by Andrew S. Cairncross (London: Methuen, 1956).
    King Henry VIII, edited by R. A. Foakes (London: Methuen, 1956).
    King Richard II, edited by Peter Ure (London: Methuen, 1956).

(New Cambridge Shakespeare):

    Othello, edited by Alice Walker and John Dover Wilson (Cambridge University Press, 1957).

    Pericles, edited by J. C. Maxwell (Cambridge University Press, 1956).

(The Pelican Shakespeare):

    Hamlet, edited by Willard Farnham (Baltimore: Penguin Books, 1957).

    King Henry IV, Part One, edited by M. A. Shaaber (Baltimore: Penguin Books, 1957).

    King Henry IV, Part Two, edited by Allan Chester (Baltimore: Penguin Books, 1957).

    King Henry V, edited by Louis B. Wright and Virginia Freund (Baltimore: Penguin Books, 1957).

    King Richard II, edited by Matthew W. Black (Baltimore: Penguin Books, 1957).

(Shakespeare Quarto Facsimiles):

    No. 9. *Henry the Fifth, 1600*, edited by W. W. Greg (Clarendon Press: Oxford University Press, 1957).

    No. 10. *Love's Labour's Lost, 1598*, edited by W. W. Greg (Clarendon Press: Oxford University Press, 1957).

SHROEDER, JOHN W. *The Great Folio of 1623: Shakespeare's Plays in the Printing House* (Hamden, Connecticut: The Show String Press, 1956).

STAMM, RUDOLF. *Englische Literatur* (Bern: A. Francke, 1957).

WILSON, H. S. *On the Design of Shakespearian Tragedy* (University of Toronto Press, 1957).

ZBIERSKI, HENRYK. *Shakespeare and the "War of the Theatres" (A Reinterpretation)* (Poznań: Państwowe Wydawnictwo Naukowe, 1957).

INDEX

INDEX

Webster, Margaret, **1**, 112; **3**, 116;
 4, 123–4; **5**, 116; **6**, 124; **8**, 122;
 10, 89 n., 131
Weelkes, Thomas, **1**, 68
 Ballets and Madrigals, **1**, 69, 70
Weever, John, *Epigrammes*, **4**, 87
Weigelin, Ernst, **5**, 134
Weilgart, Wolfgang J., *Shakespeare Psychognostic. Character Evolution and Transformation* reviewed, **8**, 145
Weir, Anthony, **9**, 119
Weisinger, Herbert, **10**, 137
Welde, Humphrey, **1**, 28
Welles, Orson, **2**, 131; **7**, 146 n.; **10**, 121, 122
 production of *Othello* reviewed, **6**, 145–6
Wellington, Duke of, **3**, 100
Wells, H. W., **4**, 18; **5**, 81, 83, 86, 89; **10**, 3
Wellstood, F. C., **1**, 86
 Catalogue of…Shakespeare's Birthplace, **3**, 2
Welsford, Enid, **4**, 19; **6**, 13; **10**, 135
 The Fool, **2**, 143
Welsh, C., **1**, 35 n.
Welth, and Helth, Enterlude of, **3**, 45
Wendell, Barrett, **2**, 119
Wenger, B. V., **8**, 4
Wentersdorf, Karl, **6**, 159, 160, 170; **8**, 142–3
Werder, Karl, **9**, 2, 4
Wertham, Frederic, **9**, 13
Wertham, James, **4**, 11
West, Benjamin, **6**, 61
West, E. J., **10**, 150
West, Hon. James, **4**, 72–3; **5**, 57
West, Robert H., **8**, 150; **10**, 138
West, William, *Symbolaeographie*, **4**, 41–3
Westall, **10**, 73
Westbrook, P. D., **2**, 140 n.; **10**, 5
Westminster Boys, *see under* Theatre, Elizabethan, companies
Westmorland, Mildmay Fane, Duke of, *see under* Fane, Mildmay
West Riding Repertory Company, *see under* Theatres
Westward Ho!, *see under* Webster, John
Whateley, Anne, **3**, 9, 139; **5**, 139 n.; **7**, 139
Whateley, Thomas, **2**, 109
Wheatley, H. B., **1**, 2, 35 n., 36 n.
Wheeler, Charles B., **9**, 135
Wheler, Robert Bell, **1**, 82, 86, 87 n.; **9**, 100 n.
Whetstone, George, **3**, 15; **7**, 104
 Promos and Cassandra, **3**, 54, 73; **4**, 26–7
 tale of Rinaldo and Giletta, **8**, 4

Whistler, James Abbot McNeill, **10**, 75
Whitaker, Virgil K., **9**, 132; **10**, 5, 25 n.
 Shakespeare's Use of Learning reviewed, **8**, 146–7
White, **10**, 73
White, D. M., **3**, 33
White, Thomas, *A Sermon Preached at Pawles Crosse*, **1**, 68
White, W. A., **1**, 58, 69
Whitefriars Theatre, *see under* Theatres, Elizabethan
Whitehall, *see under* London
Whitehouse, Lorna, **1**, 101, 102
Whiter, Walter, **4**, 18, 19; **7**, 8; **8**, 30
Whitgift, John, Archbishop of Canterbury, **8**, 101–2
Whitney, Geoffrey, **1**, 63
Whittington, Robert, **1**, 68
Whole contention betweene the two famous houses Lancaster and Yorke, The, *see under* 'Contention betweene the two famous houses Lancaster and Yorke, The Whole'
Whorf, Richard, **4**, 123; **8**, 122
Wickert, Maria, **8**, 145; **10**, 5
Wickham, Glynne, **9**, 133
Widmann, W., **9**, 110 n.
Wieland, Christoph Martin, **4**, 126, 127; **9**, 94, 96, 97, 100 n.
Wigert, Knut, **7**, 114
Wilbye, John, **1**, 68
Wilcox, John, **1**, 8; **4**, 141 n.; **10**, 10
Wilde, Oscar, **4**, 104; **6**, 136; **8**, 131; **10**, 141
Wilder, Thornton, **1**, 97
Wildgoose, William, **4**, 82, 83
Wildhagen, Heinz D., **6**, 120
Wildi, Max, **7**, 115
Wiles, R. M., **3**, 137
Wilkins, George, **3**, 30; **5**, 39; **6**, 165; **7**, 65–6; **8**, 56
 Miseries of Enforced Marriage, **1**, 46
 The Painfull Adventures of Pericles Prince of Tyre, **3**, 45, 151–2; **5**, 26, 39–45; **8**, 158
Wilkinson, Allan, **5**, 150
Wilkinson, C. H., **4**, 96 n.
Wilkinson, L. P., **10**, 146 n.
Wilkinson, Norman, **2**, 7; **8**, 80
Willcock, Gladys D., **4**, 9; **7**, 5, 11 n.; **9**, 134, 141; **10**, 135
 'Shakespeare and Elizabethan English', **7**, 12–24
Willet, Andrew, *Ecclesia Triumphans*, **2**, 70
Willey, Basil, *The Seventeenth-Century Background*, **3**, 7
Williams, Charles, **4**, 6, 146; **8**, 9, 12, 36
Williams, David, **10**, 124
Williams, Emlyn, **10**, 131, 133–4

Williams, Frayne, *Mr Shakespeare of the Globe*, **3**, 9
Williams, George W., **4**, 161, 163; **5**, 134; **10**, 155
Williams, Harcourt, **2**, 14, 16; **9**, 20; **10**, 75
Williams, Iolo A., **2**, 21
Williams, John, **2**, 24, 25, 26, 27, 32, 34
Williams, Philip, **3**, 152; **4**, 157, 162, 163; **5**, 144, 145; **7**, 149; **8**, 11, 154, 155; **10**, 155
Williams, Tenessee, **6**, 140; **10**, 100
Williamson, Audrey, **6**, 163 n.
Williamson, Hugh Ross, **4**, 148, 156
Willis, John, *Stenographie*, **5**, 151
Willman, Noel, **10**, 123
Willoughby, Sir Ambrose, **8**, 7
Willoughby, E. E., **1**, 75, 77 n.; **4**, 88; **5**, 47, 144, 147; **7**, 152; **8**, 153, 154; **10**, 88 n.
Willoughby, Henry, *Willobie his Avisa*, **3**, 10, 54; **4**, 88
Willymat, William, **2**, 70, 72
 A Loyal Subject's Looking-Glasse, **2**, 70; **4**, 40
 A Prince's Looking-Glass, **4**, 40
Wilson, Arthur, *The Swisser* (MS.), **3**, 52
Wilson, E. C., 'Shakespeare's Enobarbus', **2**, 135
Wilson, F. P., **1**, 12, 122; **2**, 152; **3**, 69; **4**, 9, 25, 50, 67 n., 88, 149; **5**, 137; **6**, 57, 63 n.; **7**, 5, 51, 55 n., 132, 142, 147; **8**, 2, 11, 18; **9**, 32, 34 n., 138 n., 146; **10**, 14, 15
 'Shakespeare's Reading', **3**, 14–21
 The Plague in Shakespeare's London, **3**, 6
Wilson, Harold S., **8**, 140
Wilson, J. Dover, **1**, 9, 10, 12, 13, 94, 114; **2**, 57, 58, 84, 108, 113, 140, 148; **3**, 3, 6, 10, 18, 21 n., 23, 24, 26, 27, 28, 75, 80, 82, 137, 141, 152; **4**, 8, 10, 36, 44, 88, 161, 162; **5**, 4–5, 61, 139, 148, 150, 152; **6**, 7, 10, 11, 12, 13, 14, 18, 155, 157, 159, 168, 169; **7**, 3, 6, 8, 82–3, 107, 136, 151; **8**, 2, 14, 22, 23, 101–2, 110; **9**, 4–6, 7–9, 12, 13, 15, 26, 27, 31, 32, 33 n., 44–5, 48 n., 50, 51, 150, 152, 153; **10**, 2, 3, 5, 9, 10, 39, 49 n., 70 n., 71–2, 138, 158
 'Ben Jonson and *Julius Caesar*', **2**, 36–43
 edition of *King Henry VI* (3 parts) reviewed, **7**, 139–40, 147–9
 edition of *Titus Andronicus* reviewed, **3**, 143–4, 145
 Henry IV and *Henry V* reviewed, **1**, 127–30